MW00844734

Democratic Institution Performance

Research and Policy Perspectives

Edited by Edward R. McMahon
and Thomas A.P. Sinclair

Westport, Connecticut
London

Library of Congress Cataloging-in-Publication Data

Democratic institution performance : research and policy perspectives / edited by
Edward R. McMahon and Thomas A.P. Sinclair.
    p. cm.
    Includes bibliographical references and index.
    ISBN 0–275–97788–9 (alk. paper)
    1. Democracy. 2. Democratization. I. McMahon, Edward R., 1956– II. Sinclair,
Thomas.
    JC423.D441753   2002
    321.8—dc21   2002070856

British Library Cataloguing in Publication Data is available.

Library of Congress Catalog Card Number: 2002070856
ISBN: 0–275–97788–9

First published in 2002

Praeger Publishers, 88 Post Road West, Westport, CT 06881
An imprint of Greenwood Publishing Group, Inc.
www.praeger.com

Printed in the United States of America

The paper used in this book complies with the
Permanent Paper Standard issued by the National
Information Standards Organization (Z39.48–1984).

10 9 8 7 6 5 4 3 2 1

Contents

Tables and Figures

Preface and Acknowledgments

The issue of how to improve the functioning of democracy around the world is multi-faceted and complex, and yet in the contemporary world, it is of increasing importance. In fact, it can quite literally become a question of life or death. The Center on Democratic Performance (CDP) was founded at Binghamton University for the purpose of promoting research and interaction between the research and academic communities on these issues. This led to a conference in June 2001, which brought together leading practitioners from both communities to discuss some of the key issues involved in the democratization challenge. Participants subsequently produced the edited chapters that form this volume.

The breadth of issues addressed in this volume is purposefully broad. As such, they provide an indication of the challenges inherent in furthering human understanding of what democracy is and how it functions. There clearly is some truth in Churchill's oft-repeated maxim that democracy is the worst form of government except all others. It is left up to us to try to perfect it, even though perfection is alien to the human spirit. What gets lost sometimes, however, is that it is the search that is important, not the attainment of the final goal. Democracy will never be a set of finished institutions; a sign of a successful democracy is one that changes as the people who make it up do so. This volume is designed to provide a stop in the way along that search.

As with any work of this magnitude, a team effort has been required to produce the volume. We would like to extend our sincerest appreciation to the contributors to the volume, who may have established a record in avoiding deadline slippage. We also wish to thank Michael Hermann and his colleagues at Praeger Publishing for working together with us and providing wise advice throughout the process. Editorial assistant Brian Nussbaum helped to ensure the completeness and quality of the manuscript. Finally and most importantly, this project could not have been brought to fruition without the dedication, hard work, and attention to detail of CDP's executive associate, Grace Cheung Schulman. Grace is a consummate professional who dealt with the myriad details with calmness and order.

Abbreviations

AARP	Formerly the American Association of Retired Persons
AB	Afrabarometer
AFL-CIO	American Federation of Labor and Congress of Industrial Organizations
ANC	African National Congress
ARD	Associates in Rural Development
CDIE	Center for Development, Information, and Evaluation
CIA	Central Intelligence Agency
CIO	Congress of Industrial Organizations
COE	Council on Europe
CPP	Cambodian People's Party
CSC	Congolese Confederation of Trade Unionists
CSCE	Commission on Security and Cooperation in Europe
DG Center	Democracy and Governance Center
DOD	Department of Defense
DOS	Department of State
ECOMOG	Economic Community of West African States Cease-fire Monitoring Group
EU	European Community
FEP	foreign economic penetration
FH	Freedom House

FMLN	*Frente Farabundo Martí para la Liberación Nacional*
Frelimo	*Frente de Libertação de Moçambique*
FUNCINPEC	National Union Front for an Independent, Neutral, Peaceful, and Cooperative Cambodia
FY	fiscal year
GDP	gross domestic product
GOLD	Governance and Local Development Project
GPRA	Government Performance and Results Act
HDZ	Croat Democratic Party
IAD	institutional analysis and development
ICFTU	International Confederation of Free Trade Unions
ILO	International Labor Organization
IMF	International Monetary Fund
International IDEA	International Institute for Democracy and Electoral Assistance
IR	intermediate result
IRI	International Republican Institute
JSTOR	Journal Storage—The Scholarly Journal Archive
KIPP	Independent Election Monitoring Committee
LDC	less-developed country
MNC	multinational corporation
MPLA	*Movimento Popular de Libertação de Angola*
NAACP	National Association for the Advancement of Colored People
NAFTA	North American Free Trade Agreement
NAMFREL	National Citizens' Movement for Free Elections
NATO	North Atlantic Treaty Organization
NDI	National Democratic Institute
NGO	nongovernmental organization
NLD	National League for Democracy (in Burma)
OAS	Organization of American States
OAU	Organization of African Unity
ODIHR	Office of Democratic Institutions and Human Rights
OECD	Organization for Economic Cooperation and Development
OPEC	Organization of Petroleum Exporting Countries

OSCE	Organization for Security and Cooperation in Europe
PAIS	Public Affairs Information Service
PE	political economy
PR	proportional representation
PRC	People's Republic of China
PRI	*Partido Revolucionario Institucional*
PTA	Parent–Teacher Association
R4	Results Review and Resource Request
REDSO	Regional Economic Development Services Organization
Renamo	*Resistência Nacional Moçambicana*
SDA	Party of Democratic Action
SDS	Serb Democratic Party
SO	strategic objective
UK	United Kingdom
UN	United Nations
UNDP	United Nations Development Program
UNFREL	University Network for Free Elections
UNITA	*União Nacional para a Independencia Total de Angola*
UNTA	National Union of Angolan Workers
U.S.	United States
USAID	U.S. Agency for International Development
USG	U.S. Government
WTO	World Trade Organization
WVS	World Values Survey

Part I

Introduction

Chapter 1

The Paradox of Democracy

Edward R. McMahon and Brian Nussbaum

Democracy has never been more widely practiced than in our present time. Recent years have clearly seen an unprecedented expansion of democratic governing institutions around the world. This is a shift captured by Samuel Huntington's famous Third Wave simile.[1] To use a highly aggregated set of figures, according to the nongovernmental human rights organization Freedom House, 12 percent of the world's population in 1900 lived in countries that could be broadly considered democratic; today that figure is approaching two-thirds of the world's population. With the decrease of overtly authoritarian states in the post–Cold War world, the democratic project has become a worldwide governance ideal. "[D]espite fits and starts—human liberty has been on an upward trajectory throughout the twentieth century. When viewed from the perspective of the century as a whole, democracy and civil liberties have made important and dramatic progress."[2] Others have made similar arguments regarding the progress of democracy and liberalism. Plattner, for example, in *The Global Resurgence of Democracy*, echoes the argument Francis Fukuyama made in "The End of History?" that we may be witnessing "the end point of mankind's ideological evolution and the universalization of Western liberal democracy as the final form of human government."[3]

Even though the Freedom House figures must be treated carefully due to definitional considerations about what constitutes a functioning democracy, it is indisputable that a wealth of raw data and experiential information has accrued in recent years. We know more now than ever about how democratic institutions are created, how they function, why they fail in some cases, and what is necessary for them to take root and become consolidated.

However, at the center of the study of democracy is a paradox. Elements of democracy have played a role in governing societies for over 2,000 years, and clearly democracy and civil liberties have made important and dramatic recent progress. A rich body of literature on issues such as election systems, presidential versus parliamentary systems, decentralization, and civil society, and institutional choices confronting nascent democracies have begun to emerge. However, while we may have greater knowledge about democracy now than at any time in the past, overall, our understanding of how it is practiced and perpetuated remains quite limited. New challenges such as Zakaria's exposé of illiberal democracy or countries with the formal trappings of democracy but not their real functioning, crop up.[4] As Brunell and Calvert have noted, recent years have seen the coining of

a rich lexicon of terms—"democracy with adjectives"—denoting differences of type, degree and interpretation, for example: semi-democracies, quasi-democracies, and neo-democracies. There are also pseudo-democracies where political contestation exists but is not conducted on a wholly fair or non-fraudulent basis, and "defective democracies." Then there are "guided democracies," "façade democracies" and "proto-democracies." ... [T]here is an old saying that if a glass is half empty, then by the same token it is also half full—and even qualified democracy is an achievement of sorts.[5]

Obviously, many examples also exist of various institutions and frameworks that have fostered democratic development in some contexts but that have spelled disaster or otherwise failed in others.

This inability to predict what choices are most appropriate for a particular nation at a given time continues to challenge democratic practitioners and scholars alike. This can lead to serious problems. "The 'right' choices are politically appropriate and must command society's respect as well as being technically sound. Bungled attempts at constitutional engineering and ill-suited electoral rules, for instance, can ultimately prove near fatal if they go uncorrected."[6]

As is implicit in the Third Wave concept, neither is it necessarily a foregone conclusion that democratic institutions will continue to consolidate. History is replete with examples of democracies that have succumbed to military coups, civil unrest, domination by foreign powers, or other causes. It is true that in absolute terms this number has declined in recent years, but this is no predictor of medium- to long-term sustained democratic consolidation.[7]

Some questions that generally generate more debate than consensus include, When and under what conditions is democracy likely to take root? What is the relationship of political to economic development? How can we increase the likelihood that democracy will be successfully consolidated? To what extent does the impetus for democratization come from internal forces, and to what extent is it the product of international suasion or pressure? What particular sets of democratic institutions are most appropriate in what contexts, and what are the elements that determine this? To what extent do regional cultural, social, historic, and other differences need to be considered? How can the rights of majorities and minorities best be balanced?

Our ability to answer these types of questions and incorporate predictive analysis into the functioning of democracy is still modest. At a 1999 conference on constitutional development, a political scientist asserted that his discipline was currently at a stage roughly analogous to that of astronomy some 500 years ago. By this he meant that whereas at that time, astronomy was viewed as being something in the realm of the occult and subject to forces beyond a person's understanding, it is now seen as responding to a set of fixed laws. His implication was that the same will happen to the discipline of political science. This line of reasoning therefore suggests that at some point we will be able to scientifically determine whether, when, and how a country will democratize.

This perspective may or may not be true. Political development is at least partly subject to the vagaries of human nature or acts of God and thus cannot be captured quite so neatly. Most observers would agree, however, that the future development of democratic institutions can be informed and aided by analysis of prior and comparative experiences. This process of improving our understanding of how institutions function is not an abstract exercise. While academic research may be viewed as the identification, selection, and testing of hypotheses, in the "real" world, the failure of a hypothesis test—wherever it may come from—can cost thousands of people their lives. In Burundi in 1993, for example, the idea that power could be transferred brusquely and in a negative sum, albeit democratic, fashion from the minority Tutsi to majority Hutu was disproven at the cost of untold human suffering.

The expansion of democracy, therefore, does not lead immediately to the establishment of stable, consolidated democratic institutions. In fact, a critical argument regards whether a country possessing some of the accoutrements of democratic institutions is necessarily on the path of democratic development. Many observers believe that the mere existence of the form of democratic institutions—skeptics would call this the current fad of the international community—does not ipso facto mean that the spirit of democracy is embraced.

The explosion in a number of countries that have undertaken some form of democratic development is undeniable. In addition, the development of democracy is not a Western-centric issue, as elements of democracy are found in many different cultures, indigenous African traditions that reflect in part the communitarian aspects of democracy, for example. The institutions of *ganwaa* (alternance in power) in the Oromo of Ethiopia, *khotla* (consultation) in Botswana, and *gacacca* (administration of justice and dispute resolution) in Rwanda are some elements of traditional African governance that can be integrated into more "modern" democratic systems.

The need for greater understanding of democratic institutional performance requires closer examination of the performance of the institutions themselves: the political economy, the civil society, elections, and legislatures, to name a few. A better understanding of how these institutions function can serve to underpin improved analytic and policy approaches to building democratic institutions. This is the task undertaken in this volume. This volume also reflects democracy's global reality through its discussion of the international nature of democratic development in general and by its chapters on specific democratic development in sub-Saharan and North Africa and in Indonesia.

Events such as those surrounding the 2000 U.S. presidential election in Florida should also remind us that the gulf between developing democracies and "consolidated" democracies may not be as wide as many, especially those in the older democracies, may think. In fact, the lesson from Florida may be a healthy one—that the developing versus consolidated democracy conceptual framework should give way to a more fluid recognition that all democracies are continually evolving. A recurrent undercurrent throughout this volume is that in addition to more recent democracies' being able to learn from those that have longer experience dealing with questions of consolidation, countries from that latter category have much to learn from the former. To cite just one example, as the Florida example and Eric Bjornlund's chapter suggest, rigorous monitoring of elections by credible, nonpartisan civic organizations may not be appropriate simply for emerging democracies.

The issues to be addressed in examining the complex and complicated phenomena of democratization are myriad. This volume identifies a number of the key variables and seeks to shed theoretical and practical light on how they affect, and have been affected by, the democratization project. These issues are extremely varied and cut across many different "practical" and academic disciplines. This volume also reflects a methodological pluralism that demonstrates the breadth of tools and approaches available to contemporary scholars.

As John W. Harbeson points out, this book undertakes, in effect, to bridge three distinct dimensions of democratization whose interconnectedness has rarely been explored, to the detriment of progress in all three areas: first, the concept of democracy itself; second, the empirical strength and viability of newly initiated democratization processes in many world regions; and third, the effectiveness of externally assisted programming in support of its development. Responsibility for relative inattention to the interconnectedness of these dimensions rests with constituencies of academics, practitioners in donor agencies, and activists on the ground, many of whom have lacked the incentive, resources, or institutional encouragement to work closely with each other fully to integrate the three dimensions in their work on democracy. Harbeson notes that the advancement of democracy hinges, in no small measure, upon more effectively integrated consideration of all three dimensions of democratization by all three constituencies. The selection of contributing topics is designed to underscore the importance of combining internal perspectives with external approaches as well as presenting the frameworks employed by those engaged in delivering democratic assistance as well as those studying democracy. This volume seeks to provide an original contribution given its particular combination of policy and research perspectives.

CIVIL SOCIETY

Civil society has been defined as "an intermediate associational realm between state and family populated by organizations which are separate from the state, enjoy autonomy in relation to the state and are formed voluntarily by members of society to protect or extend their interests or values."[8] As such, civil society plays a critical role in serving as the soil in which democracy can take root and prosper.

Kristi Andersen's chapter addresses issues dealing with civil society, focusing on the important role that political parties play as facilitators for civic engagement. By addressing the way in which parties affect U.S. civic involvement, she paints a picture of the effect that parties can have on both the building and maintenance of civil society institutions. Rather than viewing parties as merely partisan interests, Andersen provides a clear picture of the ways in which parties fit into the larger public arena.

John W. Harbeson's chapter also examines this topic, especially in terms of its conceptualization in the international donor community. He reviews civil society, discussing the various ways in which it is defined and described, as a precursor to an influential critique of the definition accepted by international donors. Arguing for a broader, more culturally relevant conception of civil society, Harbeson offers important insights into aspects of civil society that are too often overlooked or even ignored by the donors.

PUBLIC OPINION

Public opinion is a vital element of the functioning of any democracy. Leaders must know what people are thinking in order to be responsive to and address the needs of the population as a whole, and yet, public opinion is an amorphous concept at the best of times. Who are "the people"? What are "they" thinking about? How is this to be translated into public policy? A separate set of operational questions bedevils this issue in developing world societies, where the ability to gather information is greatly constrained.

Michael Bratton's chapter reflects the key role that public sentiment plays in democratization and consolidation. It shows this linkage by reporting the findings of an extensive public opinion survey that was carried out in twelve African nations. This cross-national survey data led Bratton to conclude that large-scale popular support for democracy and its institutions is not deeply ingrained in the region. This chapter gives very valuable insight into the level of the African attachment to democracy, which is a key factor in any attempt to spread democratization on the continent.

INTERNAL INSTITUTIONS

Two chapters focus upon country-specific challenges for democratization. An important example of these internal institutions blocking the fluid functioning of democracy appears in Ali A. Mazrui's chapter. Mazrui's examination of the sometimes problematic integration of Muslim Sharia law and democratic institutions offers a timely and fascinating insight into democracy's compatibility with cultural institutions. The interaction between traditional culture and democracy is an often overlooked facet of democratization that is becoming more and more relevant in a world facing increased interaction and global interdependence.

Another internal challenge that can plague nascent democracies is, as Howard G. Brown shows, transitional justice. His chapter is an enlightening glance at the problem of transitional justice during the French Revolution. This chapter is a most compelling historical look at the problems facing many nascent democracies today. Not only does this chapter put problems of modern-day transitions in an important historical context, but it also clearly demonstrates that even the Western democracies, which are considered most consolidated, experienced serious "growing pains" during their democratization.

INTERNATIONAL STANDARDS

Emerging international norms and standards for what constitutes democratic functioning are currently undergoing an important evolution. There are also challenges posed by balancing the internal requirements of democratizing nations with external perspectives, including the expectations of other nations and international organizations that are increasingly adopting common international standards for democratic performance.

Eric Bjornlund's chapter adds an important viewpoint to the attempt to establish international democratic standards. He discusses the impact of aid to election monitoring groups and their subsequent impact on democratization, specifically in the case of Indonesia. This chapter is part of a growing literature that contributes to the work of both the real-world practitioners and academic theorists concerned with democracy.

Elizabeth Spiro Clark's chapter examines from a broader perspective the question of evolving international standards and their future effects for individual nations and the democratization movement as a whole. By presenting some important trends that have come to shape many nascent democratic elections, Clark provides a valuable and provocative look into the future emerging framework of democratic standards.

ELECTIONS

Elections are a key part of any democracy. Often the role that they play is even greater than simply electing officials. Successful democracies must somehow mediate conflicts and integrate societies while at the same time perpetuating some conflicts as an intrinsic part of elections. Terrence Lyons discusses the important role of postconflict elections in terminating wars, contributing to democratization, and restructuring the role of international organizations in peace-keeping and delivering aid. This chapter demonstrates the way in which elections can serve as a terminal point for conflict and a starting point for democratization. By examining the phenomena of postconflict elections, Lyons shows an important and often overlooked role that elections sometimes play. Useful both for actual war termination and for legitimating postconflict governance, these elections prove invaluable to many nascent democracies. Finally, Lyons shows the ways in which the international organizations can make use of postconflict elections in peacekeeping and aid delivery.

GLOBALIZATION

Two chapters delve into the complex and emerging relationship between globalization and democratization. Globalization plays an important role in David L. Cingranelli's chapter, which examines the effects of increasing global economic integration and democratization on workers' rights. Globalization has stirred controversy in terms of its perceived negative effect on workers, which Cingranelli argues is largely a myth. His chapter showcases the positive effects on workers' rights that have resulted from economic integration and democratization. Presenting evidence that globalization has, over time, created a "leveling up" of workers, Cingranelli makes an important and timely contribution to the literature addressing workers' rights at the global level.

Nicolas van de Walle examines the effect of globalization on the development and consolidation of the democratic politics in low-income nations. His chapter focuses on the interplay between the simultaneous phenomena of globalization and the Third Wave of democracy. Much controversy has arisen as to the way in which globalization involves and affects low-income nations, and van de Walle makes a valuable contribution to the debate by exploring the ways in which increased economic integration impacts democratization in the Third World. Many nascent democracies are trying to contend with both institutionalizing democracy and at the same time thrusting themselves into the world economy. This chapter examines these two impulses with the aim of deciding whether they are opposing or compatible.

INTERNATIONAL AID AND ACADEMIC RESEARCH

Scholars and practitioners operate in different domains; the questions that they ask and the knowledge that their works generate often fail to link together. At the extremes, academicians are accused of being out of touch with real problems, while practitioners are debunked as atheoretical and, therefore, driven by political whims. Two chapters confront the issue of the relationship between the international aid community and academic research. Harry Blair's chapter gives the reader a glimpse of the complex relationship between academic research and international aid policy. By examining how research contributes to recent trends in the democratic assistance provided by the U.S. Agency for International Development (USAID), he shows the way in which academe can play an important role in shaping or at least guiding that agency. This examination of how institutional research is put into real-world use shows the increasingly important interconnectedness of theory and practice when it comes to democratic assistance.

Shaheen Mozaffar also contributes an important piece regarding the relationship between academic research and international aid. His chapter emphasizes the responsibility of academics to provide research that is "policy-relevant," meaning useful and applicable to real-world decision making. He posits that research that is overly theoretical or esoteric is irresponsible in the face of the myriad needs of the democratic assistance community.

CONCLUSION

Edward Friedman's concluding chapter, entitled "The Art of Democratic Crafting and Its Limits," provides considerable food for thought about the nature of democratic development and its future. Like any powerful conclusion, this chapter raises more questions than it answers. Friedman reviews paradigm shifts in the way that democratization has been conceptualized, noting that until perhaps fifteen years ago (i.e., well into democracy's Third Wave), underlying economic and/or social cultural factors were seen as the primary determining forces regarding democratic development. It was assumed that countries had to have reached a certain stage of economic development in order to develop democratic institutions. In addition, an underlying bias toward Anglo-Saxon Protestant cultures suggested that a correlation existed between such environments and democratic development; however, with the spread of democratization to poorer countries such as India or Catholic countries such as Spain and much of Latin America, the utility of these generalizations was reduced.

The 1990s sought increased emphasis on institutional choices' playing a key role in determining the success of the democratic project. These included issues such as whether a country should have a presidential or parliamentary system, whether election systems should be majoritarian or proportional, and whether a multiplicity of parties or fewer parties would be healthier for a country's democratic development. This approach has also come to be seen to have its limits, especially as the specter of illiberal democracy and questions of ethnicity and regionalism in many emerging democratic contexts have not been resolved.

Friedman's conclusion brings us back to this book's starting point. Democracy and how to best promote it retain much of a paradoxical nature. It is important not to be too scientific and prescriptive. The core of the issue of democratic development still contains a heavy dose of art.

Nonetheless, there are many useful insights contained in this volume. The improvement of the human condition does not come about through, in effect, throwing one's hands up in the air and saying that elements are out of our control. The essential nature of the human race is to continually struggle against what was once thought of as being beyond the realm of understanding. Thus, even Friedman posits that some important lessons have been learned, for example, that sequencing of decisions is important and that a country's democratic transition agenda should not be overloaded at the beginning. In this view, democratic development takes time and cannot be accomplished in one fell swoop. The democracy paradox may remain, but it is getting smaller.

NOTES

1. Huntington's explanation of trends in democratization in *The Third Wave: Democratization in the Late Twentieth Century* (Norman: University of Oklahoma Press, 1991) posits that the current high tide, or wave, of democracy began around 1974.

2. Freedom House, *Freedom in the World* (New York: Freedom House, 2000), 7.

3. Francis Fukuyama, "The End of History?" *The National Interest* 16 (Summer 1989): 3.

4. Fareed Zakaria, "The Rise of Illiberal Democracy," *Foreign Affairs* (November–December 1997): 22–43.

5. Peter Burnell and Peter Calvert, eds., *The Resilience of Democracy* (Portland, OR: Frank Cass, 1999), 2–3.

6. Ibid., 13.

7. See Thomas Carothers, "The End of the Transition Paradigm," *Journal of Democracy* 13, no. 1 (2002): 5–21.

8. Gordon White, "Civil Society, Democratization and Development (I): Clearing the Analytic Ground," *Democratization* 1, no. 3 (Autumn 1994): 379.

Part II

Domestic Aspects of Democratization

Chapter 2

Political Parties and Civil Society: Learning from the American Case

Kristi Andersen

The ways that citizens can make their voices heard and have some impact on important collective decisions have multiplied and changed in recent years. Obviously, changes in communication technology—which are not discussed here— have altered mass-elite relations; the U.S. Congress, for example, has recently been struggling with ways to cope with and respond to the deluge of E-mail that its members receive. The extent to which decisions made by legislatures or bureaucratic agencies must be open to citizen review and input has increased substantially in recent years, and, of course, the role of nonstate actors in political decision making at all levels is increasingly significant. In this context the relationships among political parties ("first among equals" in terms of voluntary associations, in Nancy Rosenblum's term[1]) and other groups are critically important.

New—or at least reconfigured—theoretical approaches are necessary to allow us to understand and analyze the new landscape of civic engagement. The scholarship in American politics probably lags somewhat behind that in international and comparative politics in coping with some of these changes. Nonetheless, this chapter relies primarily on research in American politics and American political development to begin thinking about the relationships among political parties and other kinds of organizations and associations, including what are variously termed "interest groups," "civic associations," "social movements," or "nongovernmental organizations."

At what level should we be theorizing about "nonstate, nonmarket actors"?[2] How we conceptualize these entities depends to a certain extent on our theoretical perspective. If we are Tocquevillians—or followers of Robert Putnam— we see parties, civic associations, and so forth as arenas where citizens can come together and construct a civil society. Those who are primarily concerned with social change and the role of social movements in producing such change may see social movements and related entities as vehicles for the expression and working out of social conflicts and/or as sites for resisting state authority. On the other hand, nonprofit organizations are often seen as collaborating with or providing supplements to state action.

Political scientists have tended to focus on interest groups, at times seeing them in a positive light as the embodiment of pluralism, at other times criticizing "special interests" and reinforcing societal inequities. Paul Burstein has argued persuasively that we should examine "interest organizations" (in which category he includes both conventional "interest groups" and social movement organizations[3]) and parties *together* in the context of theories of democratic politics—that we should pay more attention to the relationship between groups' expression of political demands and the ways that these demands are perceived by elected officials.[4] If this stance is adopted, clearly, political parties become central to understanding group behavior and civic life in a democracy.

In the recent upsurge of research on the state of American civic life, including research on the historical roots of the patterns of American civic engagement, political parties are not very visible. From bowling leagues, to the League of Women Voters, to the Parent–Teacher Association (PTA), to the Order of the Eastern Star, attention has mostly been focused on growth and decline of civic associations. Even though one frequently voiced criticism of Putnam's and similar perspectives is that their framework is apolitical, researchers have not yet devoted much effort to understanding the ways that healthy civic life is a function of *links* between formal institutions of government and "nonpolitical" civic associations—or to the role of political parties in helping to forge these links.[5]

Moreover, when groups (whether conceived of as "interest groups" or civic associations or social movements) are discussed, they are usually seen as possibly competing with (or even replacing) parties in terms of their functions. That is, they *compete* with parties in mobilizing citizens, defining policy options, recruiting leaders, and so on. Looked at this way, the *connections* between parties and groups are easily obscured.

This chapter briefly discusses some of the literature relating to the various sorts of nonstate, nonmarket actors, with particular attention to (1) their role in facilitating citizens' involvement in public life and collective decision making, a central quality of high-performing democratic systems; and (2) categories that we might use to analyze and compare how these actors operate on the assumption that political parties are particularly critical to democratic performance and should thus be at the center of any inquiry about citizens' associational involvement.

PARTIES AND ASSOCIATIONS

The propensity of Americans to form associations and groups of all types, noted and admired by Tocqueville, has been extensively documented. Recent concerns about the decline of civic life have produced a new boom in scholarship on associations. Skocpol, Gamm and Putnam, and others describe the development of increasingly larger and frequently federated organizations. This growth began in the second quarter of the nineteenth century and reached its peak in the later years of that century. Other sorts of groups, professional associations, for example, emerged and grew during the twentieth century. Hall's study of New Haven, Connecticut, documents the gradual enlargement of the domain of nonprofit organizations—in the arts and culture, education, and social welfare provision. A number of scholars have joined the debate about the implications of changes in the forms of civic associations (e.g., declines in large cross-class organizations) and the putative decline in citizen involvement in such groups.[6]

Meanwhile, political parties, evolving from informal caucuses of notables and legislators in first decades of the republic, took on many of the structural characteristics familiar today (e.g., conventions) during the Jacksonian period. The Progressive reforms, including the Australian ballot and the primary, arguably produced a decline in the centrality of parties to politics; and the party reforms of the late twentieth century, along with the rise of candidate-centered elections, have resulted in institutions quite different in shape from those of 50 or 100 years ago. A persistent characteristic of American parties, however—in contrast to parties in other democracies—is multiple centers of power and multiple levels of organization. Political party organizations of varying degrees of influence and coherence are to be found at the local, county, state, and national levels, and links between parties and other sorts of groups take place at all of these levels. The following sections provide a typology, probably neither mutually exclusive nor exhaustive, of the party–group linkages, along with brief mention of the literatures that touch upon them.

Groups as Information Channels

The parties' candidates and elected officials speak to groups, meet with representatives of groups, and address concerns of groups through their promises and their behavior once in office. Candidates' and officials' sense of their constituency is shaped by the constellation of organized groups in their district or city. "[A] key asset for a local level challenger . . . is early support from political active groups . . . these include . . . labor unions, civic associations, and special-interest groups like environmentalists, feminists, and others. They serve as an organizational base."[7]

Information flows the other way, too, of course. Groups ranging from labor unions, to environmental groups, to the PTA publish legislative newsletters covering current issues and advocacy strategies and maintain Web sites with, among other things, links to congressional representatives. These organizations, in increasing numbers, keep track of and publish information on congressional and state legislative voting records.

Finally, civic associations have acted to create information channels—of particular note is the role of the League of Women Voters and other politically concerned but nonpartisan groups that sponsor forums and candidate debates, publish surveys of candidate positions, and engage in other forms of voter education around elections.

Groups as Mobilization Channels

Parties work through and use groups to mobilize new voters, sometimes helping to create groups but more often using groups already in existence. There are numerous examples of this. In the 1930s, Franklin D. Roosevelt's campaign worked effectively through nonparty groups such as the Labor Non-Partisan League in Ohio and the Good Neighbor League.[8]

One of the most written-about instances of party building through the mobilization of existing organized groups is that of Anton Cermak's Chicago Democratic machine in the 1920s and 1930s.[9] Cermak—and later elements of the state and national parties allied with FDR—worked with existing ethnic organizations, both political and nonpolitical, to build Democratic attachments. Cermak (and Al Smith in 1928) spoke to these groups, worked with their leaders, and received their endorsements.[10] The mobilization of ethnic and working-class Chicagoans was accomplished in part through nonparty organizations. Such entities as the Polish Democratic Club of the 7th Ward or the Lithuanian Democratic League "proved to be crucial conduits providing new members and resources" to the Democratic Party.[11]

As these examples show, the groups were often quasi-partisan organizations. Joel Silbey says that "partisan clubs, ethnic and otherwise, from the Tippecanoe Clubs of 1840 to the Republican Wide Awakes to Irish volunteer fire companies, engaged in electioneering activity at every level."[12] When late-nineteenth- and early-twentieth-century urban politicians wanted to strengthen their positions, they developed "a local coalitional politics that pivoted on ethnic and religious self-consciousness."[13] Jo Freeman's recent book on women in the parties describes the numerous Republican women's clubs that were active during the mid-twentieth century (sometimes under conditions of conflict with the "regular" party organizations), and, of course, there are the familiar examples of the urban "reform clubs" that arose during the 1950s.[14]

Groups as Campaign Resources

Nonparty groups can provide parties and candidates with valuable resources—both money and volunteers—during election campaigns. Cotter, Gibson, Bibby, and Huckshorn asked state party leaders which "non-party groups" in their states were "closely aligned with the party and provide significant levels of assistance to the party and its candidates."[15] The two parties in 1980 varied in this regard, with the Democratic chairs all mentioning such groups—mostly labor unions but also teachers groups, social action groups, and business, farm, or professional organizations. A third of the Republicans, in contrast, mentioned no extraparty organizations—most who did acknowledge such relationships mentioned business, farm, or professional organizations or party auxiliary groups. The parties received support in the areas of fund-raising, volunteers, and efforts to get out the vote.

In elections in the 1990s the Christian Right supplied thousands of campaign workers for conservative Republican candidates.[16] "Citizen groups," said Berry and Schildkraut, "are often very involved in political parties as well—they are not a distinct set of politicos who disdain party politics. Campaign organizations are full of citizen group activists, and party conventions at the state and local level are filled with delegates who are representatives of various interest groups."[17]

Parties as Channels for Demands

Groups of various sorts—sometimes organized and professional enough to be termed interest groups, sometimes not—express their opinions to and make demands on parties. We see this most clearly in recent years at the platform hearings at the national level. References in candidates' acceptance speeches to interest groups also increased over time, from 1948 to 1992.[18] These kinds of interactions may happen at the local level as well. Paul Kleppner's research suggests that party–group connections may vary according to political structure. He argues that the territorial nature of Chicago's political structure (fifty wards) encouraged even small groups to become politically active, since if they were predominant in one or a few wards, they could elect or influence a city council member.[19]

Samuel Eldersveld's description of party organization in Detroit[20] remains the most vivid portrayal of the coalitional nature of local politics and of party leaders' constant dealings with clubs, groups, and associations of all kinds. "Let's take this district here," said one leader. "There are two major racial groups, the Negroes and the Jews. But it is not only nationality groups but also political groups—for example, we have the Young Democrats and the CIO [Congress of Industrial Organizations]." Or another: "There are 26 clubs in my district. Mine is a continuing job to maintain harmony."[21] His data show that the "subcoalitions" that he identifies (based on combinations of race, nationality, class, and labor affiliation) were strongly reflected in the local party hierarchies. A striking finding is the interconnectedness of group and party via the perceptions of supporters. That is, "the more one is attached perceptually to his party, the more likely also that he will be aware of his subcoalitional loyalties. . . . He will exhibit more tendencies to discuss politics with subgroup members, to feel the subgroup should articulate political positions."[22]

Kweit and Kweit's more recent research shows the group-connection changes in the parties by looking at "new" (young or recently switched into the party)

party members. They find that in the 1960s the Democratic Party benefited from new members concerned about woman's rights and civil rights and from those who were members of professional and public interest groups. Republicans had just begun (in the 1980s) to recruit new members who were affiliated with religious and antiabortion groups.[23]

Parties as Targets of Organizations

Groups organized to push for particular policies or protest certain conditions may eventually become third parties. In turn, there is an extensive literature on the impact of third parties on the major parties, particularly during the period preceding the Civil War and during the era of agrarian and populist discontent and organization in the 1880s and 1890s. Mary Ryan notes that the eventual impact of antebellum African American associationalism (including militia companies, newspapers, and fraternal orders), while little noted, included "the realignment of a major party," as well as the Civil War and the end of slavery.[24]

Recent efforts of the Christian Right illustrate another possible relationship between civic associations or groups and parties, in that the groups have attempted to gain control of Republican Party institutions. The success of these attempts has varied with the political opportunity structure, being greater where the state parties are electorally weak or factional and underregulated by state law. "The Christian Right," conclude Green, Guth, and Wilcox, "offers the GOP potent activist resources and access to a significant voting bloc."[25]

Zisk's study of environmental and peace groups found a few efforts by members of these groups to gain office; more common was service as party delegates or members of party caucuses; even more frequent was providing formal endorsement, financial help, or volunteer help to candidates nominated by the parties.[26]

THE IMPORTANCE OF PARTY–GROUP CONNECTIONS

Tocqueville observed that "civic associations . . . facilitate political association," while "political association singularly strengthens and improves associations for civil purposes."[27] There are a number of reasons to agree with Tocqueville, perhaps to worry about the implications of historical changes in both parties and in the shape of America's associational life and to ponder the role of political parties in the civic landscape of other democracies.

Americans' well-known proclivity to form clubs and associations of all kinds has had numerous effects on our public and private lives—and it has also affected the political parties. Three significant kinds of connections might be suggested. First, pressures from citizen groups may shape the organizational structure of political parties. Second, political parties may help to foster associationalism, making organizational affiliation more meaningful for citizens.

Third, citizen groups may provide a form of legitimacy for political parties, thereby authenticating the democratic element of party organizations.

One of the clearest ways in which citizen groups have affected the structure of party organizations is through efforts to make the national conventions more representative of the population as a whole. The 1964 conflict over the Mississippi delegation is one of a number of instances in which party insiders were forced to accept a broader demographic constituency at the party convention.

In a more general sense, parties are often influenced by the informal and voluntary clubs that exist within them. In particular, the "reform clubs" formed by both Democrats and Republicans—usually upper-middle-class and well educated—in the 1960s were described at length by Wilson and others. Clearly, the activity of these groups had a number of effects on the established parties in their states and locales, including pushing for reformist policy positions, providing candidates with substantial volunteer support, and raising issues related to the accountability of public officials. Women's clubs and women's divisions were an important means of mobilizing women voters between the 1920s and the 1960s and also had pushed the parties to create more opportunities for women within the parties and to select more women to run for public office and for political appointments.[28]

Thus, to the extent that we value organizational openness and flexibility, a positive aspect of the synergy between associationalism and partisanship is this possibility of organizational change *within* parties. This is consistent with the general point made by Elisabeth Clemens that to the extent that parties and groups are connected and in contact, they influence one another with regard to organizational structure and repertoires.[29]

A related "contextual effect"—and perhaps close to Tocqueville's point that political associations "improve" civic associations—is that a healthy party system with durable party organizations, accountability, and competitive elections helps to create a context in which joining organizations and, through them, taking part in public discourse and public controversies become more meaningful. Zisk, in her study of environmental and peace groups, says, "[L]ittle has been written about the impact of campaigns on activists and potential members,"[30] though the recent studies by Rahn and others on the contribution of elections to social capital would seem to support this point.[31] Jeremy Weinstein's recent research looks at the role of political institutions—particularly parties—in facilitating social capital formation. He finds that competitive parties and party mobilization (measured by survey responses about party contact on the American National Election Studies) are significant predictors of political engagement across states.[32] Thus, at a general level, we might expect that the more integrated into the community a party organization is, the higher the rate of political participation (in all forms) will be. In other words, if the social and associational networks of the community are tightly connected to party organizations, it is likely that more individuals will be prompted to participate in politics. On the other hand, if party organizations are weak, and the dominant social networks in the community are devoid of party activists, there is a greater likelihood that overall participation will be low.

Finally, despite the criticism directed at the national Democratic Party over the past several decades for being a "collection of special interests," it can be argued that close ties at various levels with groups of various sorts help to legitimize parties. Eldersveld's findings—that group loyalty coexists with party loyalty and that members of party "subcoalitions" see value in working through parties—suggest that group–party connections help to legitimate the party system and the representative system more generally. In a more recent study of state convention delegates, about half of the delegates said that a single issue caused them to be involved in the 1980 campaigns. This implies a direct relationship whereby individuals' interests or commitments are activated by a group, which then encourages them to connect that interest to the political system via the parties. But only a minority of delegates in organizations devoted to particular issues was motivated by that issue. For example, among Democrats active in woman's rights groups, 62.8 percent are participating because of specific issues, but only a fifth of those say that the issue is woman's rights. Thus, group membership facilitates broad political activism and expression, not merely narrow interest-based activism. This is consistent with Eldersveld's conclusion that group and party loyalty are not mutually exclusive and may even be reinforcing.[33]

The decline of social capital and the attendant consequences for civic life and political engagement are cause for concern. However, we must recognize that important intervening institutions connect civic participation to the political process. Political parties, in particular, have been and continue to be critical to the flow of information between citizens and their elected officials. Certainly, in discussions of how to build social capital—in the United States or elsewhere—we should remain cognizant of the role that parties have played in the past and of the possibilities for their role in the future.

What lessons might be drawn from this brief catalog of ways that parties and other groups (quasi-party organizations, interest groups, nonprofits, civic associations, and so on) have related to one another throughout U.S. history? One is that the development of civil society—that is, of organizations that nurture civic skills and bring citizens together to solve collective problems—should not be thought about in isolation from the development of political parties. This is particularly important if it is the case, as suggested here, that interest groups and other organizations, on the one hand, and parties, on the other, are mutually strengthening as well as—in some aspects—competitive. Moreover, the U.S. experience suggests that it is important to think about a large range of possible ways that parties and other sorts of groups and organizations interact. These range from situations of formal inclusion (e.g., unions as part of the British Labour Party), to organized groups that attempt to influence political parties (e.g., trade associations, groups that represent particular demographics such as the National Association for the Advancement of Colored People [NAACP] or

AARP [formerly known as the American Association of Retired Persons]), to groups that help to communicate party platforms to voters (e.g., the League of Women Voters). In turn, this raises questions of state regulation of associations, particularly regarding their tax status and constraints on their activities. These issues should not be considered independently of issues regarding laws establishing and governing parties and elections.

NOTES

The author is grateful for the contributions of McGee Young, who coauthored an earlier, more extensive version of this chapter (Kristi Andersen and McGee Young, "How Political Parties and Voluntary Organizations Interact in Shaping Civil Society," paper presented at the meetings of the American Political Science Association, 2000).

1. Nancy L. Rosenblum, "Primus Inter Pares: Political Parties and Civil Society," *Chicago Kent Law Review* 75, no. 2 (2000): 494; see also Nancy L. Rosenblum, "Political Parties as Membership Groups," *Columbia Law Review* 100, no. 3 (2000): 813–844.

2. The author is indebted for this phrase and much of the immediately following discussion to Elisabeth Clemens.

3. The approach here is in substantial agreement with Paul Burstein, "Interest Organizations, Political Parties, and the Study of Democratic Politics," in *Social Movements and American Political Institutions*, ed. Anne N. Costain and Andrew S. McFarland (Lanham, MD: Rowman and Littlefield, 1998) on the conceptual indistinguishability of interest groups, civic associations, and social movement organizations.

4. Burstein, "Interest Organizations," 51.

5. Robert Putnam, *Bowling Alone: The Collapse and Revival of American Community* (New York: Simon and Schuster, 2000); Theda Skocpol and Morris P. Fiorina, eds., *Civic Engagement in American Democracy* (Washington, DC: Brookings Institution, 1999); Richard M. Vallely, "Couch Potato Democracy?" *The American Prospect* (March–April 1996): 25–26.

6. Theda Skocpol, "How Americans Became Civic," in *Civic Engagement in American Democracy*, ed. Skocpol and Fiorina; Gerald Gamm and Robert D. Putnam, "Association-Building in America, 1840–1949," *Journal of Interdisciplinary History* 29, no. 3 (1999): 511–557; Peter Dobkin Hall, "Vital Signs: Organizational Population Trends and Civic Engagement in New Haven, Connecticut, 1850–1998," in *Civic Engagement in American Democracy*, ed. Theda Skocpol and Morris P. Fiorina (Washington, DC: Brookings Institution, 1999). For some of the major points in the "civic life" debates, see Putnam, *Bowling Alone*; Skocpol, "How Americans Became Civic"; Vallely, "Couch Potato Democracy?"; and Sidney Tarrow, "Making Social Science Work across Space and Time: A Critical Reflection on Robert Putnam's Making Democracy Work," *American Political Science Review* 90, no. 2 (1996): 389–397; Everett C. Ladd, "The Data Just Don't Show Erosion of America's 'Social Capital,' " *Public Perspective* 7, no. 4 (1996): 5–22.

7. Stephen A. Salmore and Barbara G. Salmore, *Candidates, Parties, and Campaigns: Electoral Politics in America* (Washington, DC: CQ Press, 1985), 92. Also see Richard F. Fenno Jr., *Home Style: House Members in Their Districts* (Boston: Little, Brown, 1978).

8. Thomas T. Spencer, "Auxiliary and Non-Party Politics: The 1936 Democratic Presidential Campaign in Ohio," *Ohio History* 90 (1981): 114–128.

9. John M Allswang, *A House for All Peoples: Ethnic Politics in Chicago, 1890–1936* (Lexington: University Press of Kentucky, 1971); Harold F. Gosnell, *Machine Politics: Chicago Model* (Chicago: University of Chicago Press, 1937).

10. Allswang, *A House for All Peoples*, chapter 8.

11. Lizabeth Cohen, *Making a New Deal: Industrial Workers in Chicago, 1919–1939* (Cambridge: Cambridge University Press, 1990), 362–363.

12. Joel Silbey, "Party Organization in Nineteenth Century America," in *Parties and Politics in American History: A Reader*, ed. L. Sandy Maisel and William G. Shade (New York: Garland, 1994), 94.

13. Paul Kleppner, *Chicago Divided: The Making of a Black Mayor* (DeKalb: North Illinois University Press, 1985), 19.

14. Jo Freeman, *A Room at a Time: How Women Entered Party Politics* (Lanham, MD: Rowman and Littlefield, 1999); James Q. Wilson, *The Amateur Democrat: Club Politics in Three Cities* (Chicago: University of Chicago Press, 1962); Alan Ware, *The Breakdown of Democratic Party Organization, 1940–1980* (Oxford: Oxford University Press, 1985).

15. Cornelius P. Cotter et al., *Party Organizations and American Politics* (New York: Praeger, 1984), 138.

16. John C. Green, "The Christian Right and the 1994 Elections: A View from the States," *PS: Political Science and Politics* 28 (1995): 5–8.

17. Jeffrey M. Berry and Deborah Schildkraut, "Citizen Groups, Political Parties, and Electoral Coalitions," in *Social Movements and American Political Institutions*, ed. Anne N. Costain and Andrew S. McFarland (Lanham, MD: Rowman and Littlefield, 1998), 141.

18. Ibid., 145.

19. Kleppner, *Chicago Divided*, 21.

20. Samuel J. Eldersveld, *Political Parties: A Behavioral Analysis* (Chicago: Rand McNally, 1964).

21. Ibid., 74–75.

22. Ibid., 86.

23. Robert W. Kweit and Mary Grisez Kweit, *The Life of the Parties: Activists in Presidential Politics*, ed. Ronald B. Rapoport, Alan A. Abramowitz, and John McGlennon (Lexington: University of Press of Kentucky, 1986).

24. Mary P. Ryan, "Civil Society as Democratic Practice: North American Cities during the Nineteenth Century," *Journal of Interdisciplinary History* 29 (1999): 578.

25. John C. Green, James L. Guth, and Clyde Wilcox, "Less Than Conquerors: The Christian Right in State Republican Parties," in *Social Movements and American Political Institutions* (Lanham, MD: Rowman and Littlefield, 1998), 134.

26. Betty H. Zisk, *The Politics of Transformation: Local Activism in the Peace and Environmental Movements* (Westport, CT: Praeger, 1992), 106.

27. Alexis de Tocqueville, *Democracy in America*, trans. Henry Reeve (New York: Knopf, 1945), 123–124.

28. Freeman, *A Room at a Time*, chapter 5.

29. Elisabeth S. Clemens, "Organizational Repertoires and Institutional Change: Women's Groups and the Transformation of American Politics, 1890–1920," in *Civic*

Engagement in American Democracy, ed. Theda Skocpol and Morris P. Fiorina (Washington, DC: Brookings Institution, 1999).

30. Zisk, *The Politics of Transformation*, 105.

31. Wendy M. Rahn, John Brehm, and Neil Carlson, "National Elections as Institutions for Generating Social Capital," in *Civic Engagement in American Democracy*, ed. Skocpol and Fiorina.

32. Jeremy M. Weinstein, "Abandoning the Polity: Political Parties and Social Capital in American Politics," paper presented at the meeting of the American Political Science Association, Atlanta, 1999.

33. John G. Francis and Robert C. Benedict, "Issue Group Activists at the Conventions," in *The Life of the Parties: Activists in Presidential Politics*, ed. Ronald B. Rapoport, Alan A. Abramowitz, and John McGlennon (Lexington: University Press of Kentucky, 1986); Eldersveld, *Political Parties*, chapter 4.

Chapter 3

Assessing Civil Society Performance: The Interface of Concept and Practice

John W. Harbeson

This chapter starts from the premise that it is for the citizens of a country and their leaders to shape models defining basic rules of the political game to suit local circumstances and belief systems. Dialogue between academe and policymakers in the area of development policy and practice has immense potential value. But it is important that this interface not be conducted in such a way as to screen out the influence of countries and peoples who are the subject of this dialogue, the less-developed countries. The chapter begins with an exposition of the difficulties underlying realization of these general principles. It then explores an unfortunate tendency in American academic discourse to undermine this principle and undervalue the concept of civil society, even in the promotion of democracy. This chapter examines selected recent American academic treatments of the subject that reduce its generic meaning to be synonymous with the design of civil society strengthening assistance by the U.S. Agency for International Development (USAID). The chapter concludes with recommendations for reforming the conceptual dialogue among academic, donor agency, and host country political actors so as to enhance the legitimation of civil society as a generic element of contemporary political theory and practice.

TOWARD A GLOBAL THEORY OF DEMOCRACY

A fundamental issue underlying this enterprise is whether and/or to what extent the concept of democracy requires not only clarification but some degree of reinvention as a precondition for assessing its impact globally in immensely diverse contexts. In the first place, it is axiomatic—even if the axiom is frequently overlooked in practice—that an empirical theory of democracy must be grounded in the experiences of democratic initiatives in *all* world regions, not just those of Western European and North American countries. The axiom implies the emergence of a truly comparative study of democratization that extends to its conceptualization as well as its practice across world regions.

The problem is that democratic *practice* globally has expanded far more rapidly and extensively since the end of the Cold War than has any broader comparative examination of basic democratic *architectures*. The obvious imperfections and infirmities of Third Wave democratic practice in many countries, when measured against a Western-evolved standard, must certainly be attributed in significant measure to the failings of the practitioners and to inhospitable socioeconomic and cultural terrains in which they have labored. They may also, however, be attributable at least in part to inertial, often somewhat hasty borrowing of available Western practices under varying degrees of external pressure at the expense of deeper quests for contextually appropriate democratic designs.

A significant risk embedded in circumstances in which democratic practice outpaces and outflanks contemporary reflection on the concept of democracy itself and important components like civil society is that weaknesses in its design and practice in a range of new and distinctive environments will be attributed to the concept itself, at least in those settings. This is particularly harmful in the case of democracy because, fundamentally, almost by definition, a government established of, by, and for the people obliges them to *define* how that government shall be designed and to adapt it to their circumstances, not just blindly take off the shelf and implement any preexisting models. Examining the quality and effectiveness of democratic institutions in a global perspective means, therefore, that inquiries into any given country's democratic performance cannot be disengaged from attentiveness to contextually inspired creativity in its design of democratic institutions. Slow, nonlinear progress in this enterprise cannot, therefore, be fairly and automatically attributed to the relevance of the concept itself in those new environments. Yet that is precisely what has begun to happen in the academic debate on civil society as a key element of the democratic process.

Thus, *participants in the democratization processes themselves are inescapably partners in the design of democratic institutions as well as the assessments of democratic performance along with academics and assessment practitioners.* In their visions of how they would develop their countries, the first postindependence generation of political leaders may have erred on the substance of those designs, but they were not wrong in insisting on incorporation of local content in those designs. At least for the last two decades, Western countries and Western-led multilateral agencies have erred in barely, if at all, lending even lip service to this imperative.

A further fundamental problem lies in a familiar conundrum underlying the whole enterprise, one that is necessary to negotiate as artfully as possible—even if escaping it altogether is probably impossible—the inseparability of normative and empirical meanings of concepts like civil society and democracy because each entails assumptions concerning the other. Western liberal political philosophy, in particular, rests on identifiable, at least potentially falsifiable empirical assumptions potentially constraining its utility in broader geographical and historical contexts. Similarly, the quest for empirical theory to undergird the study and assessment of democracy and democratization cannot be undertaken without reference to normative presuppositions enabling the observer to "recognize civil society when s/he sees it." An inquiry into democracy, which at least takes seriously the quest for theory distilled from the circumstances and constitutional designs present in *all* world regions, is most likely to mitigate the danger and the error of judging one country's performance by the experience and values of another. The more such an error occurs in the study of democratic performance, the more our inquiries become philosophically at war with the subject studied.

The foregoing perspectives on assessing democratic performance are singularly applicable to examining civil society performance and its relationship to overall processes of democratization. The reason is that the global relevance of civil society beyond its European birthplace has been intensely questioned, while the global meaning of democracy has not been similarly challenged for reasons that have not been adequately explored. In an inquiry into the conceptualization of civil society in a global context in relationship to democracy, it is necessary at least to acknowledge that democracy could be examined on the same basis.

CONCEPTUALIZING CIVIL SOCIETY

The hypothesis of this chapter is that assessment of the quality and effectiveness of civil society in newly democratizing countries has been singularly impaired by insufficient clarity concerning the concept itself. Assessments of "the effectiveness of civil society in a democratic system" are impossible, it can be argued, absent progress in addressing controversies raging over its conceptualization. Those controversies are rooted in the conundrum, just recalled, arising from the inescapable dependence of empirical and normative theory upon each other.

The recent resurgence of interest in civil society as a factor that is important, even indispensable to the progress and sustainability of democracy's Third Wave has generated an opposite and at least equal literature that seriously questions its utility for that purpose. That deep skepticism has extended to even the *possibility* that it may be susceptible to refinement as a globally relevant concept that is sensitive to a bewildering diversity of cultural and socioeconomic contexts. That issue must be addressed before dealing with equally serious doubts concerning *how* it may be possible to do so. Only after some satisfactory working, if tentative, responses to these issues have been formulated is it possible to reach the issues related to assessing how effectively, if at all, civil society has related empirically to democratization in less-developed country circumstances.

A principal objective of this chapter is to begin to try to disentangle the conceptual issues concerning civil society that stand in the way of developing bases for appraising its effectiveness with respect to democratization processes outside Western Europe. Because the controversies surrounding the global applicability of the concept have remained largely within the province of academics, this volume offers a rare and important perspective. It provides consideration, on the one hand, of how lessons gleaned from support for civil society in democratization contexts function in practice. It also includes the reflections of academics on the subject of civil society in relationship to democracy, particularly the effectiveness of civil society in relationship to democracy.

A Democratic versus a Generic Concept of Civil Society

Civil Society and the State in Africa bears some responsibility for generating the ongoing conceptual controversy.[1] On the one hand, as critics have observed, the setting for the conference from which the book emerged was the first, optimistic beginnings of post–Cold War democratization superimposed on continuing external pressures for economic liberalization in sub-Saharan Africa. Thus, the book did assert that its central hypothesis was that "civil society is a hitherto missing key to sustained political reform, legitimate states and governments, improved governance, viable state–society and state–economy relationships, and prevention of the kind of political decay that undermined new African governments a generation ago."[2]

On the other hand, its core argument was that civil society is a *generic* factor in state–society relations. Its contention was that civil society was a variable (or set of variables) whose importance in the renaissance of African political orders and processes of socioeconomic development had been underexamined.

It is at the deeper level of state reconstruction that the importance of the idea of civil society becomes apparent. At this level the issue is not the *form* of the state—for example, democracy v. authoritarianism—but the legitimacy of the state itself; not the rationalization of the forms of state and society *in the abstract* but the basic *empirical* determination of 1) the true parameters of evolving African societies, and 2) the type of states commensurate with the predominant values those societies embody.[3]

Thus, the book proposed that civil society's utility in understanding the dynamics of state–society relations was not just as a Western export that African peoples should accept in the service of their accommodation of Western styles of development but as a tool in the understanding of *any* society's interface with *whatever* state form may be extant. Indeed, the book argued that "civil society *by definition* [emphasis added] roots political values in culturally specific value systems, and is thus of singular value in *overcoming* and counteracting ethnocentrism."[4] It offered that civil society's generic functions include defining, or at least wrestling with, what a society's defining rules of the political game *should* be, that is, whatever any given society might determine that they should be.

The book envisaged a comparative study of civil society, across countries and world regions, centering on similarities and differences in terms of the structure of participation in this process, the interests and motivations juxtaposed in any particular civil society area, the manner in which civil society bridges state–society relations, the ways in which civil society processes may be institutionalized, the manner of civil society's creation and dissolution, patterns of consensus and conflict within civil society, and modes of reciprocal interaction between government and society at large. In essence, the book proposed that civil society was an *arena* defined and characterized by a society's processes of attempting to determine or shape the rules of the game by which it is to be governed.

It can be hypothesized that the appropriateness and utility of evaluating civil society's effectiveness in practice hinges on whether or not *Civil Society and the State*'s claim that civil society is a *generic* element of state–society relations can be upheld. To be useful, civil society must be successfully conceptualized, not just as those actors and organizations that espouse and play by democratic rules but as an arena in which those actors and organizations contest with others for influence in defining and shaping the political rules of the game. Unless one is an unabashed devotee of globalization of "McWorld," in Barber's terms, one must show that civil society is an arena with distinctive functions in *any* country's state–society relations and not a captive of its origins in the philosophies and social "science" of a particular corner of the globe.[5] It is an imperative of twentieth-first-century social science that it become truly grounded, conceptually as well as empirically, on insights from *all* world regions. The fundamental issue, therefore, is whether or not civil society can be fashioned as a generic, culturally neutral, analytic category that is useful for that purpose.

Civil Society and the Practice of Democracy

A fundamental problem in the contemporary controversies over civil society's conceptualization has been that its intimate association with the theory and, in at least some respects, the practice of *democratic* reform has been allowed to eclipse the deeper claim to being a generic arena within which not only societal demands for reform per se are advanced or *opposed* but the basic rules of the political game are established, shaped, and fought over. Civil society's theoretical importance in the literature of Western democratic philosophy has been appropriated as an ideal toward which external donors have urged new democracies to aspire and work with their external support. Its potential validity as a *generic* component of state–society relations has been impeached because the idealized democratic model describes so little of political practice and reality.

A multifaceted irony has resulted from the appropriation of civil society as a key dimension of democratic reform in less-developed countries. Civil society may have gained greater acceptance as a globally useful analytic category in the world of development practitioners than it has among those within the academy concerned with the politics of developing countries. At the same time, that acceptance in development practice has been within the framework of essentially unabashed promotion of a conceptualization of democracy that owes everything to European and North American experience and little or nothing to that of any other world region. The final dimension of the irony is that, at least within sub-Saharan Africa, the recipients identified by Western donors as the heralds of incipient African civil society have tended to be individuals and groups that have generally appeared to internalize Western *conceptions* of civil society, however their political *practices* may be characterized.

Although the usefulness of promoting civil society is beginning to be questioned in the world of development practice, it has enjoyed a high priority for several years. A working definition of civil society in practice, adopted by USAID, has been "those non-state organizations which are engaged in or have the potential for championing the adoption and consolidation of democratic governance reforms."[6] It recognized as civil society nongovernmental organizations (NGOs) those that "engage in public advocacy, analyze policy issues, mobilize constituencies in support of policy dialogue and, most importantly, act as agents of reforming, strengthening and broadening democratic governance."[7] USAID's concept could be read as one of support for organizations intent on achieving democratic governance rather than democratizing the *sector* itself, that is, working horizontally with organizations of *all* stripes to build a sector in which tolerance and mutual respect for advocacy of most interests become the norm. USAID's approach is perfectly reasonable except insofar as it is susceptible to interpretation as meaning that civil society is coextensive only with groups that are already democratic in structure, purposes, and behavior.

The enmeshing of civil society with the cause of democratization in developing countries has tied it to prevailing conceptualizations of democratization that have been unabashedly, if implicitly, founded on Western European and North American experience.[8] This state of affairs has appeared to be very important in influencing some academics to seriously challenge civil society's utility as an element of a less ethnocentric, globally fashioned social science. Those challenging civil society's pretensions to status as a generic component of political processes have contended that the concept (1) is perhaps irretrievably unfocused and incoherent even within Western political philosophy and European experience; (2) inherently engages in ethnocentricism in screening out non-Western expressions of civil society rather than incorporating them; and (3) imposes an idealized pluralist model, flawed even in the West, that does not relate to non-European circumstances and may even be counterproductive in them. Two of the more important, Africa-focused works mounting these critiques have been John and Jean Comaroff, eds., *Civil Society and the Political Imagination in Africa*, and Nelson Kasfir, ed., *Civil Society and Democracy in Africa*.[9]

Civil Society and Democratic Norms

Kasfir and his collaborators challenge, on both empirical and analytic grounds, the validity of a linkage between a Western democratic conception of civil society and the promotion of an equally Western conception of democracy in a variety of sub-Saharan African circumstances. The key to their argument hinges on Kasfir's interpretation of the first quote earlier from *Civil Society and the State in Africa* contending that "civil society is a hitherto missing key to sustained political reform, legitimate states and governments."[10] Kasfir asks, "Which organized representatives of social interests must be kept out to achieve these reforms?" The short answer should be, "None." But Kasfir assumes an affirmative answer. In essence, he chooses to assume that because civil society *may* be a venue for pursuing democratic governance reform, it is *synonymous* with organizations having that purpose, excluding all others. He overlooks the book's argument for a larger and more generic understanding of civil society as the arena within which nonstate actors and organizations seek to define and influence the basic rules of the political game and to hold state actors accountable to them. He overlooks the ways in which the working rules of that arena itself may or may not approximate the democratic ideal.

The same point applies to Kasfir's presumption that what he defines as the "conventional" view of civil society restricts membership to those organizations that observe a democratic ideal of "civil behavior." In fact, a generic understanding of civil society would imply a definition in functional terms as the arena wherein nonstate actors of *all* stripes contend with each other to define, establish, or shape the basic rules of the political game. Civil behavior, as democrats understand it, becomes not a defining characteristic of civil society but an objective to be pursued in reforming it.

Similarly, Kasfir questions the view that appears to limit civil society to those groups that challenge or confront the state, for example, those seeking to move authoritarian governments to become more democratic. Bayart does in fact appear to conceptualize civil society in that way, as "society in its relation with the state . . . in so far as it is in confrontation with the state."[11] But that is neither a necessary nor even a prevalent view. Walzer's definition avoids the problem by positioning civil society as "the space of uncoerced human association and also the set of relational networks—formed for the sake of family, faith, interest and ideology" in the space between the government and the family.[12] A narrower, more explicitly political conception of civil society as advocated in this chapter can center on the activities envisaged in Walzer's definition when and to the extent that such groups seek to influence the basic rules of the political game.

Finally, Kasfir questions the possibility and also desirability of civil society autonomy vis-à-vis both society-at-large and the government. He argues that civil society organizations can scarcely be autonomous of the socioeconomic and cultural interests within the society that they purport to represent. Similarly, he both raises the possibility of civil society autonomy from governments that seek aggressively to limit it and suggests that too much autonomy might actually endanger or presume the weakness of governments on which they are ultimately dependent. Conceding that some formulations of civil society may be of questionable realism for the reasons that Kasfir suggests, the real point here is less one of autonomy and more of identity and capacity. A generic understanding of civil society would recognize that nonstate actors and organizations exercise a distinctive role in seeking to influence the basic rules of the political game and require the capacity to be able to do so. Somewhat analogous to political parties, nonstate actors require the capacity to aggregate and articulate the political agendas of the interests that they represent and to resist suppression or co-optation by governments.

In short, he attacks the unrealism of a prescriptive, pro-democratic definition of civil society, but he tends to assume that those he criticizes *define* civil society in practice as synonymous with their normative prescriptions for it, thereby excluding from membership all groups that do not conform to those prescriptions. It would appear to be clearly possible, however, to distinguish normative prescriptions for civil society from a generic and empirical definition of civil society as an arena in which nonstate actors contend within each other to influence the basic rules of the political game.

Generic Civil Society or Concept with No Fixed Meaning

John and Jean Comaroff pose a deeper challenge to the proposition that a generic, useful, empirically assessable concept can be extracted from the history of the idea in political philosophy and in practice. They are less concerned with its capture and co-optation by the promotion of democratization in practice than what they consider the idea's intrinsic incoherence. "The Idea of civil society has proven impossibly difficult to pin down," the Comaroffs complain.[13] In their view, civil society—whatever it is—lacks even stable ontological status. "Is it a social domain? A type of institution or practice? A normative condition? A moral ideal?" they ask. Lacking intrinsic, fixed, or coherent meaning, they conceive civil society as a kind of empty vessel into which changing historical and varied cultural content is emptied—"an immanent construct whose materiality exists only to the extent that it is named, objectified, and sought after."[14]

The Comaroffs and their collaborators suggest, however, that in its contemporary iteration, civil society is diminished "by the burden of its parochial roots in the European Enlightenment." In that form and in African circumstances, they perceive civil society to be intrinsically self-contradictory—privileging some peoples and excluding others, "hybridizing and compromising identities," and substituting "future-oriented memory" for historical realities, while purporting to represent political empowerment, inclusiveness, and validation.[15] These very characteristics of civil society, they conclude, embody simultaneously not just the foregoing liabilities but its power and possibilities—it may yet speak to and empower the political imagination and ultimately inspire a generation of truly African conceptions of civil society.

Does the Comaroffs' critique of the "Idea" of civil society invalidate it as a distinct and generic factor in state-society relations? The key to a negative answer lies in what they do *not* question. In a word, they do not challenge the possibility of comparative politics, the identification of functions, roles, and processes common to political orders across cultures and historical periods. The danger to which their analysis points lies in labeling the processes by which nonstate actors compete to influence the basic political rules of the game with such a culturally and historical freighted term as civil society.

Moreover, their analysis impeaches not the importance of those processes but inequities in the terms, conditions, and qualifications for participation in them growing out of ethnocentric and contradictory superimposition of one culture's ideals on the realities of another. But the case for a generic understanding of civil society advanced here treats the process of nonstate actors' contestation to influence the basic rules of the political game as the given, the terms and conditions of participation as the variable. *How and on what terms* the contestation takes place are a major dimension of what the contestation is all about.

TOWARD ASSESSING CIVIL SOCIETY EFFECTIVENESS

In the area of democracy promotion, civil society has been perhaps the most profoundly contested conceptually, as summarized in the preceding section. The issue then becomes what impact, if any, the controversy at the conceptual level should have upon the empirical assessment of civil society effectiveness.

The conclusion of the preceding section was that civil society can be rescued from its detractors by positing it as a generic element of state–society relations centered on nonstate actors' contestation to influence the basic rules of the political game. The critics tend to interpret empirical promotion of civil society in less-developed countries by implicitly reading into it a working presumption that the boundaries of civil society are synonymous with those actors who promote a *democratic* civil society and who themselves behave *democratically*. They respond by surveying the range of societal actors and associations outside civil society, so defined, and implicitly accusing external promoters of civil society of ethnocentrism, a neocolonial mentality, and engaging in an incoherent, illogical, and futile exercise. As suggested in the preceding section, the critics falsely interpret civil society programming and, thus, level charges that are very wide of the mark. Nevertheless, the critics identify some important areas for improved assessment of civil society effectiveness. Stated somewhat differently, the critics provide answers to the question of "effectiveness with respect to what?" that the promotion and assessment of civil society should take seriously.

First, civil society promotion should focus more explicitly on civil society as a *sector* of democracy-promoting actors and organizations in isolation as it has been interpreted as doing to date. The civil society sector should be defined to include *all* organizations and actors, regardless of political orientation, to the extent that they seek to influence the basic rules of the political game. While it is natural and appropriate that donors seek to work through actors and organizations committed to democratization, support for and assessment of their effectiveness should center more *horizontally* on coaxing nonstate actors and organizations of other persuasions and divergent interests to contend with each other over the basic rules of the political game in peaceful, tolerant ways that are the hallmark of democracy, even though they may not be themselves internally democratic and have agendas and interests other than democracy. While civil society is not exclusively a liberal project, even within Western political philosophy, the criticism of civil society promotion is not that it promotes democracy but that it excludes actors and organizations other than those that specifically focus on democracy promotion.

Second, civil society promotion should focus on dialogue between actors and nonstate organizations concerning the basic rules of the political game; that is, they should focus horizontally on dialogue with each other as well as vertically with the government on these questions. There is no harm in such a dialogue's duplicating what transpires in political society, that is, among those formally engaged in politics via political parties, legislatures, and cabinets. But it might extend to informal rules of the game beyond the scope of constitutional or legislative provisions, for example, what it should mean for nonstate organizations to be inclusive and interact with each other democratically. These rules also focus on developing and promoting alternative dispute resolution processes, especially with respect to conflicts between their members. The emphasis here should be on process first, rather than substance; on procedural democracy, even if the outcomes of such dialogues do not entirely accord with Western norms.

Third, emphasis on the horizontal dialogue among civil society actors might center on confidence-building measures to increase trust among them, especially between more and less powerful actors in order to strengthen norms of inclusiveness.

Fourth, the agenda of civil society *sector* strengthening might focus on accountability issues in several different ways. It might include initiatives to promote accountability by those in power to the *sector as a whole*, not just to individual organizations in respect of their particular interests. While some observers may be overly concerned about a civil society sector so powerful that it might threaten the state or otherwise run amok, civil society sector strengthening might include measures to promote checks and balances, transparency, and accountability within the sector itself.

CONCLUSION

Since its revival over the last decade, civil society has been perhaps the most controversial element of democracy promotion. The activities of civil society are central to theories of democratization within academe as they have been to external support for democratization. But among academics, the prevailing conceptualization of civil society has been under attack for its allegedly exclusionary, ethnocentric, illiberal, even neocolonial implications. This chapter has suggested that these attacks are centered on a conception of civil society attributed to its advocates under which the civil society sector is presumed to include only those nonstate actors and organizations that actively espouse democracy and democratization. It suggests that this is not a necessary, or perhaps even a prevalent conceptualization among civil society's defenders: that a more generic conceptualization is both possible and intended by at least some of its advocates. This chapter has suggested, however, that it is important for the effectiveness of civil society, in fact, to be inclusive of *all* nonstate actors and organizations to the extent that they engage in attempting to influence the basic rules of the political game. It concludes that the effectiveness of civil society should include a focus on civil society as a *sector*, its inclusiveness, the quality of democratic dialogue among its members, progress in building interorganizational trust and respect, and its effectiveness in promoting accountability both of government and within its own ranks.

NOTES

1. John W. Harbeson, Donald Rothchild, and Naomi Chazan, eds., *Civil Society and the State in Africa* (Boulder, CO: Lynne Rienner, 1994).

2. Ibid., 2.

3. Ibid., 9.

4. Ibid., 27.

5. Benjamin R. Barber, *Jihad v. McWorld: How Globalism and Tribalism Are Reshaping the World* (New York: Ballantine Books, 1996).

6. United States Agency for International Development (USAID), *Civil Society and Democratic Reform: Strategic Approaches for International Donors* (Washington, DC: USAID, 1995), 3. USAID is currently in the process of a new review of its civil society programming. It is worth observing that gaining initial support for civil society programming did not come entirely from an agency accustomed to working with African governments and Western NGOs but less so with developing *African* NGOs.

7. Harbeson, Rothchild, and Chazan, *Civil Society*, 4.

8. Robert Dahl's *Polyarchy: Participation and Opposition* (New Haven, CT: Yale University Press, 1971) defined a minimalist, empirically grounded conceptualization of democracy centered on electoral processes. The most influential works on democratic transitions appeared implicitly to have followed Dahl's teaching. These include Samuel Huntington, *The Third Wave: Democratization in the Late Twentieth Century* (Norman: University of Oklahoma Press, 1991); Guillermo O'Donnell and Philippe Schmitter, *Transitions from Authoritarian Rule: Tentative Conclusions about Uncertain Democracies* (Baltimore: Johns Hopkins University Press, 1986); Juan D. Linz and Alfred Stepan, *Problems of Democratic Transition and Consolidation: Southern Europe, South America, and Post-Communist Europe* (Baltimore: Johns Hopkins University Press, 1996).

9. John L. and Jean Comaroff, eds., *Civil Society and the Political Imagination in*

Africa (Chicago: University of Chicago Press, 1999); Nelson Kasfir, ed., *Civil Society and Democracy in Africa: Critical Perspectives* (London: Frank Cass, 1998).

10. Harbeson, Rothchild, and Chazan, *Civil Society*, 2.

11. Jean-Francois Bayart, "Civil Society in Africa," in *Political Domination in Africa: Reflections on the Limits of Power*, ed. Patrick Chabal (Cambridge: Cambridge University Press, 1986), 112.

12. Michael Walzer, "The Idea of Civil Society: A Path to Social Reconstruction," *Dissent* 38, no. 2 (Spring 1991): 293.

13. Comaroff and Comaroff, *Civil Society*, 5.

14. Ibid., 6.

15. Ibid., 5.

Chapter 4

Wide but Shallow: Popular Support for Democracy in Africa

Michael Bratton

In his pocket guide to democracy, Dahl asks a disturbing question: "Might what is called 'democracy' become both broader in reach and shallower in depth, extending to more and more countries as its democratic qualities grow ever more feeble?"[1] As Przeworski and colleagues have reminded us, the consolidation of democracy cannot be depicted by mere quantities such as the number of countries that hold elections or the span of years that elected governments survive.[2] At heart, regime consolidation involves qualitative change within political institutions and political cultures, processes that Diamond has described as democratic deepening.[3] In different ways, all of these authors wonder whether the global expansion of the formal institutions of political competition, elections, and popular sovereignty is simply a veneer. Beneath the surface, are democratic preferences, procedures, and habits actually taking root?

In addressing this question, this chapter draws on a grand tradition of comparative research on mass attitudes to democracy and extends it into uncharted territory. It applies and adapts to sub-Saharan Africa, approaches used in Norris' "world-wide audit of support for representative democracy at the end of the twentieth century."[4] Via the test case of African public opinion, it is possible to observe how broadly and deeply popular attachments to democracy have spread under conditions that are among the least propitious in the world. Preliminary results from a large-scale, systematic survey research project, known as the Afrobarometer,[5] show that impressively large proportions of people in Africa's new multiparty regimes say that they support democracy. They especially value the political liberalization that has recently occurred in their countries, especially when comparing present political arrangements with previous ancien régimes. But, for many reasons analyzed below, their support is partial, formative, dispersed, and conditional. In short, while expressed support for democracy in Africa may be wide, it is also shallow.

This argument is made with reference to six claims, each supported with survey and other evidence:

1. Popular conceptions of democracy are tractable;
2. Enclaves of nondemocratic sentiment remain;
3. Rejection of authoritarian alternatives does not amount to support for democracy;
4. Democratization is far from complete;
5. Support for democracy is dispersed; and
6. Liberalization does not amount to democratization.

DEMOCRACY ENJOYS A WIDE BASE OF POPULAR SUPPORT

First, the good news: democracy enjoys a wide base of popular support in those parts of Africa that have recently undergone electoral transitions. The Afrobarometer asks a standard question about support for democracy using wording often employed to track such commitments. Because the merits of this question are debatable, it is worth quoting in full. It asks, "Which of these three statements is closest to your own opinion? A. Democracy is preferable to any other form of government. B. In certain situations, a non-democratic government can be preferable. C. To people like me, it doesn't matter what form of government we have." This question has been asked in similar form in the Eurobarometer, the Latinobarometer, and the World Values Survey, thus inviting broad cross-national and cross-continental comparisons.[6]

By this measure, two out of three citizens (69 percent) in twelve African countries say that they prefer democracy to other forms of government (see Table 4.1, row 1). This distribution marks a solid base of pro-democracy sentiment in posttransition regimes on a continent that is usually held to lag behind the rest of the world in indicators of democracy and development. The mean score on support for democracy for the Afrobarometer countries falls squarely between the mean scores for Western Europe (82 percent in the 1990s) and Latin America (59 percent in 2000).[7] As in Latin America, however, cross-country variance in country scores is wider than in Western Europe, suggesting an African region whose populations have yet to fully agree about the virtues of democracy.[8]

Nevertheless, a majority of citizens expresses support for democracy in eleven out of twelve Afrobarometer countries, with the residents of Tanzania, Botswana, and Nigeria being the most supportive (above 80 percent). Tanzania's high score is raised by the Zanzibar islands, where fraud and violence in recent elections have apparently served only to strengthen the population's preference for (real) democracy.[9] Expectations for democracy in Nigeria, which were meas-

Table 4.1
Popular Attitudes to Democracy, Selected African Countries, 1999–2001 (percentages of national samples, including "don't knows")

	Bot	Gha	Les	Mwi	Mal	Nam	Nig	Saf	Tan	Uga	Zam	Zim	AFRO
SUPPORT FOR DEMOCRACY													
"Democracy is preferable to any other kind of government."	83	77	39	66	60	57	81	60	84	80	74	71	69
"In certain situations, a non-democratic government can be preferable."	7	9	11	22	16	12	9	13	12	8	9	11	12
"For someone like me, it doesn't matter what form of government we have." (percentage choosing these options)	6	15	23	11	24	12	10	21	5	8	12	13	13
UNDERSTANDINGS OF DEMOCRACY													
"What, if anything, do you understand by the word 'democracy'?" (percentage able to offer a meaning)	68	74	51	92	70	66	94	90	83	69	74	70	77
(percentage saying civil and political liberties)	24	37	15	68	21	46	28	49	48	25	56	24	36
SATISFACTION WITH DEMOCRACY													
"Overall, how satisfied are you with the way democracy works in [your country]?" (percentage saying "fairly" or "very" satisfied)	75	54	38	57	60	63	84	52	70	62	58	18	58
REJECTION OF AUTHORITARIAN RULE													
Military rule.	85	88	69	82	70	58	90	75	96	89	94	79	81
One-man rule.	86	87	69	87	73	56	84	67	92	84	89	78	79
One-party state.	78	78	51	77	74	63	88	56	60	53	80	74	69
Traditional leaders.	74	71	59	71	47	54	74*	64	88	80	80	63	69
Reject authoritarian rule (all 4 alternatives) (percentage disapproving these forms of rule)	65	56	37	52	35	39	61*	40	52	43	72	52	51
EXTENT OF DEMOCRACY (Our country is)													
"A full democracy."	46	(69**	24	34	24	29	17	26	19	21	24	9	23
"A democracy, but with minor problems."	36	)	13	28	21	41	33	34	35	27	38	18	27
"A democracy, but with major problems."	8	13	13	23	37	15	46	24	28	27	20	17	21
"Not a democracy." (percentage choosing these options)	5	12	17	12	6	3	1	8	8	5	7	38	10

*In Nigeria, rejection of traditional rule is measured as percentage of respondents rating traditional rule between 1 and 5 on a scale of 1 to 10.

**This question was asked only in binary form in Ghana (i.e., "In your opinion, is Ghana today a democracy or not a democracy?").

ured less than a year after a historic founding election, may be inflated by transition euphoria.[10] Despite these reservations, however, the form of government commonly called democracy clearly attracts wide support in various sub-Saharan African countries.

The Africans whom we interviewed also claim to understand the meaning of democracy. Three out of four survey respondents (77 percent) can venture a definition of the term, with the remainder saying that they "don't know" or have "never heard of democracy" (see Table 4.1, row 2). Perhaps unexpectedly, fully one-third offers universal and liberal definitions, associating democracy with civil liberties (28 percent), notably, freedom of expression and political rights (8 percent), that is, the right to participate in competitive elections.[11] Liberal notions of democracy are especially common in Malawi and Zambia (and above average in South Africa, Namibia, and Ghana), perhaps reflecting the extent to which the old regimes in these countries stifled dissent and denied real choices at the polls.

Support for democracy in the abstract is also accompanied by satisfaction with democracy in practice, though at reduced levels (Table 4.1, row 3). Asked, "How satisfied are you with the way democracy works in [your country]?" a slight majority gives a positive response, averaging 58 percent across twelve countries. Satisfaction is again high in Nigeria and Tanzania, in part for the idiosyncratic reasons already discussed. The encouraging results from Botswana (75 percent satisfied) probably represent a mature public contentment with the capable developmental performance of elected governments over almost forty years. Zimbabwe lies at the other end of the scale: barely 18 percent of respondents say that they were satisfied with democracy, clearly revealing the extent to which the performance of elected government in that country is now deemed to have fallen short of expectations.

The Zimbabwe case casts light on the quality and depth of democratic commitments in African countries. There is striking dissonance in Zimbabwe between support for democracy (71 percent) and satisfaction with democracy (18 percent). This gap suggests that citizens can demand democracy even when they are not being supplied with it. Although democracy does not presently work well as an instrument for fulfilling current needs, people can remain intrinsically attached to it as a preferred form of government. More than half of all Zimbabweans feel this way (59 percent). Yet the proportion of "dissatisfied democrats" (whom Norris calls "critical citizens"[12]) is far lower for all twelve African countries in our sample (19 percent) (see Table 4.2). Because other elected regimes in Africa have not sunk as far as Zimbabwe into political and economic crisis, the extent of intrinsic citizen attachments to democracy has not been fully tested and revealed in these other places. Overall, one in five Africans interviewed is willing to extend support to democracy, even while being dissatisfied with its results. This suggests that there is a reservoir of popular goodwill toward democratically organized regimes that has yet to be fully tapped.

We turn now to the bad news. Any generalizations about widespread, liberal,

Table 4.2
Cross-Tabulation of Support for, and Satisfaction with, Democracy (percentage of respondents in 12 African countries, n = 18,526*)

| | | Satisfied with Democracy | |
		Yes	No
Support Democracy	Yes	57% satisfied democrats	19% dissatisfied democrats
	No	12% satisfied nondemocrats	12% dissatisfied nondemocrats

*Excludes "don't knows."

and intrinsic forms of support for democracy must be qualified in several important respects. When taken together, the following reservations point to the incompleteness of expressed popular commitments to democracy in Africa.

POPULAR CONCEPTIONS OF DEMOCRACY ARE TRACTABLE

Liberal democrats may welcome the discovery that many Africans seem to define democracy in terms of universal human rights. But, since the unfamiliar notion of a popular African liberalism runs against the grain of the literature on political culture on the continent,[13] it requires further interrogation. Attitudes about democracy that individuals venture in a public opinion survey may be half-formed, self-censored, or readily subject to change. The Afrobarometer data already contain several items of counterevidence that demonstrate the popularity of contending versions of democracy and the fragility of any apparent liberalism.

First, while civil and political liberties may be the most common popular way of thinking about democracy overall, the survey sample contains considerable cross-country variation. In the twelve countries surveyed, this liberal definition ranked first in only nine. In Nigeria and Lesotho, people were more likely to define democracy as "government by, for, and of the people," and in Botswana, people were equally likely to opt for this definition as for one based on individual rights. When transferred to African contexts, the meaning of Lincoln's Gettysburg definition is open to interpretation. Since it correlates with respondents' level of education, it may be a learned response absorbed through formal schooling.[14] Alternatively, "government by, for, and of the people" may reflect more collectivist interpretations of democracy that run counter to standard liberal versions. Such meanings are certainly more consistent with Jerry Rawlings' populist cry of "power to the people" or Julius Nyerere's communitarian recollections of "talking until we agree."[15]

Second, citizens attach distinctive, homegrown meanings to democracy in certain countries. Although indigenous conceptions are invoked less frequently than universal rights, they nevertheless impart local flavor to popular definitions. In Uganda, democracy is seen as a regime of "peace and unity" (14 percent, third-ranked meaning) in a context where genocidal conflicts were the order of an earlier day. In South Africa, where democracy is associated with "equality and justice" (13 percent, second-ranked meaning), people look to the new regime as an antidote to apartheid and a device to rid the country of humiliating discriminations. In Mali, respondents draw on traditional values when reading democracy as "mutual respect" (4.2 percent, fifth-ranked meaning), a norm that smoothes the way to discussion, decision making, and peace building at the community level.

Thus, the meaning of democracy is tractable. It can be bent to mean what people want it to mean. Because the term has positive moral connotations, it can be stretched to cover a wide range of preferred political systems.[16] Thus, some Afrobarometer survey respondents regard democracy vaguely as the obverse image of the prior political order, while others use the term to portray the imagined advantages of a precolonial past. We also suspect that alongside those "democrats" who are attached to the new regime because of a normative acceptance of principles, others simply recognize pragmatically that, in a post–Cold War world, there is no feasible alternative.[17] To the extent that democracy can mean all things to all people, however, it risks losing a core identity of its own. Nor is it clear whether ideals like peace, unity, and equality can be easily reconciled with expressed desires for individual liberties. If the former values ever take precedence, the type of democracy preferred in Africa could well become a nonliberal one.

Finally, mass political attitudes are not fixed and can be easily molded. The Afrobarometer instrument contains a small test of the effects of question wording on the meanings attached to democracy. We first ask, in completely open-ended fashion, "What, if anything, do you understand by the word 'democracy'?" Respondents are free to say anything that comes to mind, their answers are recorded verbatim, and coding of responses takes place after the fact. This inductive approach gives rise to the distribution of responses reported in Table 4.1 (row 2) in which civil and political liberties rank first overall. We follow up with a closed-ended question that asks respondents to rate the "importance" of certain given attributes "in order for a society to be called democratic," ranging from political procedures like "the majority rules" to substantive outcomes like "everyone enjoys basic necessities like shelter, food, and water." When the question is posed this way, people continue to associate democracy with civil and political liberties; for example, strong majorities think that "freedom to criticize the government" (75 percent) and "regular elections" (74 percent) are important in a democratic society. But even larger majorities associate a democratic society with "jobs for everyone" (86 percent) and "equal access to education" (88 percent).

In principle, one sets greater store by the results of open-ended questions than of structured questions that can lead respondents toward predetermined answers. Nevertheless, when primed to think in terms of the delivery of socioeconomic goods (jobs, education, etc.), interviewees clearly broaden their initial conception of democracy to include positive (social and economic) as well as negative (civil and political) rights. This pattern of responses is consistent across all twelve countries. Thus, while many Africans seem prone to think of democracy first as a set of freedoms (like the protection of rights and voting in elections), they may also be easily persuaded that socioeconomic development is actually more important than political liberty.

ENCLAVES OF NONDEMOCRATIC SENTIMENT REMAIN

Pro-democratic sentiments have not won the day in all the countries in the Afrobarometer sample. For example, the survey conducted in Lesotho in August 2000 revealed that only a minority of the electorate (39 percent) prefers democracy (see Table 4.1, row 1). Instead, Basotho profess considerable cynicism and confusion about the sustainability of various political arrangements for their country, with one-quarter saying that the form of government "doesn't matter" and a further one-quarter (24 percent, higher than in any other country) saying that they "don't know" their own regime preferences. Such detachment is directly traceable to the country's disputed general election of May 1998, in which opposition forces rejected the ruling party's victory, and a government was installed by armed South African intervention.[18] These chaotic events created an atmosphere of instability and uncertainty that is reflected in a profile of public opinion that is clearly skeptical of democracy.

In other places, respondents actively express support for authoritarian alternatives. For example, more than one out of five Malawians (22 percent) consider that "in certain situations, a non-democratic government can be preferable." This appears to be a considered opinion since it coexists with one of the highest levels of democratic literacy in the sample (92 percent of Malawians, second only to Nigerians, can offer a meaning for democracy). These sentiments are most prevalent in Malawi's Central Region, the homeland and political base of Dr. Hastings Kamuzu Banda, the country's former strongman. In South Africa, willingness to entertain authoritarian alternatives is also above average; in this case, it is significantly concentrated among whites.[19] In both these countries, support for nondemocratic alternatives appears to be an expression of regret for an old regime among persons who previously possessed—but who have now lost—access to the levers and spoils of power.

Both political disengagement and authoritarian nostalgia coexist in yet other countries. In Mali, almost one-quarter of its largely rural and poorly educated population withdraws from tendering an opinion when asked to compare political regimes. A further 16 percent flirts with the idea of a nondemocratic alternative, perhaps remembering the way that a transitional military government under Amadou Toumani Touré served as midwife to the birth of a democratic regime in 1991–1992. In Namibia, equal proportions are disengaged from evaluating regime options and tempted by nondemocratic alternatives (and many others "don't know"), leading to a well-below-average level of popular support for democracy. In all these places, though each for different reasons, new democratic regimes remain at risk for want of more wholehearted popular commitments.

REJECTION OF AUTHORITARIAN ALTERNATIVES DOES NOT AMOUNT TO SUPPORT FOR DEMOCRACY

One of the shortcomings of transitions to democracy in Africa during the 1990s was that political protesters knew what they were against but did not have a clear vision of what they were for. They were against dictatorship, with all its attendant repression, mismanagement, and corruption. They said they were for democracy, but more as a slogan than as a fully comprehended institutional system for dividing and balancing power and for demanding accountability. In fact, people seemed ready to accept political "change," however defined, provided it led them away from the political status quo, which had long been deemed unacceptable. As such, mass movements for political transition were generally "antiauthoritarian" rather than specifically "pro-democratic."

The Afrobarometer provides evidence that this tendency persists (Table 4.1, row 4). Respondents were asked whether they approved of various ways in which their country could be "governed differently." These alternatives included military rule, one-man rule, one-party rule, and traditional rule "by kings, chiefs, . . . [or] a council of traditional elders."

Importantly, more people reject authoritarian alternatives than express support for democracy. Military rule is highly unpopular (repudiated by 81 percent of all Africans interviewed), closely followed by one-man rule (disavowed by 79 percent).[20] Several decades after political independence, citizens in many African countries appear to have arrived at the conclusion that government by military or civilian strongmen is no longer tolerable. Popular rejection of soldiers as governors is most pervasive in Tanzania, a country that has never suffered a successful military coup. But it is also widespread in Nigeria and Ghana, where the army has repeatedly wrested control of government from civilians. In all these countries, antimilitary sentiment is more widespread than support for democracy.

Authoritarian temptations vary by country. One-man rule remains a viable popular option in only one place in our sample: Namibia, where Sam Nujoma has stamped his personal authority on the political regime by pushing through a constitutional amendment to allow himself a third presidential term. Whereas only a bare majority opposes one-man rule in Namibia (56 percent), an overwhelming majority does so in Zambia (89 percent), where Frederick Chiluba decided to forgo his own bid for a third term in the face of resistance in Parliament, in his own party, and from civil society. If nothing else, these contrasting examples suggest that incumbents take public opinion into account when judging the prospects for clinging to power.

An institutionalized one-party regime retains greater appeal in Africa than a personal, one-man show. In three countries, citizens barely reject single-party government: Lesotho (51 percent), Uganda (53 percent), and South Africa (56 percent). This alternative regime remains attractive in Lesotho and Uganda because multiparty competition in these places is presumed to have given rise to political violence, against which single-party rule seems to promise greater stability. Perhaps South Africans do not rule out one-party government because this system comes close to what they already have; the African National Congress (ANC), the main vehicle of the country's democratic transition, retains overwhelming popular support within a dominant party system.[21]

Lastly, some Africans remain enamored of traditional forms of government. In Mali, respondents were equally split on whether government by a council of elders would be an acceptable form of contemporary governance. This result raises the question as to whether the exercise of hereditary authority by older male community leaders is seen as compatible with democracy. If accompanied by "mutual respect," some Malians apparently think that democracy and patrimonialism can be reconciled. Tanzanians seem to disagree; 88 percent reject rule by chiefs or headmen, no doubt because a one-party government has systematically undermined the powers and challenged the legitimacy of traditional leaders. The contrasting cases of Mali and Tanzania help to highlight the fact that, in the popular imagination, traditional rule and one-party rule remain the most tenable alternatives to multiparty electoral democracy in Africa.

To reveal the depth of democratic commitments, let us examine the proportion of citizens who reject all authoritarian alternatives.[22] The Afrobarometer shows that barely half the respondents across twelve countries reject all four alternatives presented above (i.e., military, one-man, one-party, and traditional rule). Some 66 percent reject two alternatives, and some 62 percent reject three; but only 51 percent consistently reject all four.[23] In other words, about half of all Africans interviewed, including many of those who say that democracy is "always preferable," retain residual attachments to nondemocratic systems.

The summary indicator of "rejection of authoritarian rule" divides African countries into three groups (see Table 4.1, row 4). In the first group, in which democratic attachments are deepest, more than six out of ten citizens completely reject all authoritarian alternatives; countries in this group include Zambia (72 percent), Botswana (65 percent), and Nigeria (61 percent). In a regime popularity contest, citizens in these countries seem to be fairly well wedded to democracy. The second group contains countries in which only slim majorities eschew all authoritarian temptations; included here are Ghana (56 percent) and Malawi,

Table 4.3

Cross-Tabulation of Support for Democracy and Rejection of Authoritarianism (percentage of respondents in 12 African countries, n = 18,554*)

		Reject Authoritarianism	
		Yes	No
Support Democracy	Yes	43% committed democrats	32% proto-democrats
	No	9% proto-nondemocrats	15% committed nondemocrats

*Excludes "don't knows."

Tanzania, and Zimbabwe (all 52 percent). The populations of these countries could go either way if faced with a tough choice between democracy and some form of authoritarian rule. The third and largest group contains five countries that lack a majority of convinced antiauthoritarians: Uganda (43 percent), South Africa (40 percent), Namibia (39 percent), Lesotho (37 percent), and Mali (35 percent). Other things being equal, these latter countries would appear to be the places where the greatest challenges persist in building popular commitment to democracy.

If (negative) rejection of authoritarian rule were evolving into (positive) support for democracy, we would expect these popular sentiments to be strongly correlated. Although the relationships run in the predicted direction and are statistically significant, the correlations are not particularly strong.[24] These results suggest that African opposition to dictatorship has yet to fully deepen into an unshakable commitment to democracy. Indeed, only a minority of the people whom we interviewed (43 percent) can be described as "committed democrats" (see Table 4.3) in that they consistently say that they both support democracy and reject all four authoritarian alternatives. Others express discordant views, simultaneously saying that they support democracy and harboring nostalgic feelings for more forceful forms of rule. This group, who at best are "protodemocrats," constitutes almost one-third (32 percent) of all survey respondents.

Because popular rejection of authoritarian rule is incomplete, sober assessments are warranted about the depth of democratic attachments in sub-Saharan Africa. Not only is support for democracy apparently shallow, but even the degree of antiauthoritarianism can be easily overstated.

DEMOCRATIZATION IS FAR FROM COMPLETE

Africans may still be engaged in political learning, but they already recognize that the versions of democracy offered by their own leaders are incomplete. To tap the extent of democracy, the surveys asked whether each respondents' country was "a full democracy," "a democracy, but with minor problems," "a democracy, but with major problems," or "not a democracy" at all. The distribution of responses by country is shown in Table 4.1 (row 5).

By this measure, the survey respondents have rather realistic impressions of recent political progress. Overall, less than a quarter (23 percent) are willing to venture that the regime in their country has consolidated itself into a full-fledged democracy. Whereas almost half of all Botswana (46 percent) consider democratization to be complete, very few Zimbabweans do (9 percent). Indeed, almost two out of five (38 percent) think that the current regime is not a democracy at all.

In between these extremes, the largest group of respondents (48 percent) recognizes that African neodemocracies are partial and incipient. The electoral regimes that have emerged from founding and second elections in Africa are beset by the challenge of constructing the multiple political institutions required in a functioning democracy. Taking a hardheaded look at the national political context, some 21 percent of all respondents think that they live in a democracy facing "major" problems of regime consolidation. Nigerians (46 percent) recognize more frequently than other Africans the enormous challenges of governing multicultural societies with untested democratic institutions. But reflecting a political optimism detected elsewhere in the surveys, even more citizens—some 27 percent overall—think that the problems faced by their democracy are "minor" and therefore, presumably, resolvable. By this criterion, Namibians are the most optimistic of all.

SUPPORT FOR DEMOCRACY IS DISPERSED

Of all the popular political attitudes considered here, support for democracy is the most difficult to explain. Statistically speaking, one cannot account for much of its variance using demographic indicators or other attitudinal predictors. Democratic commitments are elusive precisely because they are not concentrated among a few distinctive social segments or opinion leaders. Instead, they are widespread, being broadly distributed across a variety of demographic and opinion groups.

One may be tempted to conclude that support for democracy is therefore "diffuse," but this runs the risk of implying, as David Easton once did, that support for democracy is deeply rooted, having been absorbed, like mother's milk, as part of a population's shared socialization experience during childhood.[25] But, in new democracies, citizens are unlikely to possess a reservoir of favorable affective dispositions arising from a lifetime of exposure to democratic norms. Since democratization is a novel experience in these countries, how could such formative indoctrination have taken place? Thus, to repeat the theme of this chapter, the widespread popular support for democracy that we have discovered in Africa is also recent, tentative, and shallow.

Instead of bestowing "diffuse support" on reformed political regimes, African citizens are highly pragmatic: they fall back on performance-based judgments of what democracy actually does for them. Thus, there is a counterpart to the expectation that attitudes of support for democracy will be so dispersed as to be difficult to model statistically: attitudes toward the performance of new regimes—such as satisfaction with the way that democracy actually works—will be much easier to predict. Both these expectations are now tested using ordinary least squares regression models. The presentation is summarized in Table 4.4 and intentionally kept brief for the general reader. Specialists who wish to examine the models more closely or explore other lines of analysis may refer to the Appendix, which describes how all dependent and explanatory variables are measured.

As Table 4.4 confirms, support for democracy is hard to explain. An array of nineteen explanatory variables accounts for only 7 percent of the variance (adjusted R square = .073) in support for democracy across twelve African countries. The model does help, however, to discern the origins of popular democratic support by distinguishing explanatory factors that are statistically significant (highlighted in Table 4.4).[26] At the risk of simplification, just three findings are noted. First, support for democracy is not explained by demographic factors because it is spread across all social groups regardless of gender, age, education, and residential location (urban or rural). In other words, Afrobarometer surveys unearth no evidence of any sociological segment that consistently opposes democracy.

Second, economic factors are somewhat more important in explaining support for democracy. The higher an individual's assessment of "overall government performance" (measured on an index that includes its performance at managing jobs, prices, crime, health, and education [see Appendix]), the more likely he or she is to also support democracy. The more that people support economic structural adjustment (measured on an index that includes support for policies of market pricing, user fees, civil service reform, and privatization), the more likely they are to also support democracy.[27] Third, political factors nevertheless carry most of the burden in explaining support for democracy. Some of these factors refer to the political psychology of citizens, such as their sense of personal political efficacy, whether they are interested in politics, and whether they feel like winners (i.e., if their party won the last election). Other political factors refer to the political performance of the new regime, especially whether it is seen as being responsive to all citizens and whether it has delivered political goods like free speech, freedom of association, and a choice of candidates at the polls. Although much remains unexplained, political considerations apparently matter most for support for democracy.[28]

Greater explanatory leverage can be obtained over other mass political attitudes. The results of the second model in Table 4.4 confirm that mass antiauthoritarianism in Africa is more fully formed than popular support for democracy. Regressing the same set of predictor variables on rejection of authoritarian rule (measured as an index of rejection of one-man, one-party, military, and traditional rule), it is possible to double the amount of variance explained (from 7 to 15 percent). Moreover, when the extent of democracy is entered as a dependent variable (measured as a single item that records whether the respondent thinks that his or her country is a non-, partial, or full democracy), further explanatory gains are achieved (up to 21 percent). To be sure, these public attitudes are also dispersed across society in the sense that they are not concentrated in any particular demographic group. But they derive more consistently from persons who are psychologically prepared to engage in politics and who base their support for political regimes on performance considerations. It is worth noting that, while antiauthoritarianism is driven largely by judgments of political performance, assessments of the extent of democracy are shaped by considerations of performance generally, both political and economic.

Finally, two models of satisfaction with democracy are presented. This concrete attitude—which, to repeat, measures how satisfied people are with "the way democracy works in [your country]"—is much more cohesive and less scattered than support for democracy. When a standard set of nineteen demographic, economic, and political predictors are regressed on satisfaction with democracy, it proves possible to explain over one-third (37 percent) of its variance. When respondent perceptions of the extent of democracy are added to the list of predictors, variance explained rises to 42 percent. In other words, the Africans interviewed are likely to be satisfied with democracy if they think that their country is a full democracy or something approaching that consolidated status. Satisfaction with democracy is driven primarily by economic considerations, although political factors continue to remain important. An individual's expectations about the economic future stand out in both models; the higher one's hopes that democracy will begin to deliver prosperity in the year ahead, the more likely one is to be satisfied with the performance of democracy today. Interestingly, education is the first demographic factor to attain statistical significance; the fact that its sign is negative in both models, however, indicates that education makes people harder to satisfy. Educated people remain skeptical that democracy will meet popular economic expectations.

LIBERALIZATION DOES NOT AMOUNT TO DEMOCRATIZATION

This chapter concludes by considering how Afrobarometer indicators compare with other standard measures of democracy and what such comparisons portend

Table 4.4
Multiple Regression Estimates of Popular Attitudes to Democracy, Selected African Countries, 1999–2001

	Support for Democracy		Rejection of Auth. Rule		Extent of Democracy		Satisfaction w. Democracy 1		Satisfaction w. Democracy 2	
	Beta	Sig.	Beta	Sig.	Beta	Sig.	Beta	Sig.	Beta	Sig.
Constant		.000		.000		.000		.000		.033
DEMOGRAPHIC FACTORS										
Gender	-.018	.128	-.010	.533	.026	.020	-.008	.425	-.017	.076
Age	.016	.187	.036	.028	.027	.019	-.001	.959	-.002	.868
Education	.010	.437	.022	.204	.025	.040	-.033	.003	-.037	.000
Residential location (urban/rural)	-.019	.133	-.002	.917	.068	.494	-.004	.728	-.003	.736
ECONOMIC FACTORS										
Overall government performance	.054	.000	-.047	.020	.145	.000	.157	.000	.121	.000
Satisfied with national economy	.024	.100	-.049	.028	.066	.000	.074	.000	.056	.000
Past economic satisfaction	.027	.111	-.018	.439	.004	.776	.058	.000	.060	.000
Future economic expectations	.044	.011	-.020	.367	.029	.063	.180	.000	.165	.000
Relative deprivation	.001	.953	-.018	.343	.002	.860	.088	.000	.086	.000
Support structural adjustment	.041	.001	.111	.000	.023	.043	.004	.687	.009	.373
Perceive economic inequality	.037	.002	.129	.000	.100	.000	-.047	.000	-.017	.085
Delivery of economic goods	.009	.566	-.066	.001	.029	.036	.065	.000	.058	.000

POLITICAL FACTORS										
Interested in politics	.070	.000	.084	.000	.011	.313	.015	.124	.009	.367
Political efficacy	.083	.000	.108	.000	.038	.001	.066	.000	.056	.000
Political winner	.066	.000	.166	.000	.019	.080	.053	.000	.051	.000
Government responsiveness	.088	.000	.059	.005	.082	.000	.087	.000	.066	.000
Trust government institutions	.017	.193	.008	.653	.159	.000	.068	.000	.025	.017
Perceive corruption	-.006	.655	-.010	.585	.132	.000	.077	.000	.040	.000
Delivery of political goods	.059	.000	.258	.000	.099	.000	.107	.000	.066	.000
Extent of democracy	-	-	-	-	-	-	-	-	.283	.000

R	.275	.400	.464	.612	.651
R square	.076	.160	.216	.375	.424
Adjusted R square	.073	.155	.213	.373	.422
Standard Error of the Estimate	.660	.646	.808	1.123	1.059

for the quality of emergent political regimes in Africa. As is well known, Freedom House provides annual estimates of the extent of civil liberties and political rights and the status of freedom for over 190 countries in the world, including our twelve African cases.[29] The methodologies for constructing Freedom House (FH) and Afrobarometer (AB) indicators differ markedly. Whereas the FH estimates are expert judgments by a small number of qualified country specialists, the AB data are based on the lay opinions of a large number of citizens of each country. The opportunity thus arises to test whether measures of the extent of democracy derived by different methods validate one another.

The extent of democracy as measured by the Afrobarometer turns out to be strongly and significantly correlated with status of freedom as estimated by Freedom House.[30] It is even more strongly associated with the FH civil liberties and political rights scores.[31] Consider a couple of examples: Botswana ranks first on ranked country lists for both the Afrobarometer indicator of the extent of democracy and the Freedom House measure of civil liberties (see Table 4.5). Zimbabwe in 2000 consistently ranks dead last.[32] These findings suggest that Western academic experts and lay African citizens arrive at roughly similar judgments about the level of democracy that pertains in any given country.

We can push this inquiry further by examining processes of political change like political liberalization and democratization (as opposed to political outcomes like the extent of liberty or democracy).[33] Do AB indicators match FH scores when the object of inquiry is political change over time? Again, the answer is affirmative. The AB indicators of political liberalization and democratization are strongly and significantly correlated with the respective FH indicators.[34] As Table 4.5 shows, the rank order distribution of countries is very similar: five countries share rankings on liberalization, and four share rankings on democratization (Table 4.5; see highlights).[35] Most remaining countries differ across measurement methods by only a rank or two.

Indeed, the same two cases are mainly responsible for observed deviations in country rankings on both liberalization and democratization: Nigeria and South Africa. Interestingly, the divergence between popular and expert opinion runs in opposite directions in these two African giants. In AB surveys, Nigerians perceive more political liberalization than do experts on FH panels. This finding tends to confirm that the mass public in Nigeria, perhaps caught up in transition euphoria, sees more political change than do foreign-based Afro-pessimists, who tend to project onto Nigeria their worst fears for the African continent. By contrast, South Africans who participate in AB surveys think that less political liberalization has occurred in their country than do FH experts. In South Africa, racial minorities pull down the country's scores on the perceived degree of liberalization and democratization. In this instance, outsiders (particularly Americans) are prone to celebrate the political progress made by South Africa in the 1990s and to project onto that country their highest hopes for the continent as a whole. For Nigeria and South Africa, therefore, I put more faith in the Afrobarometer data than in the Freedom House estimates.

Table 4.5
Democracy, Political Liberalization, and Democratization: Comparative Rankings of Afrobarometer and Freedom House, Selected African Countries, circa 2000

Extent of Democracy			Political Liberalization		Democratization	
AB Rank	**FH CL Rank**	**FH PR Rank**	**AB CL Change Rank**	**FH CL Change Rank**	**AB PR Change Rank**	**FH PR Change Rank**
Botswana	**Botswana**	S. Africa	Malawi	S. Africa	Malawi	S. Africa
Malawi	S. Africa	**Botswana**	Nigeria	Malawi	Mali	Malawi
Namibia	Malawi	Malawi	**Mali**	**Mali**	Nigeria	Mali
S.Africa	Namibia	Lesotho	Ghana	Nigeria	**Ghana**	**Ghana**
Zambia	Mali	Namibia	Namibia	Ghana	**Namibia**	**Namibia**
Mali	Zambia	Mali	Tanzania	Namibia	S. Africa	Tanzania
Lesotho	Lesotho	Tanzania	S. Africa	Tanzania	Zambia	Lesotho
Uganda	Tanzania	Nigeria	**Zambia**	**Zambia**	Tanzania	Nigeria
Tanzania	Nigeria	Zambia	**Botswana**	**Botswana**	Lesotho	Zambia
Nigeria	Uganda	Uganda	**Lesotho**	**Lesotho**	**Zimbabwe**	**Zimbabwe**
Zimbabwe	**Zimbabwe**	**Zimbabwe**	**Zimbabwe**	**Zimbabwe**	**Botswana**	**Botswana**

AB = Afrobarometer; FH = Freedom House; CL = Civil Liberties; PR = Political Rights.

Finally, a comment is required about the strong observed relationship between the AB indicator of the extent of democracy and the FH civil liberties indicator. This seems to confirm that the Africans interviewed understand and appraise democracy at least partly in liberal terms. But it also raises the troubling prospect that African conceptions of democratization stop short at liberalization. We have already seen that, when defining democracy, the Africans interviewed put more emphasis on expressive liberties than on electoral rights. Yet, if democratization is a long-term, institution-building project, then attention also must be devoted to ensuring not only that the quality of elections is maintained but that other essential institutions such as civilian control of the military, the dispersal of executive powers, and the sovereignty of the law are guaranteed for the long run. It is far from clear, however, that, beyond demanding liberty from an overweening state, African citizens are ready to dedicate themselves to these projects.

This point has theoretical implications. So far, the literature on the deepening of democracy in Africa has been concerned about the fallacy of electoralism, namely, the danger that a formal facade of multiparty contests will mask a persistent atmosphere of civil rights violations.[36] I propose that there might be an equally important, but unacknowledged, fallacy of liberalization. This fallacy derives from a public attitude that free speech is all that is necessary for democracy. It assumes that movements for political reform need go no further than wringing political openings from authoritarian regimes. It overlooks the fact that contestation over the rules of the political game does not end with electoral transitions. It misses the point that democratization is an ongoing, long-term, intergenerational process that requires continued political struggle in multiple, partial arenas, including the arena of public opinion. Unless wide popular commitments are substantially deepened, democratization in Africa could easily stall at the stage of the liberalization of authoritarian regimes.

APPENDIX: NOTES TO TABLE 4.4

Coding of Dependent Variables

Support for Democracy. This standard variable asks respondents to choose between three options and is coded as follows: 3 = "Democracy is preferable to any other form of government," 2 = "In certain situations a non-democratic government can be preferable," 1 = "To people like me it doesn't matter what form of government we have."

Rejection of Authoritarian Rule. This variable is an index constructed of four items concerning acceptance or rejection of presidential rule, one-party rule, military rule, and traditional rule. Having learned that "some people say that we would be better off if the country was governed differently," respondents were asked: "What do you think about the following options?" "We should get rid of elections so that a strong leader can decide everything," "We should have only one political party," "The army should come in to govern the country," and "All decisions should be made by a council of traditional elders." Responses were coded as follows: 1 = strongly agree, 2 = agree, 3 = disagree, 4 = strongly disagree. To construct an index of rejection of authoritarian rule, scores for all questions were added together and divided by four.

Extent of Democracy. This variable is measured by a single item that asked: "In your opinion, how much of a democracy is [your country] today?" The interviewer inserted the name of the country. Responses were coded as 0 = not a democracy, 1 = a democracy, but with major problems, 2 = a democracy, but with minor problems, 3 = a full democracy. In Ghana, the item asked only whether "Ghana today is a democracy"; "yes" was recoded as 2 in order to include Ghana in this part of the analysis.

Satisfaction with Democracy. A standard item was also used here, namely, "Generally, how satisfied are you with the way democracy works in [your country]?" Again, the name of the country was inserted. Response categories included 1 = very dissatisfied, 2 = somewhat dissatisfied, 3 = neither satisfied nor dissatisfied, 4 = somewhat satisfied, 5 = very satisfied. The middle category was used in Southern Africa but not in East or West Africa. Because some respondents insisted, we added a category during fieldwork of 0 = "This country is not a democracy" for those who wished to use it.

Coding of Explanatory Variables

Demographic Factors

Gender. 1 = male, 2 = female.
Age. Raw age in years at the time of the survey. Range = 18–100.
Education. A four-point ordinal scale with the following ranks: 0 = no formal education, 1 = primary schooling (any or all), 2 = secondary schooling (any or all), 3 = any postsecondary education.
Residential Location. 1= urban, 2 = rural.

Economic Factors

Overall Government Performance. This summary measure captures public assessments of government performance across five policy areas. The question asked, "How well would you say the current government is handling the following problems: Creating jobs, keeping prices stable, reducing crime, addressing educational needs, improving basic health services?" For each of the five subitems, respondents chose among 1 = very badly, 2 = fairly badly, 3 = fairly well, and 4 = very well. An index of overall government performance was then constructed for every respondent by adding together responses to each item and dividing by five.

Satisfied with National Economy. A standard item: "How satisfied are you with the condition of [your country's] economy today?" Responses could be arrayed among 1 = not at all satisfied, 2 = not very satisfied, 3 = somewhat satisfied, 4 = very satisfied.

Past Economic Satisfaction. "How do economic conditions in your country compare with one year ago?" While the question was asked from a sociotropic perspective in the seven Southern African countries, it was posed from an egocentric viewpoint in East and West Africa: "When you look at your economic conditions today, how satisfied do you feel compared with one year ago?" To create a single variable, answers were merged onto a shared five-point scale from "much worse/much less satisfied" to "much better/much more satisfied."

Future Economic Expectations. "What about in twelve months time? Do you expect economic conditions in [your country] to be worse, the same, or better than they are now?" Once again, the question was asked from a sociotropic perspective in the seven Southern African countries but posed from an egocentric viewpoint in East and West Africa: "When you look forward at your life's prospects, how satisfied do you expect to be in one year's time?" To create a single variable, answers were merged onto a shared five-point scale from "much worse/much less satisfied" to "much better/much more satisfied."

Relative Deprivation. "Now let's speak about your personal economic conditions. Would you say they are worse, the same, or better than other [citizens of your country]?" This item is measured on a 5-point scale from 1 = much worse to 5 = much better.

Support Structural Adjustment. This summary measure is an index of the number of adjustment policies supported by respondents. Four such policies were considered: market pricing of consumer goods, user fees for health or educational services, job reductions in the civil service, and privatization of public corporations. Support was scored if respondents "strongly" or "somewhat" agreed with a pro-reform position. Support for an adjustment policy was scored as a 1 and opposition as a 0. The index is additive over four policies and ranges from 0 to 4.

Perceive Economic Inequality. A single item asked respondents to choose whether "the government's economic policies" have "A . . . helped most people" or "B . . . hurt most people." Respondents were asked to indicate the strength of their position on a standard five-point scale from 1 = strongly agree with statement A to 5 = strongly agree with statement B.

Delivery of Economic Goods. "We are going to compare the present system of government with the former system of rule. Please tell me if the following things are better or worse now than they used to be: People have an adequate standard of living." Scored on a standard five-point scale from 1 = much worse to 5 = much better.

Political Factors

Political Efficacy. A single item that asked respondents to choose between "A. No matter how you vote, it won't make things better in the future" or "B. The way you vote could make things better in the future." Once strength of opinion is factored in, the item was scored on a standard five-point response scale.

Government Responsiveness. "We are going to compare the present system of government with the former system of rule. Please tell me if the following things are better or worse now than they used to be: Everybody is treated equally and fairly by the government." Scored on a standard five-point scale from 1 = much worse to 5 = much better.

Political Winner. Proxy measure for vote in last election. Derived from party identification, that is, "Do you feel close to any political party?" If yes, "which one?" Respondents were coded into 1 = winner, 0 = loser, 0.5 = neutral, according whether their preferred party won the last presidential, legislative, or general election before the date of the survey.

Interested in Politics. "How interested are you in politics and government?" 1 = not interested, 2 = somewhat interested, 3 = very interested.

Trust Government Institutions. An index derived by the same method as previous indexes from trust in four institutions: police, courts of law, army, and electoral commission. The response scale for the items and the index run from 1 = I do not trust them at all/never to 4 = I trust them a lot/just about always.

Perceive Corruption. Two different items were combined into a single indicator. In Southern Africa, "How many officials are involved in corruption?" In East/West Africa, "Do you agree or disagree: Bribery is not common among public officials in [your country]." Each was measured on a four-point scale from 1 = None/agree strongly to 4 = All/disagree strongly.

Delivery of Political Goods. "We are going to compare the present system of government with the former system of rule. Please tell me if the following things are better or worse now than they used to be: A. People are free to say what they think. B. People can join any organization they want. C. Each person can freely choose who to vote for without feeling pressured." Scored on a standard five-point scale from 1 = much worse to 5 = much better, then combined into an index (all subitems added, then divided by three).

NOTES

1. Robert A. Dahl, *On Democracy* (New Haven, CT: Yale Nota Bene Books, 2000), 180.

2. In "What Makes Democracies Endure," *Journal of Democracy* 7 (1996): 39–55, Adam Przeworski, Adam Alvarez, José Antonio Cheibub, and Fernando Limongi argue that the term consolidation has no meaning apart from regime duration.

3. "Deepening makes the formal structures of democracy more liberal, accountable, representative, and accessible—in essence, more democratic." See Larry Diamond, *Developing Democracy: Toward Consolidation* (Baltimore: Johns Hopkins University Press, 1999), 74.

4. Pippa Norris, ed., *Critical Citizens: Global Support for Democratic Governance* (Oxford: Oxford University Press, 1999).

5. The Afrobarometer is a collaborative, cross-national research program that inves-

tigates public attitudes and behaviors toward democracy, economic reform, and civil society. Round 1 of the Afrobarometer was conducted between July 1999 and May 2001 and includes interviews with over 21,500 respondents across twelve countries: three in West Africa (Ghana, Mali, and Nigeria), two in East Africa (Tanzania and Uganda), and seven in Southern Africa (Botswana, Lesotho, Malawi, Namibia, South Africa, Zambia, and Zimbabwe). To varying degrees, all these countries have undergone transitions to multiparty electoral democracy, a precondition both for conducting meaningful surveys and for measuring popular support for democracy. They are therefore fairly typical of Africa's struggling new multiparty systems; in no sense, however, do they represent the parts of Africa that remain gripped by autocrats or mired in civil war.

6. See Russell J. Dalton, "Political Support in Advanced Industrial Democracies," in *Critical Citizens*, ed. Norris, 69; Marta Lagos, "Between Stability and Crisis in Latin America," *Journal of Democracy* 12, no. 1 (January 2001): 138; Hans-Dieter Klingemann, "Mapping Political Support in 1990s: A Global Analysis," in *Critical Citizens*, ed. Norris, 46.

7. Dalton, "Political Support," 70; Lagos, "Between Stability and Crisis," 139. The Western Europe scores are derived from the Eurobarometer and World Values Survey (WVS) for 1993–1997.

8. Note that the range of country scores on support for democracy is almost identical in sub-Saharan Africa (from 39 percent in Lesotho to 83 percent in Botswana) and Latin America (from 39 percent in Brazil to 84 percent in Uruguay). In Latin America, however, all countries surveyed are neodemocracies and thus represent their continent, whereas the twelve Afrobarometer countries are an unrepresentative sample that excludes most nondemocracies on the continent.

9. Also, the popular conception of democracy in Tanzania may be distorted by the country's long experience under a dominant party.

10. When averaging country scores, the data are weighted to standardize the sample size for each country at n = 1,200. The mean figures for the twelve-country "Afro" sample reflect this weighting. Thus, even though the Nigeria survey employed a large sample (n = 3,600), its high score on support for democracy contributes no more than the score of any other country to the "Afro" mean (see Table 4.1, last column).

11. These figures include persons who "don't know" any meaning of democracy. If "don't knows" are excluded, and we consider only persons who profess to understand democracy, then 40 percent cite civil liberties, and 9 percent cite political rights. Whichever way one counts popular notions of democracy, civil liberties lead the way.

12. Norris, *Critical Citizens*, 3.

13. For example, Frederic Schaffer, *Democracy in Translation: Understanding Politics in an Unfamiliar Culture* (Ithaca, NY: Cornell University Press, 1998); Daniel Osabu-Kle, *Compatible Cultural Democracy: The Key to Development in Africa* (Peterborough, Ontario: Broadview Press, 2000).

14. Contingency coefficient = .412, p < .000.

15. Ministry of Information, *A Revolutionary Journey: Selected Speeches of Flt.-Lt. Jerry John Rawlings* (Accra: Information Services Department, 1983), 4; Julius K. Nyerere, *Ujamaa: Essays on Socialism* (Oxford: Oxford University Press, 1977).

16. See David Collier and Steven Levitsky, "Democracy with Adjectives: Conceptual Innovation in Comparative Research," *World Politics* 49 (April): 430–451.

17. Guillermo O'Donnell, "Illusions about Consolidation," *Journal of Democracy* 7, no. 2 (1996): 34–51.

18. For a definitive account of these events, see Roger Southall and Roddy Fox, "Lesotho's General Election of 1998: Rigged or de Riguer?" *Journal of Modern African Studies* 37, no. 4 (1999): 669–696.

19. Twenty-one percent of whites are nostalgic for authoritarianism versus 12 percent of blacks. Contingency coefficient = .226, p < .000.

20. Since the proportions of respondents who reject one-party rule and traditional rule (69 percent) are roughly the same as the proportion of respondents who support democracy (68 percent), we cannot say that these forms of antiauthoritarian sentiments are more widespread than pro-democratic ones.

21. To view South Africa in comparative perspective, see Hermann Giliomee and Charles Simkins, eds., *The Awkward Embrace: One-Party Dominance and Democracy* (Cape Town: Tafelberg, 1999).

22. Thanks to Larry Diamond for suggesting this procedure.

23. The two alternatives are one-man rule and one-party rule; the three-alternative option also includes military rule; and the four-alternative option adds traditional rule.

24. Pearson's rho = .194 (for military rule), .165 (for one-man rule), .102 (for one-party rule), and .094 (for traditional rule). A similar pattern applies when support for democracy is correlated with rejection of multiple alternatives: .156 (for two alternatives), .187 (for three alternatives), and .189 (for four alternatives). All p's < .000.

25. David Easton, *A Systems Analysis of Political Life* (Chicago: University of Chicago Press, 1965), 273. Also, David Easton, "A Reassessment of the Concept of Political Support," *Journal of Political Science* 5 (1975): 435–437.

26. Because of the large sample size (n = 21,398) and the multiplicity of predictor variables, a demanding standard of p < .001 was applied in order to isolate the most powerful explanatory factors. If the model contained no significant predictors, one would have to conclude that support for democracy is a "nonattitude"; that is, respondents have never thought about the issue and offer entirely random responses. The existence of numerous effective predictors, however, indicates that opinion is structured in observable ways.

27. But the inverse is not true. Because support for democracy is much more widespread than support for adjustment, political liberalism does not automatically lead to economic liberalism.

28. In an article based on preliminary data from three African countries, Robert Mattes and the author found that satisfaction with democracy was easier to explain than support for democracy. Michael Bratton and Robert Mattes, "Support for Democracy in Africa: Intrinsic or Instrumental?" *British Journal of Political Science* 31 (July 2001): 447–474. The present analysis, using data from all twelve countries in Round 1 of the Afrobarometer, confirms this and other findings from the earlier study.

29. See Aili Piano, *Freedom in the World, 2000–2001* (New York: Freedom House, 2001).

30. Pearson's r = .605, p = .049. N = 11 because the Afrobarometer question was not asked in Ghana.

31. Pearson's r = .779, p = .005 (for civil liberties), and Pearson's r = .631, p = .038 (for political rights).

32. Spearman's rank-order correlations are also all strong and significant. The author chose not to rank the Freedom House status of freedom scores because of the limited variance on this variable among Afrobarometer countries.

33. Political liberalization is measured as follows: by an AB question on whether

"things are better" since the political transition in terms of whether "people are free to say what they think" and by the change in FH score on the civil liberties (CL) indicator from 1988 to 2000. Democratization is measured as follows: by an AB question on whether "things are better" since the political transition in terms of whether "people are free to choose who to vote for without feeling pressured," and by the change in FH score on the political rights (PR) indicator from 1988 to 2000.

34. Pearson's $r = .862$, $p = .001$ (for political liberalization), and Pearson's $r = .602$, $p = .050$ (for democratization). $N = 11$ because the Afrobarometer question was not asked in Uganda.

35. Spearman's rank-order correlations are also strong and significant.

36. See, for example, Marina Ottaway, "Should Elections Be the Criterion of Democratization in Africa?" *CSIS Africa Notes* no. 145 (Washington, DC: Center for Strategic and International Studies, 1993).

Chapter 5

Shariacracy and Federal Models in the Era of Globalization: Nigeria in Comparative Perspective

Ali A. Mazrui

In May 1999, a new president was sworn into office in Nigeria—the first elected civilian president of Nigeria since the military coup of 1983. Retired General Olusegun Obasanjo was also the first *non-Muslim* to be popularly elected president nationwide since Nigeria's independence.[1]

Nigeria has the largest concentration of Muslims on the African continent. It has more Muslims than any *Arab* country, including Egypt.[2] In the fifteen months (approximately) since Olusegun Obasanjo became president, some predominantly Muslim states in the Nigerian federation have taken steps toward implementing the Sharia in their own states, although the country as a whole is supposed to be a secular republic.[3] This has caused consternation among non-Muslim Nigerians. Indeed, in Kaduna state, this Christian consternation exploded into intercommunal riots that cost hundreds of lives earlier in the year 2000.[4] But the momentum for Shariacracy still continues.

GLOBALIZATION AND ISLAMIC REVIVALISM

Many different reasons have been advanced for the rise of Sharia advocacy and Sharia implementation in Northern Nigeria. One explanation is that the Nigerian federation is getting more decentralized, and part of the decentralization is taking the form of cultural self-determination. In Yorubaland this cultural self-determination is taking the form of Yoruba nationalism. In Igboland it is taking the form of new demands for confederation. In the Muslim North cultural self-determination is taking the form of Shariacracy.

Another explanation for the rise of Sharia militancy is to regard it as a political bargaining chip. As the North is losing political influence in the Nigerian federation, it is asserting new forms of autonomy in preparation for a new national compact among contending forces.[5]

What has not been discussed is whether the rise of Sharia militancy is itself a consequence of globalization. One of the repercussions of globalization worldwide has been to arouse cultural insecurity and uncertainty about identities. Indeed, the paradox of globalization is that it both promotes enlargement of economic scale and stimulates fragmentation of ethnic and cultural scale.[6]

The enlargement of economic scale is illustrated by the rise of the European Union and by the North American Free Trade Agreement (NAFTA). The fragmentation of cultural and ethnic scale is illustrated by the disintegration of the Soviet Union, the collapse of Czechoslovakia into two countries, the rise of Hindu fundamentalism in India and Islamic fundamentalism in Afghanistan, the collapse of Somalia after penetration by the Soviet Union and the United States, and the reactivation of genocidal behavior among the Hutu and Tutsi in Rwanda and Burundi.

Because globalization is a special scale of Westernization, it has triggered identity crises from Uzbekistan to Somalia and from Afghanistan to Northern Nigeria. Fragile ethnic identities and endangered cultures are forced into new forms of resistance. Resisting Westernization becomes indistinguishable from resisting globalization. In Nigeria the South is part of the vanguard of Westernization and therefore the first to respond to globalization. When, in addition, the South appears to be politically triumphant within Nigeria, alarm bells are sounded in parts of the North. This may not necessarily be Northern distrust of Yoruba or Igbo cultures. It may be Northern distrust of Westernization. Is Southern Nigeria a Trojan horse for globalization? And is globalization in turn a Trojan horse for Westernization?

The Sharia under this paradigm becomes a form of Northern resistance—not to Southern Nigeria but to the forces of globalization and to their Westernizing consequences.[7] Even the policy of *privatization* of public enterprises is probably an aspect of the new globalizing ideology. Privatization in Nigeria may lead either to new transnational corporations establishing their roots or to private Southern entrepreneurs outsmarting Northerners and deepening the economic divide between North and South. Again the Sharia may be a Northern gut response to these looming clouds of globalization.

In Nigeria the Sharia is caught between the forces of federal democratization and the forces of wider globalization. Let us look more closely at the complexities of globalization and the intricacies of democratic federalism.

GLOBALIZATION: ECONOMIC AND CULTURAL

Two forms of globalization have affected Nigeria in contradictory ways— economic globalization, on the one hand, and cultural globalization, on the other. The forces of economic globalization in the world as a whole have deepened the marginalization of Nigeria. The forces of cultural globalization, on the other hand, have substantially penetrated and assimilated much of Nigeria.

On attainment of independence, the economic marginalization of Nigeria was partly due to the fact that colonialism had created an elite of consumption rather than an elite of productivity. The postcolonial Nigerian elite was more adept at making money than at creating wealth. Money could be made in a network of capital transfers without generating genuine growth. The Nigerian elite had learned the techniques of circulating money without a talent for creating new wealth.[8]

The colonial impact in Nigeria had generated urbanization without industrialization, fostered Western consumption patterns without Western productive techniques, cultivated among Nigerians Western tastes without Western skills, and initiated secularization without the scientific spirit. The stage was set for the marginalization of Nigeria in the era of globalization.

One had hoped that petroleum would enable Nigeria to join the more prosperous forces of globalization. Following the dramatic rise of the Organization of Petroleum Exporting Countries (OPEC), Nigeria became the fifth largest producer of petroleum in the world.[9] Yet the nature of the elite of consumption and the shortage of relevant skills plunged the Nigerian economy into mismanagement, corruption, and debt. Long lines at petrol stations and recurrent shortages of fuel were the order of the day. Commercial activity was often disrupted by shortages of petroleum products—diesel, kerosene, cooking gas, and other commodities. The giant of Africa was in danger of becoming the midget of the world. Africa's Gulliver was in danger of becoming the Lilliput of the globe.

On the other hand, cultural globalization had indeed substantially co-opted Nigeria to its ranks. Southern Nigeria especially has demonstrated remarkable receptivity to the forces of cultural globalization through Westernization. Although Christianity arrived in India eighteen centuries before it arrived in what is today Nigeria, the population of Christians in India is still little more than 2 percent (2.5 percent), whereas the population of Christians in Nigeria is over 35 percent.[10] In one century, Christianity made more headway in Southern Nigeria than it has done in India in nearly 2,000 years.

At least for a while, Nigeria has also been very receptive to Western education. By the beginning of the twenty-first century, Nigeria had exported more highly educated personnel to the United States (proportionally) than had any other country in the world. Of all the new immigrants to the United States, the Nigerians had the highest proportion of graduates.[11] The great majority of these immigrant Nigerians were Igbo, Yorubay, and other southerners.

In addition to religion and education as forces of cultural globalization, there has been the impact of major European languages as international media of communication. In the case of Nigeria, the impact of the English language has been relatively profound. Nigeria has produced its own simplified version of English (Pidgin) as a grassroots lingua franca.[12] But Standard English has made great strides—producing such world-class literary figures as Chinua Achebe,

Wole Soyinka, J. P. Clark, and the late Christopher Okigbo. The great majority of Nigeria's great writers in the English language are southerners—complete with the Nobel literary laureate Wole Soyinka. Once again Nigeria has shown great receptivity to cultural globalization in a European idiom.

If in global terms Nigeria as a whole was economically on the periphery, Northern Nigeria was the periphery of the periphery. The world economy had marginalized Nigeria as a country. The Nigerian economy had marginalized the North as a region. In spite of the fact that Northern soldiers had ruled Nigeria for so long since independence, the nation's economic elite was much larger in the South than in the North. The oil wealth and related industries were disproportionately located in the South. The Southern elite was, on the whole, more adept at making money than the Northern counterparts.[13]

One of the triggers of the Shariacracy movement in some Northern states was Northern resentment of being the periphery of the periphery. When the North held political power, northerners could more easily accept their economic marginality. But the federal elections of 1999 shifted political power to the South without reducing the economic marginality of the North. The politics of Shariacracy were in part a protest against regional economic inequalities.[14]

But what is *Shariacracy*? We define it *as governance according to the norms, principles and rules laid down by Islamic law*. Under British colonial rule, the Sharia was implemented for Muslims in the domain of family law and certain areas of civil suit. But the *kadhis* (or Muslim judges and magistrates) were not normally authorized to administer the criminal side of Islamic law. In each British colony in Africa with a large Muslim population, there was a triple heritage of law—indigenous, Islamic, and British-derived. Criminal law tended to be British-derived with suitable imperial and colonial amendments.[15] However, issues like marriage, divorce, inheritance, succession, and certain forms of property could be subject to either the Sharia or African customary law.

The Sharia is therefore nothing new in Northern Nigeria. What is new is Shariacracy—the adoption of the Sharia as the foundation of governance and its expansion into the domain of the criminal justice system.

While Northern Nigerians have deeply minded being economically marginal, they have *not* minded being culturally authentic. Partly because of Islam and partly because of Lord Lugard's policy of Indirect Rule during the colonial period, the Hausa-Fulani have been far less receptive to Westernization than the Southerners had been. To that extent Northern Nigeria had in any case remained more culturally authentic and less penetrated by the West even without the adoption of the Sharia law.[16]

However, the new globalization in Southern Nigeria was bound to sound cultural alarm bells in the North. In the colonial era Lord Lugard had kept Christianity at bay in the North through the shield of indirect rule.[17] Postcolonial politicians in Northern states are seeking to keep globalization at bay through the shield of the Sharia.

If modernization is a higher phase of Westernization, and globalization is a higher phase of modernization, the stage is now being set for new kinds of normative responses. Against economic marginalization, the Sharia is a form of passionate protest. Against encroaching globalization, the Sharia is cultural resistance to Westernization. Northern Nigeria is engaged in both protest and resistance through the medium of the Sharia.

Ordinary people in Africa are often ignorant of Western-derived law; but if they are Muslim, they have some prior familiarity with the Sharia. Courts of law in postcolonial African countries south of the Sahara use primarily the European imperial language for adjudication, argument, verdict, and sentencing. The legal concepts and principles invoked are in English, French, Portuguese, or Latin, as the case may be. The defendant may be quite ignorant of the particular European language as he or she stands in the dock, and terms like "accessory before the fact" or *mutates mutandis* are often beyond the comprehension of the average defendant or plaintiff in postcolonial Africa. Debates that go on between the lawyers in a Western-style courtroom in Africa are almost literally "double Dutch" to the accused.

An Islamic court in sub-Saharan Africa, on the other hand, normally uses the language of the particular community within which the court operates. An Islamic court in Zanzibar or in Mombasa, Kenya, is likely to use Kiswahili; while an Islamic court in Northern Nigeria uses Hausa. The Qur'an and the written parts of the Sharia may indeed remain in Arabic, but the legal discourse in the court is conducted mainly in the relevant African language.[18]

What is more, many of the basic phrases in the Sharia might already have entered the indigenous languages of African Muslims—Arabic words like *harem* (forbidden), *halal* (permissible), *riba* (usury), *zina* (adultery), and *hukumu* (judgment) have already entered the Swahili language.[19] Many such legal and moral terms drawn from the Sharia have also been assimilated into Hausa. The gulf that separates the language of lawyers from the language of everyday life is much narrower in a postcolonial Muslim legal system than under a Westernized African judicial order.

ASYMMETRICAL FEDERALISM: GLOBAL PERSPECTIVES

If Nigeria is a secular federation, can some constituent states nevertheless be theocratic? Is national secularism compatible with official religions at the state level?

This raises the issue of whether federations are viable if the constituent states are *asymmetrical* in their constitutional systems. Quebec in Canada has been demanding treatment as a *distinct society*. If Islamic law in Nigeria risks discriminating against non-Muslim Nigerians, language policy in Quebec risks discriminating against English-speaking Canadians. There is a built-in asymmetry in the Canadian federation when one province can give the French language special status while the rest of the country is primarily English-speaking. The French language is the "Sharia" of Quebec.[20]

Comparable asymmetry exists in the Indian Federation in which the de facto status of the Hindi language differs between Northern states and Southern states, although both Hindi and English are dejure national languages.

The United Kingdom virtually invented asymmetry as a constitutional order. Scotland has had its own law, its own currency, and more recently its own regional assembly under Tony Blair in the 1990s. On the other hand, Northern Ireland has had a separate regional assembly long before either Wales or Scotland. As for England, it has no separate regional assembly distinct from the national Parliament of the whole country. In short, the United Kingdom has never tried to have symmetrical constitutional arrangements for its main constituent regions (England, Scotland, Wales, and Northern Ireland).[21]

For much of the nineteenth and twentieth centuries, Scotland was the "Zamfara state" of the United Kingdom. Zamfara in Nigeria in the twentieth century had turned to Islamic law. Scotland much earlier had turned for guidance to Roman law as developed by the jurists of France and Holland. The legal practices and judicial institutions of Scotland were very different from those of England at that time. The law of Scotland was not based on Roman law, but there was considerable infusion of Roman principles into it.

Like Zamfara, Scotland not only had a separate legal system from the rest of the country but also declared allegiance to a different religion. Zamfara in the twenty-first century turned to Sunni Islam; Scotland continued its allegiance to a separate Church of Scotland (Presbyterian) in 1707. A separate Scottish church and a separate Scottish legal and judicial system have continued to the present day, although Scottish law has borrowed a good deal from English law in more recent times.[22]

Alongside the constitutional asymmetry, some degree of national integration was taking place among the constituent regions of the United Kingdom. The whole country was getting Anglicized and "Britishized" into a relatively coherent whole. Similarly, the decision of Zamfara, Kano, and other Northern states in Nigeria to go Islamic need not be incompatible with the wider process of Nigerianization and national integration.

A less enduring asymmetry was the ban on alcoholic drinks in the history of the United States. Initially, prohibition of alcohol was by individual states. The first state law against alcohol was passed in Maine in 1850 and was soon followed by a wave of comparable legislation in other states. This was followed by two other waves of laws at various state levels.[23]

Meanwhile, a campaign for alcoholic prohibition at the federal level had been gathering momentum. A constitutional amendment against alcohol needed a two-thirds majority in Congress and approval by three-quarters of the states. Such a constitutional change was ratified on January 29, 1919, and went into effect on January 29, 1920, as the Eighteenth Amendment of the U.S. Constitution.[24]

Just as the Sharia in Nigeria can work only where there is popular support for it, the Eighteenth Amendment of the United States worked only where public opinion was genuinely for temperance and against alcohol. Prohibition at the federal level created resentment among those states that were not against alcoholic drinks and in large cities in the United States where alcohol had long become a way of life.[25]

Bootlegging emerged as a new kind of crime—the most dramatic embodiment of which was Al Capone and his bootlegging gang (illicit alcohol underground) operating from Chicago. Prohibition at the federal level created more problems than it solved. In less than fifteen years, the United States was ready to repeal the Eighteenth Amendment. In February 1933 Congress adopted a resolution proposing a new constitutional amendment to that effect. On December 5, 1933, Utah cast the thirty-sixth ratifying vote in favor of the Twenty-first Amendment. At the federal level alcohol was legal again.[26]

A few states in the Union continued to be "dry states" and chose to maintain a statewide ban. But the disenchantment that the federal-level Prohibition had created adversely affected attitudes to temperance even in those states that had once led the way in favor of Prohibition. It is arguable that Prohibition at the state level might have lasted much longer if the original asymmetry (some states for and some states against) had been respected and allowed to continue. The Eighteenth Amendment was a pursuit of national symmetry in American attitudes to alcohol. The amendment sought a premature national moral consensus on alcohol—and thereby hurt the cause of temperance in the country as a whole. By 1966 virtually all the 50 states of the Union had legalized alcoholic drinks—though some preferred that drinking be restricted to homes and private clubs rather than be served in public bars and saloons.

The most controversial elements of the Sharia are the *hudud* (Islamic punishments for criminal offenders). In a federation like Nigeria, do different punishments for the same offense in different states violate the principle of "equal protection before the law"? Saudi Arabia has been known to put to death even a princess on charges of adultery. Zamfara has not invoked the death penalty for adultery and fornication. But this Nigerian state has flogged an unmarried girl on the evidence of her pregnancy.[27]

This author believes that such punishments are too severe and ought to be reconsidered in the light of *ijtihad*. But in this chapter, the author is focusing on the implications of having differing punishments within states for the same offense. Is such a situation a denial of "equal protection before the law"?

It is in the nature of federalism that some laws be state laws, and that some be federal enactments. Therefore, some offenses would be state offenses, and others federal felonies. The state offenses are bound to differ from state to state.

Can there really be "equal protection before the law" when a citizen can be subject to the death penalty in one state and have a light sentence in another state for the same offense? In reality, a similar asymmetry has been persistent in the United States. First, there is the fact that the death penalty has been abolished or ceased to be carried out in some American states and not in others. Texas is the leading executioner state in the Union; Massachusetts has no death penalty at all. New York state had no capital punishment when Mario Cuomo was governor but has now reinstated the death penalty under Governor George Pataki.

Even more controversial are the following twin questions. Can the death penalty be applied to mentally retarded offenders? Can it be carried out on young offenders whose crimes were committed when they were still minors? Some states have said yes to both questions—"kill them!" Surprising as it may seem, the U.S. Supreme Court ruled in 1989 that it was perfectly constitutional to execute the mentally retarded or young offenders whose offenses were committed when they were minors. In *Penry v. Lynaugh* (1989), the Court ruled that execution of a "mildly to moderately retarded" person did not violate the Eighth Amendment (cruel and unusual punishment); and in *Stanford v. Kentucky* (1989) the Court ruled that the Eighth Amendment did not prohibit the death penalty for a defendant who was sixteen or seventeen years old at the time of committing the crime.[28]

Twelve years later, in the year 2001, the issue of executing the mentally retarded was back before the U.S. Supreme Court with the case of a convicted killer whose mental capacity is that of a seven-year-old. The Court had previously said that it was constitutional to execute this very offender, but new considerations have brought the case back to the Court.[29] In a 2002 decision (*Atkins v. Virginia*), the Court held that the Eighth Amendment prohibits the execution of mentally retarded criminals.

Behind it all is a nation still divided on the death penalty, with some states upholding it and others rejecting it as "cruel and unusual punishment."

What all this means is that federalism is able to accommodate a lack of constitutional symmetry even when the areas of disagreement are about matters of life and death. The *hudud* in Nigeria and Sudan include matters of life and death. So does the debate about capital punishment in the United States.

CAN GOD'S LAW BE REVIEWED?

To Nigerian Muslims the Sharia is an *alternative* paradigm of judicial order and law enforcement. Inherited colonial traditions of law enforcement and social responsibility are not working in the country as a whole.

One solution is to go back to ancestry. For Muslim Nigerians, there are two ancient systems—African law and the Sharia. African customary law was unwritten and uncodified. Did it allow the judge too much discretion?

The Sharia is ancient and firmly rooted in sacred scriptures. Is it allowing the judge too little discretion? Muslim Nigerians have preferred too little discretion rather than too much.

To Muslims, the Sharia is God's law, but it is God's law as interpreted by human beings. Here on earth, there is no such thing as a law that is independent of human interpretation. God's law is infallible, but its human interpreters are not.

Africa was the first asylum of persecuted Islam—the pre-Hijjra *hijra* to Ethiopia of Islamized Arabs on the run from Mecca. Will Africa be the final asylum of the Sharia under persecution by materialism, secularism, Westernization, globalization, and ungodliness everywhere else in the world?

Nascent Islam in the seventh century of the Christian era found refuge in the rising plateaus of Ethiopia. Will mature but harrassed Islam in the twenty-first century of the Christian era find asylum in the grazing fields of Muslim Nigeria?

This would be a great responsibility for Nigerian Muslims—for they would be mortals entrusted with immortal law. What is crucial is that human interpreters should not act as if they were in direct communication with Allah. Humans should always allow for their own fallibility in interpreting the Sharia.

For the Sharia to survive in Nigeria, the door of *ijtihad*, or judicial review, would have to be reopened. Without saying so in so many words, the doors of *ijtihad* in Sunni Islam have in fact been closed for nearly 1,000 years.[30] They were wide open during the days of the Prophet and the first four Caliphs. But the consolidation of the four Sunni School into *madhahib* effectively closed the doors of judicial review.[31]

The question that now arises is whether Africa will eventually be the place that holds the key to the doors of *idjitihad*. Will Nigeria lead the way?

Will the Sharia survive the governors who first initiated it in Northern Nigeria? Is the Sharia in Nigeria to stay? One scenario is that it will stay, but not necessarily in the form in which it was first implemented. The doors of *ijtihad* may reopen—fresh *fatawa*, new legal interpretations of God's law.

Few public *ulamaa* today would openly proclaim that *slavery* is compatible with Islam—although slavery was tolerated in the Prophet's own time and long afterward.

Scholars like Taha Jaber Alalwani have given learned *fatawa* many of the sayings of the Prophet, and some verses of the Qur'an showed that Islam was in favour of emancipation. Islam was clearly in favor of freeing individual slaves, but was Islam in favor of abolishing the institution of slavery?

Thirteen centuries before William Wilberforce and Abraham Lincoln, Islam was on the verge of evolving from being pro-emancipation of individual slaves to being pro-abolition of slavery. What interrupted this Islam's symphony of freedom was the historical accident that the Arabs went monarchical and royalist after the assassination of Caliph Ali Ibn Abi Talib. The royalization of the Arabs under the Umayyads and the Abbasids gave class and status among Muslims a new lease on life. Slavery became part of the interplay between servitude and privilege in the succeeding millennium of Muslim history. A new *ijtihad* against servitude, a new *fatwa* against slavery, had to await the *ulamaa* of the twentieth century.[32]

Similarly a new *ijtihad* is needed about the death penalty for adultery and amputation of the hand for stealing. These Islamic punishments were first introduced when societies had no police force, no forensic science, no criminologists or psychiatrists to understand the causes of crime.

If all Muslim governments agreed today that amputating the hand of a thief is wrong, and the Prophet Muhammad had said, "My people will never agree on error," then the new Muslim consensus will outlaw amputation as punishment.

If the whole *umma* finally agreed that the death penalty for fornication or adultery is no longer acceptable, that would mean that the *ummah* had reached consensus. The Prophet had said, "My people will never agree on error." Both *idjitihad* and *idjmaa* can be sources of fundamental legal review.[33]

CONCLUSION

The globalization of the world economy has left Nigeria and much of the rest of Africa marginalized. Nigerians have been casualties of international capitalism rather than genuine partners.

Cultural globalization, on the other hand, has found ready receptivity in Nigeria. Large parts of the country were rapidly Christianized, and the English language developed a Nigerian dialect.

An earlier phase of cultural globalization was Westernization. Nigeria inherited a legal system based primarily on British law and the English judicial traditions. Moreover, the language of interpreting the Western-derived law and the Constitution was the imperial language, English.

If Nigeria as a whole was a periphery of the world economic system, Northern Nigeria was economically a periphery of the periphery. But this economic marginalization of the North was for a while camouflaged by the fact that Northerners held political power. After General Olusegun Obasanjo was elected president in 1999, the political decline of the North exposed more mercilessly the North's economic marginality. The Shariacracy initiative by some Northern states is in part a protest against economic marginalization and in part a defense against unwanted cultural globalization.

Nigeria is the only African country outside Arab Africa that has seriously debated an alternative to the Western constitutional and legal inheritance. In part, this is what the debate about Shariacracy is all about. It is an exploration of an alternative to the Western legacy. But Nigeria may need to use *ijtihad* as a process of reviewing the Sharia. After all, the Sharia is God's law as interpreted by fallible human beings.

Another problem posed by the Sharia debate is whether a federal system is able to support cultural self-determination of its constituent parts and still retain cohesion as a federation. Switzerland has conceded cultural autonomy to its constituent cantons, but in terms of *language* (German, French, and Italian).[34] Initially, the Nigerian federation allowed for neither linguistic nor religious self-determination at the state level. What the Shariacracy debate has opened up is the possibility that religion, rather than language, could be the basis of cultural differentiation in an asymmetrical constitutional order.

Nigeria has the largest concentration of Muslims on the African continent.

The population of Nigeria, as we indicated, encompasses more Muslims than the population of any *Arab* country, including Egypt. But can the Sharia be implemented at the state level without compromising secularism at the federal level?[35]

We have tried to demonstrate that in terms of theories of asymmetrical federalism, such a paradox of state theocracy combined with federal secularism is feasible. But it would work only if both political power and economic prosperity were more evenly distributed between North and South and when globalization in the wider world became more compatible with Nigeria's national well-being. No wonder there are voices sincerely pleading for the postponement of Shariacracy. In the name of Nigerian unity, should the Sharia be a dream deferred?

NOTES

This is a revised version of a presentation at the International Conference on "Restoration of Shariah in Nigeria: Challenges and Benefits," sponsored by the Nigeria Muslim Forum and held in London, England, on April 14, 2001. The first half of this lecture borrowed from Mazrui's previous writings on the Sharia in Africa.

1. For a report, see the *Washington Post*, 30 May 2000, 1.

2. Nearly 50 percent of the estimated 128 million Nigerians are estimated to be Muslims; see *Political Handbook of the World, 1999*, ed. Arthur S. Banks and Thomas C. Muller (Binghamton, NY: CSA Publications, 1999), 723; and *The World Guide 1999/2000* (Oxford: New Internationalist Publications, 1999), 429.

3. For a list of these states, consult *Africa Research Bulletin* 37, no. 8 (22 September 2000): 14–77.

4. See the reports in *The Guardian*, 22 February 2000, 1; and *Christian Science Monitor*, 26 May 2000, 1.

5. An overview of the North–South and other cleavages bedeviling Nigeria may be found in *The Economist*, 15 January 2000, 14–15; also see *The Economist*, 8 July 2000, 47. For longer analyses on earlier conflicts caused by the Sharia issue, see Toyin Falola, *Violence in Nigeria: The Crisis of Religious Politics and Secular Ideologies* (Rochester, NY: University of Rochester Press, 1998), especially 77–113; Simeon O. Ilesanmi, *Religious Pluralism and the Nigerian State* (Athens: Ohio University Center for International Studies, 1997), 174–207; M. H. Kukah and Toyin Falola, *Religious Militancy and Self-Assertion: Islam and Politics in Nigeria* (Aldershot, U.K., and Brookfield, VT: Avebury Press, 1996), 117–139; and Pat A. T. Williams, "Religion, Violence, and Displacement in Nigeria," *Journal of Asian and African Studies* 32, no. 1–2 (June 1997): 33–49.

6. Consult Benjamin Barber, *Jihad vs. McWorld* (New York: Ballantine Books, 1996).

7. For an earlier example, consult Abdullah Mu'aza Saulawa, "Islam and its Anti-Colonial and Educational Contribution in West Africa and Northern Nigeria, 1800–1960," *Hamdard Islamicus* 19, no. 1 (1996): 69–79; and Falola, *Violence in Nigeria*, 74–77.

8. Many of the fruits of Nigerian development were stolen by the elite; see A. A. Niwanko, *Nigeria: The Stolen Billions* (Enugu, Nigeria: Fourth Dimension, 1999).

9. Today, Nigeria produces about 931 million metric tons of oil, which is about 2.9

percent of world output; see John B. Ejobowah, "Who Owns the Oil: The Politics of Ethnicity in the Niger Delta of Nigeria," *Africa Today* 47 (Winter 2000): 37; also see Sarah Ahmed Khan, *Nigeria: The Political Economy of Oil* (Oxford: Oxford University Press for the Oxford Institute of Energy Studies, 1994).

10. The figure for India is drawn from a report in *U.S. News & World Report*, 25 January 1999, 40, while the figure for Nigeria is drawn from Banks and Muller, eds., *The Political Handbook of the World 1999*, 723.

11. Some interesting research on African immigrants to the United States is contained in Yanyi K. Djamba, "African Immigrants in the United States of America: Socio-Demographic Profile in Comparison to Native Blacks," *Journal of Asian and African Studies* 34, no. 2 (June 1999): 210–215.

12. On Nigerian English, see Ayo Bamgbose, "Post-Imperial English in Nigeria, 1940–1990," in *Post-Imperial English: Status Change in Former British and American Colonies, 1940–1990*, ed. Joshua A. Fishman, Andrew Conrad, and Alma Rubal-Lopez (Berlin and New York: Mouton de Gruyter, 1996), 357–372; and on regional variations, consult V. O. Awonusi, "Regional Accents and Internal Variability in Nigerian English: A Historical Analysis," *English Studies* 67 (December 1986): 555–560.

13. See, for instance, Minabere Ibelema, "Nigeria: The Politics of Marginalization," *Current History* 99, no. 637 (May 2000): 213.

14. This resentment did have precedents in the 1970s and 1980s; see Roman Loimeier, *Islamic Reform and Political Change in Northern Nigeria* (Evanston, IL: Northwestern University Press, 1997), 9–10.

15. This was due to the British discomfort with some of the harsher aspects of Islamic criminal punishment; see Kukah and Falola, *Religious Militancy and Self-Assertion*, 39–41.

16. See Michael Crowder, "Lugard and Colonial Nigeria: Towards an Identity," *History Today* 36 (February 1986): 23–29.

17. Consult Pat Williams and Toyin Falola, *Religious Impact on the Nation State: The Nigerian Predicament* (Aldershot, U.K., and Brookfield, VT: Avebury Press, 1995), 16–17.

18. For an introduction to Islamic law, see, for example, R. Gleavy and E. Kermeli, eds., *Islamic Law: Theory and Practice* (London and New York: I. B. Tauris, 1997).

19. Relatedly, consult Ali A. Mazrui and Pio Zirimu, "The Secularization of an Afro-Islamic Language: Church, State and Marketplace in the Spread of Kiswahili," in *The Power of Babel: Language and Governance in the African Experience*, ed. Ali A. Mazrui and Alamin A. Mazrui (Oxford, Nairobi, Kampala, Cape Town, and Chicago: James Currey, E.A.E.P. Fountain, David Philip, and the University of Chicago Press, 1998), 169–171.

20. Relatedly, for an interesting comparative work, see Amilcar A. Barreto, *Language, Elites, and the State: Nationalism in Puerto Rico and Quebec* (Westport, CT: Praeger, 1998).

21. For an assessment of devolution in the United Kingdom, consult Jonathan Bradbury and James Mitchell, "Devolution: New Politics for Old?" *Parliamentary Affairs* (April 2001): 257–275.

22. A discussion of the origins and development of Scottish national consciousness and constitutional developments may be found in Robert McCreadie, "Scottish Identity and the Constitution," in *National Identities: The Constitution of the United Kingdom*, ed. Bernard Crick (Cambridge, MA, and Oxford: Blackwell, 1991), 38–56.

23. See K. Austin Kerr, *Organizing for Prohibition: A New History of the Anti-Saloon League* (New Haven, CT, and London: Yale University Press, 1985), 335.

24. Consult Thomas M. Coffey, *The Long Thirst: Prohibition in America 1920–1933* (New York: W. W. Norton, 1975); and Kerr, *Organizing for Prohibition*, 185.

25. Kerr, *Organizing for Prohibition*, 275–279.

26. Coffey, *The Long Thirst*, 315.

27. However, the three men who the woman said had coerced her into having sex went unpunished; see *The Guardian*, 23 January 2001, 16.

28. These and other significant Supreme Court death penalty cases are discussed in Barry Latzer, ed., *Death Penalty Cases: Leading U.S. Supreme Court Cases on Capital Punishment* (Boston and Oxford: Butterworth-Heinemann, 1998).

29. See the *New York Times*, 22 June 2001, 17 for a report on the case.

30. On *ijtihad*, see H.H.A. Rahman, "The Origin and Development of Ijtihad to Solve Complex Modern Legal Problems," *Bulletin of the Henry Martyn Institute of Islamic Studies* 17 (January–June 1998): 7–21.

31. Consult Frank E. Vogel, "The Closing of the Door of Ijtihad and the Application of the Law," *American Journal of Islamic Social Sciences* 10 (Fall 1993): 396–401.

32. For a discussion on Islam and slavery, consult John R. Willis, *Islam and the Ideology of Slavery*, vol. 1 of *Slaves and Slavery in Muslim Africa* (Totowa, NJ, and London: Frank Cass, 1985).

33. On *ijma*, see M. N. Khan, "Ijma: Third Source of Islamic Law," *Hamdard Islamicus* 22 (January 1999): 84–86.

34. Even the vaunted Swiss system is not a perfect model; consult, for instance, Clive Church, "Switzerland: A Paradigm in Evolution," *Parliamentary Affairs* 53, no. 1 (January 2000): 96–113.

35. Both religion and ethnicity are challenging aspects to developing a satisfactory Nigerian federal system; for an account of the development of various Nigerian federal systems and the challenges, see Martin Dent, "Nigeria: Federalism and Ethnic Rivalry," *Parliamentary Affairs* 53, no. 1 (January 2000): 157–168.

Chapter 6

The French Revolution and Transitional Justice

Howard G. Brown

The late twentieth century saw scores of fledgling democracies struggle with the problems of transitional justice as liberal regimes sought to establish themselves after the collapse of repressive regimes.[1] France experienced the same struggle in the wake of the French Revolution. The central problem of transitional justice is trying to balance some form of amnesty, either tacit or explicit, with forms of selective punishment, usually given the more elevated name of retributive justice. Although the correct balance is different in every case, the objectives remain the same. Strategies for transitional justice are designed to serve two fundamental purposes: to enable the new regime and its core values to take root and to begin the process of national reconciliation. The survival of the new regime is primary, but this often depends on overcoming a legacy of violence and fear. In the late 1790s, the fledgling First French Republic had to overcome the deep civil strife and political animosities bred by the Terror of 1793–1794 and the Thermidorian Reaction, which followed in 1795. Efforts to overcome these divisions led to a constitutional republic known as the Directory (1795–1799). However, the Directory failed to create an effective transitional justice; that is, the regime itself was short-lived, and national reconciliation was delayed until after 1800. Even then, the process came with a high price tag: the abandonment of democracy under Napoleon.

The French Revolution has long been a landmark in the origins of democracy, but it has never been studied explicitly as the first country to experience the problems of transitional justice. This is partly because the five years between Robespierre and Napoleon have been the subject of far less study than the years immediately before or after. Certainly, historians are familiar with the vicissitudes of democracy in these years, but this is limited to constitutionalism, elections, and press freedom and almost wholly ignores the problem of ensconcing the rule of law in the aftermath of the Terror. For this reason, the vast literature on the French Revolution contains no detailed study of the amnesty adopted in October 1795.[2] It was a failure, and so it has been ignored. But failure can be as historically significant as success. In order to understand the significance of the amnesty, we need to trace its immediate origins, assess its consequences, and then weigh possible alternatives. Such an analysis leads us to conclude that the new liberal republic made a grave mistake by failing to provide victims of the Terror with some form of retributive justice.

ORIGINS OF THE AMNESTY

The amnesty adopted in October 1795 was the final stage of an evolutionary process unleashed by the overthrow of Robespierre fifteen months earlier.[3] This evolution can be usefully framed as four stages in the politics of justice as they were used to dismantle the Terror and then to try to end the French Revolution.

First stage: *justice as rhetoric.* On 9 Thermidor Year II (July 27, 1794), elements within the Revolutionary Government—in other words, leading members of Robespierre's own "party" (the Montagnard Jacobins)—overthrew him in order to save themselves from another impending purge. As one of them said, it was kill or be killed. The coup was not planned or executed in order to change the regime. The coup leaders had been fully involved in setting up and operating the institutions of the Revolutionary Government, and they expressly stated that it would carry on as before. However, in order to justify outlawing and immediately executing Robespierre and 100 of his closest allies without a trial, the leaders of the coup quickly invented a discursive dichotomy in which they juxtaposed terror and justice. Robespierre was soon described as a tyrant operating a "system of terror" based on arbitrary persecution of political opponents. Using the rhetoric of justice to legitimate the coup soon forced the new leaders to restore elementary forms of jurisprudence to the Revolutionary Tribunal as well as to begin releasing imprisoned "suspects."

Second stage: *justice as retribution.* Replacing the rhetoric of terror[4] with the rhetoric of justice led unavoidably to a number of deputies being punished by their colleagues as scapegoats for the "system of terror." In the autumn and winter of 1794–1795, the convention opted for highly selective antiterrorist justice by staging two great show trials. The first trial was of Jean-Baptiste Carrier, who, as parliamentary deputy on mission during the civil war in the Vendée, had overseen massive roundups and systematic drownings in the Loire River. The second trial was of Fouquier-Tinville, the public prosecutor for the Revolutionary Tribunal during Robespierre's ascendancy. The horrors revealed by these trials helped to break the hold of revolutionary discourse on the political imaginary. The Jacobins lost their influence in government and were put on the defensive throughout France. Two failed *sans-culottes* uprisings in the spring of 1795 inspired the arrest of several dozen Jacobin deputies held responsible for the "excesses" of the Terror. A handful were hastily tried and executed, others were deported to French Guyana, and yet others simply remained in prison awaiting their fate.[5]

Third stage: *justice as revenge*. Seeing a few of the *"grands coupables"* being punished, but no judicial pursuit of "terrorists" at the village level—what could be called Robespierre's willing executioners—provoked the populace into acts of revenge. In order to understand the limits on transitional justice in the French Revolution, it is important to emphasize that two centuries ago 85 percent of the French population lived in the countryside, fewer than half of them conducted their daily affairs in French, and it took a full week to cross the country by stagecoach. These conditions bred intense localism. The introduction of democracy made it extremely difficult for the central state to control local authorities. Thus, the Terror had emerged in 1793 as ad hoc responses to widespread regional resistance. The hydra of revolt began as a huge peasant rebellion in western France and grew new heads at Lyons, Marseilles, Toulon, and Bordeaux. In this climate of crisis, the National Convention authorized surveillance committees, exceptional tribunals, and *sans-culottes* militias to proliferate across the country. This was revolutionary terror organized like a cottage industry. For a while it was impossible to impose effective control over the exercise of coercive force. Insofar as there was a "system of terror," it was the fruit of a prolonged struggle to bring local instruments of state-sanctioned violence under government control while continuing to wage a life-or-death struggle with counterrevolutionaries at home and abroad. Suppression of the Vendée and Federalist revolts, including 3,000 people who perished in the sinister drownings at Nantes or the bloody mop-up at Lyons, the condemnation and execution of 17,000 victims by more than seventy military commissions and revolutionary tribunals, and the imprisonment of over 100,000 people, many only "suspects" never put on trial, combined to make the Terror the haunting memory for early-nineteenth-century Europeans that the Holocaust is today. This should not be allowed to obscure the intensely localized nature of repression during the Terror. Most departments in France experienced fewer than a dozen executions.[6]

The tension between local and national experiences of Terror naturally shaped the backlash against it. By the spring of 1795, the leadership of the National Convention had changed so much that lawmakers began to aid and abet the growing popular reaction against the Terror. A series of piecemeal laws ordered the disarming of former "terrorists," required any officials sacked since the overthrow of Robespierre to be placed under official surveillance, and even ordered the arrest and prosecution of anyone accused of unauthorized political killings in the past three years. This last decree required all ninety criminal courts to remain in permanent session. Deputies hoped that such judicial proceedings would respond to the popular demand for vengeance and thereby stem a rising tide of anti-Jacobin violence. This proved a vain hope. Furious victims refused to wait for the courts and took revenge into their own hands. In the summer of 1795, mobs massacred scores of prisoners in southern towns and cities from

Lyons to Marseilles, a region where repression had been especially bloody in 1793.[7] The spectacular slaughter of political prisoners was accompanied by hundreds of individual killings and lesser assaults.[8]

These brutal acts were committed not by lone fanatics or anarchic mobs but by groups of people bound together by a common sense of outrage at the excesses of local revolutionary militants. Those who took the lead had suffered personally during the Terror. Their targets were individuals well known in the local context. This was an extension of personal and group rivalries that had spiraled out of control until they threatened the fabric of community life. When fellow villagers perished on the scaffold, collective outrage inspired a deadly lust for revenge.[9] Once the traditional community was no longer at the mercy of an alien ideology wielded by a handful of local militants, it succumbed to an overwhelming urge to punish them for their transgressions of the unwritten communal code. Some murdered Jacobins were so well known for their excesses that their brutal deaths were described as "executions which only lack the seal of the law to make them acts of justice."[10] On the other hand, some republicans vociferated about paramilitary death squads supposedly organized and funded by counterrevolutionaries whose strings were pulled from beyond the frontier.[11] Thus, these vendetta-style killings were plausibly labeled in sharply contrasting ways. From one perspective, they constituted an orchestrated effort to bring down the republic—in short, counterrevolution. From another perspective, they were legitimate punishments for heinous crimes against the community—in other words, justice. Historians have recently come to the balanced conclusion that the so-called White Terror owed more to a popular groundswell of anti-Jacobinism than it did to explicitly counterrevolutionary activities. The sense of righteous killing far surpassed other political objectives.[12]

Fourth stage: *justice as amnesia*. The surge of revenge killings in southern France and the emergence of a large guerrilla movement in western France (known as *chouannerie*) risked bringing down the republic and paving the way for a restoration of the monarchy. Therefore, the National Convention changed tack once again. First, it quickly repealed all of its recent antiterrorist laws. This meant annulling judicial decisions that had compensated victims for revolutionary seizures of property. It also meant prohibiting all civil or criminal judgments against officials who had ordered arrests under the Law of Suspects of September 1793. Finally, it meant overtly shielding former revolutionary militants from the now revenge-minded judiciary. This involved annulling recent laws requiring administrative surveillance and disarmament of former "terrorists," banning their prosecution for acts not specified in the Penal Code, and ordering the release of anyone arrested for such ill-defined crimes as "terrorism," "harassment," "oppressing the people," and "abuse of authority."[13] Second, the National Convention subverted national elections by deciding that two-thirds of its members would continue as deputies in the new bicameral legislature. By this time, most French people were either indifferent or openly hostile to the republic. Without the two-thirds law, the new legislature would have been dominated by monarchists. Naturally, therefore, the two-thirds law provoked an antirepublican insurrection in Paris—quickly crushed by an obscure young general named Bonaparte. This royalist revolt inspired the convention to use its last days to exclude all relatives of émigrés from political office and to revive the draconian laws of 1792–1793 against émigrés and refractory priests. Such renewed extremism alienated moderates seeking a modus vivendi with the republican regime.

The expiring convention also adopted an amnesty "for all acts associated with the revolution." The amnesty put an end to all existing detentions, investigations, prosecutions, and criminal proceedings. According to the rhetoric of the moment, only pulling a veil over the past could put an end to political hatred, factional struggles, and the interminable cycle of violence that these created. Such a momentous decree was presented to the convention as "the only means of ending the revolution."[14] However, this was not an evenhanded amnesty. It excluded émigrés, deported priests, royalist insurgents in Paris, and guerrillas in western France still locked in armed struggle with the republic. No one debated these exclusions at the time. The fear of royalist reaction ensured that the amnesty favored radical revolutionaries, that is, those who had committed crimes due to "an excessive zeal and blind rage for liberty."[15] In fact, proponents of the amnesty argued that it should be adopted precisely because it was not general.[16] Thus, although the amnesty also covered the vigilante violence of 1795, it was designed primarily to protect republicans who had served the Revolutionary Government of 1793–1794. The convention hoped that giving *sans-culottes* and other radical republicans the judicial equivalent of absolution would unite all strands of pro-revolutionary sentiment behind the nascent constitutional regime called the Directory. As one set of judges put it, the amnesty was both a veil and a pardon "which we expect to result in a sincere forgetfulness of the past, a perfect union of all French republicans, and an unalterable accord for the strengthening and prosperity of the Republic."[17] Unfortunately, the nature of the amnesty crippled the Directory's ability to complete the transition from revolutionary expediency to the rule of law.

CONSEQUENCES OF THE AMNESTY

The amnesty of October 1795 followed months of harassment, beatings, mob assaults, arbitrary arrests, and prison massacres directed against Jacobins and functionaries of the Revolutionary Government throughout the country. In this light, the amnesty appears as a not unreasonable effort on the part of beleaguered republicans to protect fellow travelers from persecution. However, six years of bloody revolution had reduced the old polity to shards and discredited the republican effort to assemble a new one. Jacobin extremists, aggrieved moderates, and intransigent royalists fought one another and the government in towns and villages across the country. A crippled economy, continuous war, Catholic hostility, and generalized banditry all fed the fires of political conflict. As will be seen, rather than helping to heal these wounds of revolution, the amnesty allowed them to fester and prevented truly effective forms of transitional justice from being applied.

When the Directory took office in November 1795, it was arguably the first regime in history to face what has since become a classic dilemma for all fledgling democracies confronted by widespread violence. As a liberal democratic regime, the Directory's legitimacy depended heavily on its willingness to respect and uphold due legal process. A constitutionally based rule of law dictates that only certain means can be used to achieve political objectives, thereby placing continual constraints on political efficiency and expediency. In such a system, policies are judged as much by the procedural characteristics that they embody as by their results. Political elites often fudge or openly ignore such procedural norms, but they rarely do so with impunity. This was particularly true in France in 1795 following all the revolutionary rhetoric about the arbitrary oppression of the absolutist monarchy and especially after the republic itself had been so badly tarnished by the arbitrariness of the Revolutionary Government. This required making a dramatic shift from emphasizing ends to emphasizing means. However, the importance of adopting more scrupulous means severely limited the Directory's ability to put a swift end to endemic violence and widespread resistance. In other words, using overwhelming military force or exceptional justice to restore order was fettered by the regime's need to observe a strict constitutionalism in order to enhance its shaky legitimacy.[18]

The strategy of combining constitutionalism, amnesty, and the rule of law amounted to the rejection of any form of explicitly transitional justice. It is not surprising, therefore, that the body politic suffered severe symptoms of sudden withdrawal. Although the Directory announced that henceforth the fundamental principle of government would be "an inflexible justice and the strictest observance of the laws," the undemocratic example set by the regime's founding fathers together with the political complexion of the newly elected magistrates seriously impaired this strategy. This is hardly surprising. After all, the Thermidorian deputies who adopted the rule-of-law strategy were the same ones who flagrantly violated their new constitution in both its spirit and letter. The two-thirds law imposed on elections to the councils seriously distorted the concept of representative democracy, supposedly the bedrock of the new order. In addition, barring the relatives of émigrés from elected office clearly contravened the Constitution, as even deputies who supported the idea later conceded. Doing so *after* the elections added to the travesty of democracy. Much could be said and was said to justify these measures, but they still smacked of opportunism. In this atmosphere of uncertain legitimacy, only monumental naïveté and an exaggerated belief in the power of rhetoric[19] could explain why the government imagined that the judges and local officials elected in October 1795 would apply the spirit as well as the letter of the law. Were these men not chosen by the very voters whom the convention did not trust to choose republicans as national deputies? Why should the newly elected justices of the peace, judges, and public prosecutors uphold the highest principles of jurisprudence when the authors of the Constitution found it perfectly acceptable to adopt such a heavy-handed expedient as the law of 3 brumaire IV (October 25, 1795)? Nullifying the recent election of émigré relatives to various local offices could hardly have encouraged their remaining colleagues to forgo expedients of their own.

The magistracy elected in 1795 reflected prevailing public sentiment. Although not necessarily antirepublican, judges tended to hate Jacobins and to mistrust the new government.[20] The judicial independence guaranteed by the Constitution and the influence that local politics had on elected judges combined to make the magistracy a serious obstacle to the Directory's plan to end the Revolution through a careful application of the rule of law.[21] Where avowedly antirepublican judges gained office, such as in the violence-torn southeast, a judicial backlash took place against the new regime. Not only did they fail to apply laws against émigrés and refractory priests, but they refused to investigate or prosecute revenge attacks on former servants of the Revolutionary Government, even if they were appointed officials of the new regime.[22] However, as long as the government respected the Constitution, the "rule of law" was whatever local judges wanted to make it.

Thus, the Directory's strategy of relying on the integrity of the judiciary to restore public order and political peace largely failed. Rather than assisting with a transition to the rule of law, the amnesty subverted it. Although the amnesty favored Jacobins, it also protected the thugs and vigilantes of the White Terror. By eschewing retributive justice, the expiring convention had left both factions intact and fostered a climate of vendetta. These problems, together with technical flaws in the amnesty law itself, inspired a sporadic yearlong legislative debate on whether to repeal it or reform it.[23] Just when a much improved version of the amnesty was about to be adopted, right-wing deputies ambushed the process. They argued that if murderers and thieves could benefit from the amnesty by construing their crimes as political, then it should be extended to émigrés and their relatives, who had been deprived of their political rights simply due to their status at birth or because their fears of seeing the revolutionary regime restored had led to errors of judgment. In short, a proper amnesty would include repealing the law barring the relatives of émigrés from holding political office. This provoked two days of tumultuous debate, which derailed plans to improve the amnesty. Raucous and confused discussion continued sporadically for weeks.

In the end, the amnesty was modified to include various rebel groups (most notably, those in western France now that General Hoche had "pacified" the region). In fact, a quid pro quo was arranged in which those who had formally benefited from the amnesty would be excluded from holding political office, while Western rebels who surrendered their weapons and Parisian rioters who opposed the two-thirds law would be amnestied. The result of this sporadic, yearlong debate, therefore, was to increase the scope of national clemency to include right-wing opponents of the republic at the expense of decreasing the pool of potential republican candidates for political office. In other words, the regime sought retribution at the expense of a broad political base.[24]

During the same period, the government began a systematic police harassment of amnestied revolutionaries in order to distance itself from political pariahs on the left. This was not based on new crimes that they had committed. In fact, the government's problem in dealing with challengers on its left was their ability to stir up discontent while remaining largely within legal bounds. The flawed amnesty and an inability to reform it led the government to focus police activity on specific categories of revolutionary: former Montagnards, officers in the *sans-culottes* militias, members of surveillance committees, and so on. These groups became the subject of an increasingly sophisticated "preventive repression," both in Paris and in the provinces. In some departments, the police drew up lists of *amnistiés* and put them under special surveillance.[25] This did nothing to restore the dignity of victims of revolutionary violence and simply took the regime down the path of arbitrariness and exceptional justice.

The elections of spring 1797 produced a right-wing landslide, thereby demonstrating just how thoroughly Frenchmen repudiated the new regime. In the following months, political violence rose to levels not seen for two years. Vigilantism returned with renewed ferocity. Although the summer of 1797 lacked the spectacular prison massacres of two years before, the reactionary atmosphere and the certainty of impunity provoked a spate of murderous anti-Jacobin riots.[26] Republican hard-liners within the government responded with a coup d'état on September 4, 1797, in which they purged the legislature of cryptoroyalists and nullified elections in half the departments of France. This also launched a period of steadily escalating repression, which ended only with the death of democracy under Napoleon.[27]

The amnesty played a leading role in this tragedy. Rather than inaugurating a period of national reconciliation, the amnesty helped to prolong political violence. This enabled both extremes to preserve a dangerous purchase on national politics. Thus, the amnesty undercut the Directory's ability to win support from a wide variety of people who had suffered personal tragedy during the Revolution. Too many felt legally emasculated by the amnesty and resented the rogue republicans and vigilante killers who benefited from it. By 1799, moderate republicans despaired of achieving national reconciliation within a truly democratic Constitution and threw in their lot with Napoleon and "liberal authoritarianism."[28]

ALTERNATIVES TO THE AMNESTY

Given the Directory's failure to consolidate liberal democracy and achieve national reconciliation, it is worth considering three possible alternatives to the amnesty: a truth commission, financial compensation, and retributive justice.

Truth Commission. The promising (albeit mixed) results of truth commissions in Chile and South Africa lead us to speculate whether such an institution could have been successful in 1795. The answer is clearly no. In order for truth-telling to play a part in national reconciliation, it must occur in a public forum and be reported more or less accurately to a wider national audience. Victims of the Terror may well have found it easier to overcome their urge for revenge if they had been given an opportunity to tell their story and to provide evidence to support it. This could have been done most effectively in some type of public forum. Such a process would have enabled them to garner general sympathy as well as legitimate their claim to rightful revenge. Perhaps more idealistically, providing a forum in which to expose atrocities, excesses, and abuses of power would also have given victims the opportunity to earn respect and admiration by publicly relinquishing their right to revenge in the interests of a return to peace and tranquility. However, without a public forum in which to reestablish their dignity in the eyes of the community through an act of magnanimity, victims remained torn between an act of revenge to restore their honor and a humiliating acceptance of their impotence.

There was no way that the Directory could meet the basic needs for effective truth-telling due to the role that public denunciation had played in radicalizing revolutionary politics and to the ludicrously partisan nature of newspapers. A ubiquitous fear of plots during the years 1789 to 1794 had valorized denunciation as a civic duty. Furthermore, incorporating thousands of local political clubs into a national network made them arenas for elaborate purification rituals easily manipulated by the likes of Robespierre. Together, these practices severely eroded faith in the power of publicity to unmask traitors or constrain dangerous politicians.[29] This made a public forum for truth-telling unthinkable. In addition, no code of journalistic ethics had even begun to emerge in the 1790s. Besides, from 1795 to 1797, the press was dominated by opponents of the regime who daily tarred the republic with exaggerated claims about Jacobin misdeeds.[30] Thus, any form of truth commission was structurally impossible.

Financial Compensation. Although the amnesty law of October 1795 prohibited claiming punitive damages, it explicitly allowed victims to sue perpetrators in civil courts for the recovery of money or property illegally seized or embezzled during the Revolution. However, this provision limited claims to simple restitution and made no mention of compensatory damages. This left no recourse for people whose crops had been burned, animals killed, or buildings demolished. Besides, being able to file civil suits did not constitute the sort of justice that would have earned the Directory much-needed credibility. That depended on making a link to criminal justice and probably also on providing further enabling legislation in the realm of civil justice. As it was, the civil legislation in place in 1795 did not encourage victims to sue perpetrators, and so, apparently, they almost never did.[31] Lawmakers attempted to rectify this problem a year later by having the government compensate victims for property losses during the Terror. This had two quintessentially Thermidorian virtues: it reaffirmed property rights, and it avoided acrimonious civil suits by not blaming individuals but rather the "system of terror." However, a currency crisis and an empty treasury made this attempt to "buy public peace" utterly impossible.[32]

Retributive Justice. In lieu of granting a full amnesty for revolutionary acts, a selective but effective application of the Penal Code could have helped to establish the moral authority of the new regime. Conceptually, retributive justice can be both general and specific. In the general sense, perpetrators are punished in order to avenge crimes that injured the new regime. This was well expressed by a deputy who demanded that amnestied members of a paramilitary death squad be rearrested and punished "in the name of the constitution, for the honor of the French People, and for that of the legislative body."[33] Here retribution was demanded for the new republican polity. However, retributive justice usually has a more limited meaning, that of punishing perpetrators on behalf of their victims. Laws are not intended to eradicate revenge but rather to contain it within the channels of retribution. When justice clearly acts on behalf of individual victims as well as on behalf of society, it respects the dignity of the victim and at the same time depersonalizes the punishment. This process acknowledges the victim's position but undercuts the victim's urge to seek private revenge for wrongs suffered. This removes the motive for escalating reprisals. Thus, retributive justice rationalizes vengeance, directing it as narrowly as possible at the most appropriate target and preventing further violence.[34]

Retributive justice as an aspect of transitional regimes needs further clarification. Three features have characterized modern systems of criminal justice: a defense of the law as an essential element in preserving morality; a need to punish those who threaten the social order; and an effort to reform offenders. However, in the last generation or so, Western democracies have witnessed a return to much older concerns about basing justice (and therefore punishment) on the impact that crime has on victims. In other words, criminal justice is moving away from an exclusive focus on the law, social order, and the criminal and toward satsifying the victim.[35] The term retributive justice is often used to describe this victim-centered approach. However, providing solace to victims is only one aspect of retributive justice as it is understood in the context of a transition from authoritarianism to democracy. The other aspect is the assertion of certain supposedly universal values underpinning criminal justice, values that the previous regime did not uphold and that, therefore, may lack substantial roots in contemporary society. Therefore, retributive justice as part of a transitional regime means punishing people for what they did during the previous regime in order (1) to accord those who suffered under that regime the status of victims—rather than, for example, enemies of the "people"—and thereby restore their dignity, (2) to establish the timelessness of the values of the new regime, even if it means punishing acts that had been legal and even encouraged under the previous regime, and (3) to combine these two features as sources of legitimacy for the new regime and as a pedagogy for society.

Actually implementing retributive justice in 1795 was enormously complicated by the reality of widespread resistance to the Revolution and the internecine strife among revolutionary factions. Factional conflict between various strands of pro-republican sentiment had greatly fueled the Terror, but the repressive measures adopted in 1793–1794 were plausibly justified by genuine counterrevolutionary violence. Herein lay the greatest quandary for the liberal constitutional republic: it was being juxtaposed not to one, but to two former regimes, absolutist monarchy and revolutionary terror. This ruled out any blanket remedy. On one hand, many victims of the Revolutionary Government were either innocent bystanders or supporters of the republic who had opposed the excessive use of state-sponsored violence. The Girondins and Dantonists are obvious examples. On the other hand, many victims of the Terror were outright royalists whom the Directory rightly considered ardent enemies of the republic, not victims at all. It is appropriate to wonder just how a fledgling regime still waging foreign war and confronting widespread domestic unrest could have sorted out such complicated circumstances.

Other factors were working against retributive justice. Obviously, daily reminders of the many misdeeds committed in the name of the republic risked undermining confidence in it, even in its new constitutional form. Furthermore, many deputies sent on mission in 1793 and 1794 had relied on a mix of local militants and shady traders willing to use any means available to accomplish the Revolutionary Government's goals in the provinces. If such men were put on trial for "excesses," they would not hesitate to invoke the mantle of superior authority as their best defense. It would then be difficult to decide just where to cut the lengthy chain of responsibility leading from a village "terrorist" all the way to a former deputy in the National Convention. In order to retain control of the process, the convention decided to form its own twelve-member screening commission to sort through the many *sans-culottes* and Jacobins arrested during the recent reaction. This commission intended to distinguish between "oppressed patriots," who would be freed, and genuine "terrorists," who would be prosecuted. However, a popular outcry against such a blatant usurpation of judicial authority got the plan annulled.[36] Unable to develop a process that they could control, deputies feared the consequences of letting retributive justice take its course through the courts.

Some deputies argued that using regular courts to try supposed terrorists would be turning them over to men whose hearts contained "the seed of vengeance for the wrongs they had suffered."[37] Others raised the specter of endless repression, claiming that punishing those who had operated hundreds of scaffolds and prisons would also require hundreds of scaffolds and prisons. This overdrawn image was in fact belied by the process of punishment already under way. By the time of the amnesty debate in October 1795, the criminal court of almost every department that had experienced serious repression during the Terror was in the midst of a major trial of local "terrorists." These trials inevitably took a long time and attracted massive public attention. However, investigating a number of these trials reveals that prosecuting political crimes committed since the overthrow of the monarchy had not led to judicial severity. The transition from revolutionary justice to the rule of law restored procedural protections to the accused. This made it technically difficult to convict former "terrorists." In fact, the majority of defendants were acquitted on the grounds of lacking criminal intent.[38] It would appear, therefore, that the amnesty did not in fact save hundreds of local "terrorists" from the scaffold or prison—many would not have been convicted anyway.

Such findings lead one to suggest how history *should* have happened. This is the sort of intellectual move that historians are professionally trained to avoid; nonetheless, the purpose of this collection encourages stretching disciplinary ethics a little. Under such circumstances, one might suggest that instead of adopting a biased amnesty, the convention could have enabled the Directory to win support for the new regime by creating a limited form of retributive justice.

Despite the dangers inherent in retributive justice described above, not exercising it sacrificed important advantages. Recent experiences with transitional justice in Eastern Europe and Latin America show that it is not the sheer number of convictions, or even the percentage of convictions that makes retributive justice effective after a change of regime. The efficiency of criminal justice in obtaining convictions matters far less than the effectiveness of having some form of retributive justice to establish the new regime's credibility in moral terms.[39] The First French Republic could have achieved this only by proclaiming the principles of accountability for injustices as part of an effort to restore the dignity of victims. This concern was eloquently expressed at the time. Perès, a member of the National Convention who continued as a deputy in the Council of 500, raised just such an approach, stressing the government's potential role in restoring victims' dignity. He asked his fellow deputies,

Once back in your departments, how will you respond to these weeping widows, these grieving orphans, who will come to you demanding to know why, regardless of all laws, you have allowed their fathers' and their husbands' murderers, with their impunity, the barbarous pleasure of mocking their distress? . . . Only justice from the government can restore confidence, the true bond of social unity.[40]

This eloquently summarized the widespread demands for vindication. Perès cleverly focused on widows and orphans, that is, individuals generally unable to take revenge into their own hands, and thus highlighted the need for the government to mobilize the apparatus of justice on their behalf.

Thus, the idea of seeking retribution in the name of the new regime's key institutions could have been used to justify a selective enforcement of the Penal Code to cover revolutionary excesses that had sullied republicanism. This would have provided an effective practical as well as theoretical basis for using the criminal courts to exact retributive justice. Politicians feared that providing an opportunity for retributive justice would simply prolong factional turmoil. It is impossible to determine the extent to which the amnesty succeeded in fostering a return to normalcy by preventing a plethora of investigations and prosecutions from stirring up revolutionary hatreds. Nonetheless, there are good reasons to think that retributive justice would not have inflamed passions—at least where they were not already dangerously inflamed.

Traditional reluctance to participate in the operations of official justice due to the destabilizing effects that it had on village communities might have limited the divisiveness of prosecuting serious revolutionary excesses. Eighteenth-century villagers abhorred testifying in cases involving their neighbors.[41] Compelling villagers to testify in highly politicized trials would have forced them publicly to take sides and thereby have produced a long-standing rift in the community. On the other hand, not prosecuting men who had clearly transgressed communal norms on the limits of power left many people determined to take private revenge. Numerous assaults and murders of former local officials under the Revolutionary Government argued for the Directorial judiciary to punish perpetrators of terrorist excesses in order to end the cycle of violence. As the deputy Siméon remarked, "So you don't want any more revolution? Well then, be aware that there is no emotion more revolutionary than vengeance."[42] He might have elaborated more fully. By leaving victims no recourse other than private vengeance, the complete lack of retributive justice that accompanied the amnesty fostered greater political violence. Stifling judicial investigation forced communities to resolve the resulting discord without help from the government.

It should be obvious by now that there were no easy solutions in the autumn of 1795. The fact of having not one but two former regimes to overcome made it hard to separate true victims from the new regime's political enemies; the revolutionary experience of "party" purges and jaundiced journalism made truth and reconciliation unthinkable; legislative limits on civil liability and virtual state bankruptcy ruled out financial compensation for victims; the inability of legislators to isolate themselves from prosecution or to create a national screening apparatus left punishment for political crimes in the hands of local criminal courts; the recourse to an amnesty precluded using the criminal courts for retributive justice and therefore left victims to settle scores their own way; an independent and often hostile judiciary proved unwilling to enforce the rule of law against revenge attacks; and the new regime depended on strict constitutionalism for its legitimacy, thereby ruling out exceptional procedures that could have constituted retributive justice. All of these factors militated against an effective transitional justice. However, failure to come to terms with the aftermath of the Terror prevented the French Revolution from establishing a durable liberal democratic regime.

APPENDIX: BASIC DATES IN THE FRENCH REVOLUTION

1789

May 5: Estates General meets for the first time in 174 years.

July 14: Storming of the Bastille saves the National Assembly.

August 4: National Assembly abolishes "feudalism" and adopts Declaration of the Rights of Man and Citizen.

1790

Complete territorial and administrative reorganization of France based on elected officials.

December 26: Loyalty oath for the clergy creates widespread opposition among the people.

1791

June 20–24: Louis XVI hurts the Catholic and royalist cause by trying to flee France.

August 27: Prussia and Austria threaten France with war to protect Louis XVI.

October 1: Legislative Assembly meets, making France a constitutional monarchy.

1792

April 20: France declares war on Austria; requires mobilizing National Guard across France.

August 10: National Guards and Parisian radicals overthrow Louis XVI.

September 2–7: Parisian *sans-culottes* fear Prussian invasion and massacre 1,100 prisoners.

September 21: National Convention meets and proclaims France a republic.

1793

January 21: Execution of Louis XVI.

February 1: France declares war on Great Britain and Holland and on Spain a month later.

March 18: Counterrevolutionary revolt in western France begins Vendée civil war.

June 2: Purge of convention leads to Federalist revolt at Lyons, Marseilles, Toulon, and Bordeaux.

September 5: Convention puts "terror" on its daily agenda and encourages repression.

December: Revolutionary government defeats Vendée rebels and crushes Federalist revolt.

1794

March 24, April 6: Execution of Hébertists and Dantonists, leading opponents of Robespierre.

June 10: Judicial Terror leads to stripping the Revolutionary Tribunal of all jurisprudence.

June 26: Battle of Fleurus ends defense of France and begins wars of conquest.

July 27: Robespierre overthrown and executed; convention starts dismantling the Terror.

November 12: Conservatives close the Paris Jacobin Club.

December 16: Execution of Carrier for "excesses" of terrorism in the Vendée.

1795

February 21: Separation of church and state with limited freedom of worship.

April 1 and May 20–21: Uprisings in Paris; repression of *sans-culottes* and Jacobin "terrorists."

June: Height of the revenge killings or "White Terror" in the Rhône Valley.

October 5: Royalist uprising in Paris against election restrictions.

October 27: Start of the constitutional republic known as the Directory.

1797

April 20: Conservatives win elections and take control of the legislature in late May.

September 4: Republican coup d'état nullifies half the elections and purges royalists.

1799

November 9: Bonaparte takes power in a coup d'état and ends the Directory.

December 25: Consulate adopts an authoritarian Constitution.

1800

February 17: Democratic local government is replaced by appointed prefects and mayors.

NOTES

1. For a wide-ranging selection of documents and analyses of postwar experiences, see Neil J. Kritz, ed., *Transitional Justice: How Emerging Democracies Reckon with Former Regimes*, 3 vols. (Washington, DC: U.S. Institute of Peace, 1995), and for an attempt to theorize recent experiences of transitional justice, see Ruti G. Teitel, *Transitional Justice* (New York: Oxford University Press, 2000).

2. The only exception is Sergio Luzatto, "Comment entrer dans le Directoire? Le problème de l'amnistie," in *La République directoriale: Actes du colloque de Clermont-Ferrand, 22–24 mai 1997*, ed. Philippe Bourdin and Bernard Gainot (Clermont-Ferrand: Société des études robespierristes, 1998), 207–229. However, the author spends little time on the amnesty itself, focusing instead on the Directory's handling of former terrorists thereafter.

3. See the Appendix for a timeline of the French Revolution.

4. The two most important contributions to the rhetoric of terror were the decree of September 5, 1793 and Robespierre's speech to the National Convention on February 5, 1794, when he provided theoretical justification for the Revolutionary Government: "If the basis of popular government in time of peace is virtue, its basis in time of revolution is both virtue and terror—virtue without which terror is disastrous, and terror without which virtue is powerless." E. Desprez et al., eds., *Oeuvres complètes de Maximilien Robespierre*, 10 vols. (Paris: Aux bureaux de la Revue historique de la Révolution française, 1910–67), x. 357.

5. Bronislaw Baczko, *Comment sortir de la Terreur. Thermidor et la Révolution* (Paris: Gallimard, 1989), 191–245. A few prominent terrorists, such as members of the military commissions of Bordeaux and Orange, were also tried and condemned before the summer of 1795, but they were few and far between. Henri Wallon, *Les Représentants du peuple en mission et la justice révolutionnaire dans les départements en l'an II* (Paris: Hachette et Cie., 1890), 5: 270–301.

6. Louis Mortimer-Ternaux, *Histoire de la Terreur, 1792–1794*, vol. 8 (Paris: Lévy, 1862–1881); René Roblot, *La justice criminelle en France sous la Terreur* (Paris: Librairie de droit et de jurisprudence, 1938); Donald Greer, *The Incidence of the Terror during the French Revolution* (Cambridge, MA: Harvard University Press, 1935); Jean-Claude Petit, *Ces peines obscures: la prison pénale en France, 1780–1875* (Paris: Fayard, 1990), 90–92, 567.

7. Albert Mathiez, *La réaction thermidorienne* (Paris: A. Colin, 1929), 234; Philippe-Joseph-Benjamin Buchez and Prosper-Charles Roux, *Histoire parlementaire de la Révolution française*, vol. 36 (Paris: Paulin,1838), 429–433.

8. Michel Vovelle, "Massacreurs et massacrés. Aspects sociaux de la contre-révolution en Provence après Thermidor," in *Les résistances à la Révolution*, ed. F. Lebrun and R. Dupuy (Paris: Éditions Imago, 1987), 141–150; Richard Cobb, *The Police and the People: French Popular Protest, 1789–1820* (Oxford: Oxford University Press, 1970), 131–150.

9. Colin Lucas, "Themes in Southern Violence after 9 Thermider," in *Beyond the Terror: Essays in French Regional and Social History, 1794–1815*, ed. Colin Lucas and Gwynne Lewis (Cambridge: Cambridge University Press, 1983), 177.

10. René Moulinas, "Le département de Vaucluse en 1795: la contre-révolution en marche?" in *Le Tournant de l'an III: Réaction et Terreur blanche dans la France révolutionnaire*, ed. Michel Vovelle (Paris: Éditions du CTHS, 1997), 529–538.

11. The growing mass of returned émigrés and refractory priests lent credence to these claims. So did the occasional appearance of such confirmed conspirators as the marquis de Surville and Dominique Allier. Gwynne Lewis in *The Second Vendée: The Continuity of Counter-revolution in the Department of the Gard, 1789–1815* (Oxford: Oxford University Press, 1978), 90–98, emphasizes the conspiratorial dimension.

12. Richard Cobb, *Reactions to the French Revolution* (London and New York: Oxford University Press, 1972), 19–43.

13. J.-B. Duvergier, *Collection complète des lois*, 2e éd. (Paris: Chez A. Guyot et Scribe, 1834), viii. 255, 320 (16 fructidor III, 21, 22 vendémiaire IV); Mathiez, *Réaction thermidorienne*, 220–221.

14. Quirot in Convention on 4 brumaire, *Le Moniteur universel ou la Gazette nationale* [hereafter *Moniteur*], an IV, 174.

15. Camus in Council of 500 on 15 floréal IV (4 May 1796), *Moniteur*, an IV, 919.

16. Chénier in National Convention on 4 brumaire IV (26 October 1796), *Moniteur*, an IV, 174.

17. Archives départementales de la Haute-Saône, 368 L 11, 16 brumaire IV.

18. In a pamphlet about ending the Revolution, the Thermidorian deputy Audouin admonished his colleagues that in the future they were to be "energetic, but less in the revolutionary sense than in the constitutional sense." British Library F. 785 (7), *Achevons la Révolution, par P.J. Audouin . . .* (fructidor III), 11.

19. See the Directory's address of 14 germinal IV (5 April 1796): "Républicans du Midi, votre bonheur est aujourd'hui dans vos mains; il est surtout dans le sincère oubli

de toutes les haines, dans la renonciation bien entière, bien franche à tous ces affreux projets de vengeances et de réactions qu'un génie infernal nourrit au milieu de vous. . . . Hommes irascibles, mais bons, ouvrez au saint amour de la patrie, à l'amitié sainte . . . ces coeurs serrés, flétris, dévorés par six ans de colère et de haine!" *Réimpression de l'ancien moniteur universel,* ii. 21.

20. For regional examples of the magistracy elected in 1795, see Jean Vercier, *La justice criminelle dans le département de l'Hérault pendant la Révolution, 1789–1800* (Montpellier: Imprimerie Causse, Graille et Castelnau, 1926), 209–210, and Marcel Reinhard, *Le Département de la Sarthe sous le régime directoriale* (Saint Brieuc: Les Presses Bretonnes, 1935), 210.

21. A month after taking office, the Directory acquired the power to fill judicial vacancies until the next election cycle. Although the government used this provision to increase the number of committed republican judges, they remained an overall minority.

22. In one case in the Vaucluse, the local justice of the peace did nothing to investigate the collective murder of the *commissaire du pouvoir exécutif* at Valréas because his brutality as former head of the revolutionary committee there gave the community a right to commit "legitimate homicide," a right that the judiciary was obliged to respect! Charles Doyle, "Internal Counter-Revolution: The Judicial Reaction in Southern France, 1794–1800," *Renaissance and Modern Studies* 33 (1989): 114. See also Colin Lucas, "The First Directory and the Rule of Law," *French Historical Studies* 10 (1977): 231–260.

23. The debate was initiated by the Directory; see its messages to the Council of 500 on 14 and 19 germinal IV (30 March and 9 April 1796) in *Recueil des actes du Directoire exécutif,* ed. A. Debidour (Paris: Imprimerie nationale, 1910–1917), 4: ii, 85, 113, as well as the report from the minister of justice and supporting petitions in Archives Nationales, C 495, d. 311. See especially the debates in the Council of 500 on 10 and 22 fructidor IV, *Moniteur,* an IV (27 August and 8 September 1796): 1385, 1427–1428, 1431–1435.

24. See especially the debates of 3 vendémiaire, 30 vendémiaire, and 3 frimaire V in *Moniteur,* V, 25–28, 142–144, 146–147, and 263–275, passim. The final law came on 17 frimaire V (6 December 1796).

25. See Luzzato, "Comment entrer dans le Directoire?" 218–229; Richard Cobb, "Note sur la répression contre le personnel sans-culotte de 1795 à 1801," in *Terreur et subsistances (1793–1795)* (Paris: Librairie Clavreuil, 1964), 179–219; Isser Woloch, *Jacobin Legacy: The Democratic Movement under the Directory* (Princeton, NJ: Princeton University Press, 1970), 48–49.

26. For example, Philippe Bourdin, "Les 'Jacobins' du Bois de Cros (Clermont-Ferrand, an V): Chronique d'un massacre annoncé," *Annales historiques de la Révolution française* (1997): 249–304; Archives Nationales BB[18] 863, indictment for events at Castres and Réalmont, 30 messidor–12 thermidor V.

27. Howard G. Brown, "From Organic Society to Security State: The War on Brigandage in France, 1797–1802," *Journal of Modern History* 69 (1997): 661–695.

28. For an explanation of "liberal authoritarianism" and its place in French history, see Howard G. Brown, "Domestic State Violence: Repression from the Croquants to the Commune," *The Historical Journal* 42 (1999): 597–622.

29. Lucien Jaume, *Le discours jacobin et la démocratie* (Paris: Fayard, 1989), 192–215; Jacques Guilhaumou, "Fragments of a Discourse on Denunciation (1789–1794)," in *The Terror,* vol. 4 of *The French Revolution and the Creation of Modern Political*

Culture, ed. Keith Michael Baker (Oxford: Pergamon Press, 1994), 139–155; Colin Lucas, "The Theory and Practice of Denunciation in the French Revolution," *Journal of Modern History* 68 (1996): 768–785.

30. Hugh Gough, *The Newspaper Press in the French Revolution* (Chicago: Lyceum Books, 1988), 188–159; Jeremy D. Popkin, *The Right-Wing Press in France, 1792–1800* (Chapel Hill: University of North Carolina Press, 1980).

31. Aristide Douarche, *Les tribunaux civils de Paris pendant la Révolution (1791–1800)*, vol. 2 (Paris: L. Cerf, 1905–1907) provides a résumé of all the civil suits handled in Paris during these years, and none of them involved compensation for victims of the Terror.

32. Camus in Council of 500 on 15 floréal IV (4 May 1796), *Moniteur*, an IV, 919.

33. In Council of 500 on 16 floréal IV (5 May 1796), *Moniteur*, an IV, 931.

34. Revenge is often taken in response to a perceived harm or an offense to personal honor whereas retribution is done for a well-defined wrong. A male suitor might seek revenge when he is rejected because it is a blow to his honor, even though the girl's family had the right to reject him and has no reason to fear being legally punished for it. Perhaps most importantly, revenge is personal: either the victim or someone closely related to him or her seeks to avenge the harm done to him. In contrast, retributive justice is impersonal, carried out by people unaffected by the original harm. The personal nature of revenge gives it several other distinguishing qualities. Revenge is sweet. It has a peculiar emotional tone involving pleasure in someone else's suffering. This means that persons seeking revenge harm their enemy until they are satisfied and may not be satisfied until they have inflicted far more harm than they suffered. Achilles offers a classical example. Unlike revenge, judicial retribution is characterized by internal limits so that the seriousness of a wrong determines the extent of punishment. The lack of internal limits on revenge and the pleasure taken in the suffering of others often lead to targeting people other than the person who first inflicted harm. Thus, an innocent family member could be the target of revenge either because this would hurt the original perpetrator more or because he or she is an easier target. This spread of vengeance to innocent people could also be the result of a talion mentality, leading, for example, to retaliatory rape. Retributive justice contrasts with revenge by being directed solely at the original wrongdoer. Although people close to the perpetrator might empathize with the suffering that he or she feels when being punished or be tainted by shame for their relationship to him or her, these are not the main purposes of the punishment. Finally, revenge is case-specific and does not commit the avenger to act in the same way in similar circumstances; in contrast, judicial retribution is based on a standardized response. Thus, retributive justice gains effectiveness as a deterrent by virtue of its predictability, whereas revenge is a greater deterrent when menacingly unpredictable. In short, revenge is personal, emotional, unpredictable, and potentially unlimited in scope or intensity; judicial retribution is impersonal, dispassionate, proportional, focused, and predictable.

These distinctions have been developed from the discussions of vindication and revenge in Robert Nozick, *Philosophical Explanations* (Oxford: Clarendon Press, 1981), 363–397, and Chin Liew Ten, *Crime, Guilt, and Punishment* (Oxford: Clarendon Press, 1987), 42–46.

35. On both the dangers and promise of taking victims into account in the evolving forms of justice in Western democracies, see Antoine Garapon, "La justice reconstructive," in *Et ce sera justice: punir en démocratie*, ed. Antoine Garapon, Frédéric Gros, and Thierry Pech (Paris: Éditions Odile Jacob, 2001).

36. See the debates of early thermidor III (July 1795) in the *Moniteur*.

37. *Réimpression de l'ancien Moniteur*, xxv. 330–333 (Quirot, 6 thermidor III).

38. This generalization is based on trials conducted at Toulouse, Vesoul, Le Mans, Montpellier, and Paris. See Martyn Lyons, *Revolution in Toulouse. An Essay on Provincial Terrorism* (Berne: Peter Lang, 1978), 80–81, 97; Pierre Gérard, "L'armée révolutionnaire de la Haute-Garonne," *Annales historiques de la Révolution française* (1959): 155; Georges Fournier, "Réalité et limites de la réaction thermidorienne dans l'Hérault, L'Aude, et la Haute-Garonne," in *Tournant de l'an III*, 490; Richard Cobb, *Les armées révolutionnaires* (Paris: Mouton et Co., 1962), 704; *L'Anti-terroriste*, 17 floréal and 18 thermidor III; Archives départementales de la Haute-Garonne 7L 201 U 4, 22 vendémiaire IV; *Réimpression de l'ancien Moniteur*, xxv. 474 (24 thermidor III); Archives départementales de la Haute-Saône 368 L 11, 16 brumaire IV; Christine Peyrard, *Les Jacobins de l'Ouest* (Paris: Publications de la Sorbonne, 1996), 295–300; Vercier, *Justice criminelle dans le département de l'Hérault*, 185–187, 201–203; Joseph Duval-Jouve, *Montpellier pendant la Révolution, 1789-an VIII*, 4 vols. (Montpellier: C. Coulet, 1879–1881), iv. passim; Archives Nationales BB[18] 364, D 18; Archives départementales de l'Hérault L 6725, 2 pluviôse IV; Mortimer-Ternaux, *Terreur*, iii. 622–635.

39. John Borneman, *Settling Accounts: Violence, Justice, and Accountability in Postsocialist States* (Princeton, NJ: Princeton University Press, 1997); A. James McAdams, ed., *Transitional Justice and the Rule of Law in New Democracies* (Notre Dame, IN: University of Notre Dame Press, 1997); Kees Koonings and Dirk Kruijt, eds., *Societies of Fear: The Legacy of Civil War, Violence and Terror in Latin America* (London and New York: Zed Books, 1999).

40. In Council of 500 on 5 fructidor IV (22 August 1796), *Moniteur*, an IV, 1360.

41. Yves Castan, *Honnêteté et relations sociales en Languedoc, 1715–1780* (Paris: Plon, 1974), 69–77.

42. *Moniteur*, an IV, p. 1391.

Part III

External Aspects of Democratization

Chapter 7

Transition Elections as Ends or Means? Lessons for Democracy Assistance from Domestic Election Monitoring

Eric Bjornlund

As a new international "democracy industry" has emerged in the last fifteen years, elections and election monitoring have become increasingly important. In dozens of countries around the world, elections have been expected to initiate or consolidate democratic transitions or to help resolve long-standing conflicts. Fair elections have become an increasingly critical requirement for international legitimacy.

Election monitoring has exploded in scope and influence. Few countries can refuse or ignore international election observers. National and international media routinely report observers' findings, and the international community reacts strongly to election fraud or the refusal of losing autocrats to accept election results. In addition to international observers, nonpartisan domestic groups have organized sometimes pivotal efforts to monitor watershed elections in their own countries. In the Philippines in 1986, mutually reinforcing international and domestic election monitoring was critical to the unseating of an autocratic government and the restoration of democracy. Likewise, in 2000–2001 repressive regimes in Yugoslavia and Peru fell under the weight of domestic and international pressure after they attempted to manipulate national elections.

In more than fifty countries since 1986, national nongovernmental organizations (NGOs), civic groups, and citizen networks have mobilized broad movements for fair elections and democratic change. Paradoxically, even as such domestic monitoring groups have gained influence and international support, international democracy-building programs have sometimes inadvertently hindered them. The international community too often views elections as *ends*— particular events that are either "free and fair" or no—rather than as *means* of building democratic practices and institutions—an ongoing process that does not end when the winner is announced or an autocrat is unseated. Monitoring by domestic groups, rather than by foreigners, can ultimately make a more profound contribution to democratic transitions. But high-profile international observation teams still attract funding and news coverage, while foreign assistance to domestic monitoring efforts often misses a rare opportunity to help build sustainable political change.

Certainly, all over the world, domestic election monitors have made critical contributions to the important goal of better elections. Their improvement of the quality and transparency of electoral processes in politically uncertain environments has deterred fraud and helped reduce irregularities in election administration. They have built public confidence in the integrity of transition elections—elections that mark an important milestone in a political transition to more open, democratic politics—by encouraging fairer electoral rules, better campaign practices, and a more informed electorate. They have helped to improve the chances that all sides will accept election results. These are often critically important contributions to elections as important *ends*.

But transition elections are not only ends but also means—catalysts for the longer-term process of building democratic practices, values, and institutions. Beyond deterring fraud or helping to push out autocrats, election monitoring has encouraged and energized citizen involvement, empowered civic organizations in public affairs, and transformed the way that many citizens view national politics. Organizers of election monitoring programs can learn how to build coalitions and advocate public policy reforms in a more democratic political system. Organizations, networks, and relationships established to monitor elections prove invaluable in subsequent efforts to press for democracy in other ways, such as monitoring government performance, fighting corruption, advocating legal reform, lobbying public officials, and educating the public.

This chapter places domestic election monitoring in the context of the new industry of democracy assistance. It briefly reviews the formative domestic monitoring experience in the Philippines and then discusses how domestic monitoring can contribute to elections as both ends and means. Finally, through consideration of a more recent case, the monitoring of transition elections in Indonesia in 1999, the chapter considers how the international community might better aid democratization through its support of domestic election monitoring and, by implication, other foreign assistance programs.

THE GROWTH OF INTERNATIONAL DEMOCRACY ASSISTANCE AND ELECTION MONITORING

While American foreign policy has long sought to spread democracy, since the early 1980s, the United States has dramatically expanded and institutionalized efforts to promote democracy around the world. In 1983, Congress established the National Endowment for Democracy, and the U.S. Democratic and Republican parties, the American Federation of Labor and Congress of Industrial Organizations (AFL-CIO), and the U.S. Chamber of Commerce each set up an institute to build democratic institutions abroad. By 2000, the U.S. government budget for democracy assistance was nearly $700 million, which supported the programs of a plethora of government agencies and nongovernmental organizations.[1] Europe, Japan, and other developed countries—along with the United Nations, the World Bank, and other multilateral organizations—have likewise poured resources and diplomatic capital into this global crusade.

A broad expansion of democracy around the world has accompanied the burgeoning of democracy promotion efforts. Beginning with the political transitions in Southern Europe in the 1970s, the Third Wave of democratization[2] spread in the 1980s to Latin America and significant parts of Asia, swept through Eastern and Central Europe after the fall of the Berlin Wall in 1989, contributed to the breakup of the Soviet Union, and continued in the 1990s in Africa and elsewhere in Asia. Since the late 1980s, dozens of countries have made a transition to democracy, from Poland to Brazil and from Taiwan to Nigeria. While the impact of international democracy aid has generally been modest, it has nonetheless reinforced the trend, and in particular cases—often involving transition elections—international contributions have been considerable.

As part of the trend toward democracy and the corresponding increase in democracy assistance, the extent and influence of election monitoring by both international and domestic organizations have exploded. Since the mid- to late-1980s, election monitoring has been a major growth industry. There has been a dramatic increase in resources available from foreign assistance budgets for monitoring and otherwise supporting transition elections, including support for domestic monitoring groups.

Like other types of democracy aid, election monitoring can make a modest but nevertheless meaningful contribution to democratic transitions. Election monitoring can improve the quality of particular elections and has, on balance, increased understanding of democratic elections by policymakers, journalists, and aid providers. International election monitoring can provide meaningful moral support to democratic activists or opposition political leaders facing authoritarian regimes, and it focuses world attention on the struggle for democracy in particular countries. But domestic monitoring may be more effective than international monitoring in furthering both democratic elections and democratization in ways that are especially significant and sustainable.

THE INVENTION OF DOMESTIC ELECTION MONITORING

Domestic election monitoring began in the Philippines in the mid-1980s with the pioneering experience of the National Citizens' Movement for Free Elections (NAMFREL). Before NAMFREL exposed electoral fraud in the 1986 "snap" presidential election in the Philippines, independent national election monitoring was largely unknown. Indeed, even international monitoring was not yet common, and there was widespread skepticism about whether independent election monitoring in general was appropriate or could be effective. NAMFREL's or-

ganizers resolved to organize a volunteer citizen movement dedicated to restoring democracy in the Philippines through free and fair elections. In this way,
they embarked on a crusade that would profoundly change their country. NAM-
FREL's remarkable success in using election monitoring to capitalize on the
Philippine public's revulsion at the martial law regime of Ferdinand Marcos has
inspired many similar efforts around the world in the years since.

NAMFREL grew out of a small meeting of concerned citizens in October
1983, soon after the assassination of opposition leader Benigno Aquino. As a
result of rampant vote-buying, fraud, and violence that had plagued elections in
the Marcos era, Filipinos did not view elections as a viable way to challenge
the regime.

Drawing on crucial support from the Catholic Church—which recruited organizers, solicited funds, and provided credibility—and some parts of the business community, NAMFREL quickly grew to an umbrella organization for some
200,000 volunteers who watched about two-thirds of the polling places during
congressional elections in May 1984. Less than two years later, in the face of
significant intimidation and other obstacles, NAMFREL fielded more than
500,000 volunteer poll watchers across the country for the historic presidential
election that pitted Benigno Aquino's widow, Corazon, against incumbent autocrat Marcos.[3]

For both the 1984 and 1986 elections, NAMFREL also organized a pioneering
"quick count" to collect and tabulate results from polling places. This allowed
the organization to verify the accuracy of the official ballot count. For the 1986
presidential election, the quick count eventually collected results from 70 percent
of the polling sites. Although the NAMFREL count was not definitive or statistically reliable, it showed Aquino leading Marcos by more than half a million
votes out of more than 20 million cast[4] and thus played a critical role in per-
suading Filipinos and the international community that Aquino had in fact won
the election.

NAMFREL demonstrated that a well-trained, organized, and motivated domestic election monitoring operation could play a major role in safeguarding
the integrity of an election by combating and exposing fraud. International observers and ultimately the broader international community relied on NAM-
FREL's findings that Aquino had received more votes than had Marcos. This,
in turn, denied Marcos legitimacy for the electoral victory that he claimed.

Since the mid-1980s, domestic election monitoring organizations founded on
essentially the same ideals as NAMFREL have provided momentum for the
struggle for democracy throughout the world by playing an active role in ensuring that elections are competitive and meaningful. Other domestic actors—
election officials, political parties, candidates, and journalists—also monitor the
election process, for example, by organizing poll watchers to collect information
on election day. The unique development of the last decade and a half, though,
is the emergence of nonpartisan election monitoring conducted by organizations
from civil society rather than from the formal political sector, from government-

supported electoral authorities, or from organizations that are competing or supporting candidates in elections. Domestic coalitions of NGOs, human rights groups, professional associations, social service organizations, and others have worked effectively together to monitor important transition or otherwise controversial elections. Significant groups have been formed in every region of the world, including Bangladesh, Bulgaria, Chile, Croatia, Indonesia, Mexico, Mozambique, Nepal, Palestine, Peru, Slovakia, Sri Lanka, Thailand, Ukraine, Yemen, Yugoslavia, and Zambia.

The origins and configurations of these groups vary, and they work in diverse political contexts, but they have benefited from contact with one another. In the late 1980s and early 1990s, with substantial technical and financial support from foreign NGOs, foundations, and governments, organizers from NAMFREL and similar election monitoring organizations in Latin America and Eastern Europe traveled extensively to share their experiences and offer technical assistance to newly formed monitoring efforts elsewhere. In this way, new groups, often working in difficult political environments, were able to learn from earlier successes and failures, to adapt materials and methodologies, and to receive key moral support. These mutually supportive interactions among democratic activists across national boundaries became part of a truly global democracy movement and represent a significant innovation in international relations.[5]

ELECTIONS AS ENDS: CONTRIBUTIONS OF ELECTION MONITORING ORGANIZATIONS

Supplemented by international observers and supported by foreign aid, domestic election monitoring groups have made important contributions to democratic elections in many countries. Their contribution is particularly important for transition elections, where, typically, substantial parts of the public or political elite do not trust the authorities to be impartial or to organize fair elections. For many such elections, election monitoring organizations have contributed to more genuine processes by encouraging fairer election rules and campaign practices and a more informed electorate, as well as by deterring fraud and helping reduce irregularities on election day.

Domestic election observers have, for example, exposed vote count and other electoral fraud in many countries. As we have seen, the findings of domestic monitors about a critical 1986 election in the Philippines, ratified and amplified by international observers, denied the incumbent legitimacy for the electoral victory that he claimed. Similarly, in Panama in 1989, a church laity group and international observers detected and exposed vote count fraud under then-strongman Manuel Noriega. In Peru in April 2000, domestic monitors exposed the blatant unfairness of the electoral process, likewise depriving President Fujimori's reelection of international legitimacy.

In addition to exposing fraud as in the Philippines and Panama, the findings of domestic monitors have deterred it by convincing authoritarian incumbents to accept electoral defeats. In the 1988 plebiscite in Chile on whether the rule of President Augusto Pinochet would be extended, the release of the official vote count was delayed; it was an independent vote count based on statistical sampling conducted by a nonpartisan group that helped convince key Pinochet supporters to acknowledge the victory of the "no" campaign.

Professional, comprehensive election monitoring has also contributed to domestic and international legitimacy of elections in polarized political environments. It has convinced opposition forces in several countries to accept bitterly disappointing election results and helped defuse the possibility of violence. For Bulgaria's first postcommunist multiparty elections in June 1990, for example, the Bulgarian Association for Free Elections conducted a parallel count that confirmed the victory by the incumbent, former Communist Party; this convinced many urban supporters of the opposition that the victory was not the result of vote count fraud, which helped calm the situation and laid the groundwork for later peaceful changes of government.

Domestic organizations can organize more meaningful monitoring of events on election day because they can mobilize large numbers, speak local languages, and are familiar with the political culture and context. Nevertheless, many international observers fail to build on the findings of domestic monitors or to share the limelight with them. Effective monitoring of controversial elections requires collaboration between international and domestic groups, including international support for domestic organizations.

International support for domestic monitoring can help give domestic groups clout. In Yugoslavia in September 2000, for example, domestic monitoring groups helped expose attempted electoral fraud of long-standing autocrat Slobodan Milosevic. Backed by advice and assistance from experienced monitoring groups, private foundations, and foreign aid programs from Croatia, Ukraine, Slovakia, Western Europe, and the United States, a coalition of NGOs organized a nonpartisan campaign for democratic elections. In the face of enormous obstacles, this coordinated, well-planned movement helped create an environment in which Milosevic was forced to step aside.

ELECTIONS AS MEANS: DOMESTIC ELECTION MONITORING AS OPPORTUNITY FOR POLITICAL ORGANIZING

International advisors and donors too often fail to recognize the most important benefits of domestic election monitoring and adopt strategies that work against efforts to sustain domestic networks and the momentum for reform after elections.

In addition to contributing to the quality and credibility of important transition elections, domestic monitoring can develop and strengthen institutions essential to the survival and success of a democratic political system. Whether elections catalyze rapid political change or merely mark incremental steps, they provide an opportunity for existing political and civic groups to expand their missions and memberships and for new groups to emerge. Monitoring efforts help citizens learn organizational skills necessary to participate actively and effectively in the political life of a country between elections. In country after country, election monitoring has provided citizens with an opportunity to become involved in public affairs and has transformed attitudes about participation in politics and governance.

Groups that have formed to monitor elections have often developed into broader-based organizations, contributing to the development of civil society and political process. Virtually all of the domestic monitoring groups formed in recent years have conceived of election monitoring as a means of mobilizing support for other democratic reforms and encouraging continuing civic participation after elections. As a leader of an NGO election monitoring effort in Sri Lanka has put it, "Monitoring elections is a means to a larger end, namely, to build a broad network of people and organizations to address issues of national importance after elections."[6] Having animated civil society and engaged many citizens in political life for the first time, election monitoring organizations can build upon their momentum by advocating political reforms, conducting public policy research, promoting accountability in government, providing civic education, and monitoring the government and the legislature. This, in turn, has enhanced political discourse, increased citizen involvement in governance, and heightened public confidence in the political process. Ultimately, this is the most profound contribution that election monitoring can make.

SOME PROBLEMS WITH FOREIGN SUPPORT FOR DOMESTIC MONITORING IN INDONESIA IN 1999

For crucial transition elections in Indonesia in 1999, the international community generously and appropriately supported the efforts of domestic election monitoring groups to educate voters and mobilize poll watchers. As in other countries, however, foreign donors and advisors largely failed to appreciate the broader purpose of their support for domestic election monitoring: using elections as a catalyst for the process of building democratic practices and institutions. The focus of donors on election day inadvertently hampered the new civic organizations and the momentum for reform. Donor funding had unintended consequences, such as spurring the establishment of dozens of new monitoring groups, creating disincentives for monitoring organizations to work together, and encouraging inordinate focus on money issues rather than substance.

In 1999, working with substantial international support, nongovernmental and university-based groups in Indonesia organized the most extensive domestic election monitoring effort in the world to date. After Suharto was forced from office in May 1998, Indonesia moved to organize competitive elections as a critical step away from authoritarianism. Recognizing the profound importance of an opportunity to establish genuine democracy in the world's most populous

Islamic country, a nation of more than 200 million people, the international community moved quickly to support Indonesia's political transition by offering technical assistance and substantial funding. By early 1999, the United Nations Development Program (UNDP) and the government of Indonesia were seeking $90 million in international contributions for the elections, including programs in support of election administration, voter education and election monitoring, and dozens of international advisors had descended upon Jakarta from North America, Europe, Japan, Australia, and elsewhere.

A number of NGOs, university-based networks, religious organizations, and other civil society groups organized election day poll watchers. Three groups in particular organized genuinely national networks and mobilized tens of thousands of poll watchers: the Independent Election Monitoring Committee (KIPP), the University Network for Free Elections (UNFREL), and the Rectors' Forum for Democracy. Together, Indonesian election monitoring organizations collectively mobilized more than half a million local observers for the elections on June 7, 1999. Foreign donors, advisors, and election observers worked closely with, and relied on, these domestic efforts.

Donors wanted Indonesian monitoring groups to work together—to avoid duplication and to ensure broad, national coverage on election day—but the availability of significant funding and the plethora of international advisors actually tended to discourage coordinated monitoring efforts. By dangling the possibility of funding, donors unwittingly created incentives that balkanized existing monitoring groups and encouraged the proliferation of new ones. In the first half of 1999, establishing an election monitoring organization in Indonesia became an entrepreneurial activity akin to starting a "dot-com" business in the United States. While there had been only one recognized election monitoring organization for elections in 1997 and just three by the end of 1998, there were more than ninety accredited domestic monitoring organizations by election day in June 1999. Donors wanting to support political activity outside the nation's capital made funds available for provincial monitoring groups, encouraging the creation of autonomous regional groups. Some donors played favorites, helping groups that had no demonstrated commitment or professionalism to get a share of the available funding. Some international organizations even sided with small factions within existing monitoring groups that sought to gain control of programs and resources. All this further complicated efforts to knit together one or more national networks that could both develop a national picture of the elections and sustain future nationwide advocacy of democracy and good government.

Even as donors inadvertently created incentives that discouraged coordinated efforts around the country, some tried to force national-level domestic monitoring groups to join forces in ways that were neither effective nor sensitive to local institutional prerogatives and personalities. Donors insisted that election monitoring organizations divide election day poll watching responsibilities along geographical lines, for example. There was, however, no obvious or logical way to divide responsibilities by province, since all major groups had potential volunteers in virtually all of the country's then twenty-seven provinces if not in most of the 327 districts. Deciding which organization's poll watchers would be dispatched to which of the country's 300,000 polling stations was exceedingly time-consuming, not to mention almost impossible to do much in advance of election day. The groups would have been better served by dividing the constituencies that they sought to mobilize (e.g., students, NGO members, religious networks) or the specific monitoring activities that they planned to carry out. One group could have concentrated on verifying the accuracy of the vote tabulation process, while another focused on preelection complaints or the adequacy of the legal framework. Long before donors introduced a focus on dividing election day responsibilities, the three leading election monitoring organizations were already working together on a common effort, using media and technology, to recruit volunteers and to educate the broader public about the importance of election monitoring.

The availability of funding was at least partly responsible for the fact that election monitoring organizations spent enormous energy on developing proposals for funding and budgets rather than election monitoring strategies and tactics. Just three weeks before election day, provincial and national leaders of the UNFREL met for three days at the University of Indonesia in Jakarta, where they found themselves mired in debates over budgets and money. As the young organizers from around the country complained about inadequate budgets, criticized the headquarters for hoarding money, and made apparently specious allegations that funds had been diverted, such pressing issues as volunteer recruitment and training, communications systems, election day plans, and local political conditions were virtually ignored. The national organizers, including several university faculty members who had founded this national monitoring network with idealistic notions of building a more democratic political system and providing a vehicle for university students to constructively channel their political energies, admitted their frustration.

Other advice from international sources similarly diverted Indonesian groups from the task of building their own political movement. Rather than allowing the Indonesian groups to set their own priorities and make their own mistakes, some donors pushed hard to expand the numbers of poll watchers. The excessive focus on how many polling stations would be covered on election day tended to overshadow concerns about the training, quality, or motivations of observers. It also overemphasized the administration on election day to the detriment of efforts to monitor the process before and after that day. Similarly, in the effort to gather extensive and comparable information, donors insisted on the use of a common reporting form, an unwieldy, lowest-common-denominator checklist. This hampered other goals, such as the rapid communication and analysis of observations and organizational innovation. Such donor requirements failed to take proper account of trade-offs between values and goals that were sometimes in tension. A somewhat smaller, better trained, and more focused domestic election monitoring effort might have been a more sustainable expression of Indonesian commitment to the principle of democratic elections and thus a more meaningful contribution to Indonesian democracy in the long run.

SOME TENTATIVE CONCLUSIONS

Elections provide an important opportunity for citizens in democratizing societies to participate in the political process. But elections are, at best, periodic political events. Genuine, continuing democracy requires citizens to participate in public affairs on an ongoing basis. Involving citizens in election monitoring is one way to engage and educate them so that they have the knowledge, skills, and inclination to continue to participate in public affairs. Ongoing participation reinforces an essential tenet of democracy: rather than being the domain solely of elites, the political process belongs to the public.

As domestic election monitoring has become more widespread, it has also become increasingly sophisticated, organized, and influential. It is a reflection and a part of a burgeoning civil society. It is a form of political organization that will undoubtedly adapt to meet future challenges as millions of ordinary citizens become increasingly accustomed to the idea that they own the political system.

The international community must support domestic election monitoring's potential not only to report on transition elections but also to help build sustainable organizations and encourage democratic participation. Indeed, there are lessons for foreign assistance more generally. Foreign aid that reinforces genuinely indigenous efforts and agendas rather than that which encourages local people to further an agenda established elsewhere is more likely to have significant impact. Programs and activities that people in the country have developed and to which they are committed are more likely to be sustained than those that are imposed from outside.

It has become fashionable to point out the obvious truth that genuine democracy requires more than elections. But the Universal Declaration of Human Rights and international treaties recognize genuine elections as the basis of legitimate government. Furthermore, elections can catalyze profound political change, and transition elections, in particular, provide significant new opportunities for citizen participation. Elections will continue to be important if global aspirations to meaningful democracy are to be realized.

In the last decades of the twentieth century, democracy established itself as the world's dominant political ideal. As with all ideals, genuine democracy remains elusive. Much of the world's population has yet to enjoy democratic rights, and the commitment of many ostensibly democratic countries remains open to question. As we begin the twenty-first century, the international community still has much to learn before it can more fully realize its potential contribution to the cause of democracy everywhere.

NOTES

1. Thomas Carothers, *The Clinton Record on Democracy Promotion, Working Paper No. 16* (Washington, DC: Carnegie Endowment for International Peace, September 2000), 4.

2. Samuel P. Huntington, *The Third Wave: Democratization in the Late Twentieth Century* (Norman: University of Oklahoma Press, 1991).

3. National Democratic Institute (NDI), *Reforming the Philippine Electoral Process, 1986–1988* (Washington, DC: NDI, 1991), 47; NDI, *Making Every Vote Count: Domestic Election Monitoring in Asia* (Washington, DC: NDI, 1996), 56. See generally Kaa Byington, *Bantay ng Bayan: Stories from the NAMFREL Crusade, 1984–1986* (Manila: Bookmark, 1988).

4. NDI, *Reforming the Philippines Electoral Process*, 48; David Timberman, *A Changeless Land: Continuity and Change in Philippine Politics* (Manila and Singapore: Bookmark and Institute of Southeast Asian Studies, 1991), 147. The official election results were based on 20.1 million votes counted, or 77 percent of registered voters, but actual turnout was likely higher as these results appeared to significantly undercount ballots from areas with substantial opposition support, and turnout in previous elections had been significantly higher.

5. See Ann M. Florini, *The Third Force: The Rise of Transnational Civil Society* (Washington, DC: Carnegie Endowment for International Peace, 2000).

6. Wimal Fernando, quoted in NDI, *Making Every Vote Count*, 26.

Chapter 8

International Standards and Democratization: Certain Trends

Elizabeth Spiro Clark

INTRODUCTION

On October 10, 2001, U.S. Undersecretary of State for Global Affairs Paula Dobriansky told a conference on U.S. democracy policy that the United States would not cease to support more democratic forms of government because of the requirements of antiterrorism coalition building. "On the contrary, the US must now work even harder to ensure that peoples around the world enjoy the freedom to participate in government to vote in periodic, genuine elections, to associate freely, and to practice their religion freely."[1] On October 1, New York Mayor Rudolph Giuliani told the United Nations (UN) Special Session on Terrorism that "the best long-term deterrent to terrorism is the spread of freedom, democracy, the rule of law, and respect for human life. The more it spreads around the globe, the safer we will all be. These are very powerful ideas and once they gain a foothold, they cannot be stopped."[2] In the October 18 edition of *Newsweek*, foreign editor Fareed Zakaria said that "we have no option but to get back into the nation-building business," reversing his earlier—and highly influential—view that U.S. policy should be to help democracy only in countries where it had already taken root.[3]

Dictatorships and failed states incubate terrorism. Because of that recognition, after September 11 old ways of doing foreign policy business, while not supplanted, are no longer adequate. It no longer seems so obvious that the United States and its allies will trade off human rights and democracy goals for coalition cooperation, however much the urgent goal of combating terrorism absorbs collective energies in the immediate present. We will no longer be confident that non-democracies can produce stable coalition partnerships. Other forces at play will support a view that the U.S. government can pursue both democracy-building and antiterrorism strategies and that the two are not in conflict. Decisions by foreign governments to support U.S. antiterrorism aims are probably never fundamentally dependent on trade-offs against human rights and democracy policy tracks.

The "nation building business" that Zakaria says we will be getting back into is the same business that has been producing precedents and templates for international action over the last decade. International interventions in conflict have produced many of the most important precedents. In postconflict periods, the international action has focused on setting up electoral processes and electoral timetables. While an international autocratic style of building nations from the top down and reserving powers for international administrators has developed and worked against the goal of democracy-building in a fundamental way, lessons can be learned to enable swifter devolution of power. Putting in place mechanisms for consulting the people on what they want in these cases is the accepted paradigm and should be followed. Not many weeks into the military campaign in Afghanistan there was wide discussion of the importance of bringing the UN into a post-Taliban political settlement process and even on using an interim UN administration along the lines of East Timor or Kosovo. The assumption was that, if this role was brought into play, the UN would proceed much as it had in those two situations and that the wishes of the people of Afghanistan would be consulted, on some clear timetable, through elections.

Success in transversing the extraordinarily difficult political track in Afghanistan will depend on the skill in drawing on the international community's experience of the last decade in helping launch and sustain new democracies. In particular, there has been much positive development in strengthening and developing international democracy norms and standards, which have charted maps for global democratization. It will be more important than ever to understand these trends if the United States and, more broadly, the international community are to be effective in the nation-building business. Within the area of international standards, three quite distinct trends have important practical implications: the hardening of core democracy standards, especially around elections; the contrary proliferating of targets for democracy assistance and of ideas on how to get to the status of a fully "consolidated" democracy; and, finally, the growing bank of short-term problem-solving measures available for getting countries through the early stages of transition between nondemocratic and democratic political systems.

TREND I: HARDENING OF CORE STANDARDS

The Organization for Security and Cooperation in Europe (OSCE) states in a handbook for election monitors that the sources for "minimum" standards are international documents that include the Universal Declaration of Human Rights, the International Covenant on Civil and Political Rights, the European Convention for the Protection of Human Rights and Fundamental Freedoms, the Charter of Paris for a New Europe—Commission on Security and Cooperation in Europe (CSCE) Summit (1990), and the Document of the Copenhagen Meeting of the Conference in the Human Dimension of the CSCE (1990). In joining the UN, all members agree to adhere to the Universal Declaration. Article 21 of the Declaration states that everyone has the right to take part in the government of his or her country, directly or through freely chosen representatives; everyone has the right of equal access to public service in his or her country; and the will of the people shall be the basis of the authority of government; this will shall be expressed in periodic and genuine elections, which shall be by universal and equal suffrage and shall be held by secret ballot or by equivalent free voting procedures.

In the wake of the collapse of the Soviet Union, the UN General Assembly was spurred to pass a resolution that reinforced Article 21. The resolution, "Enhancing the effectiveness of the principle of periodic and genuine elections," stresses that such elections are "a necessary and indispensable element of sustained efforts to protect the rights and interests of the governed."[4]

The most important document for the growing universal acceptance of "hard" international core standards is the Copenhagen Document, in which the member states of the OSCE commit themselves "to ensure that the will of the people serves as the basis of the authority of government" and lay down concrete minimum standards, especially relating to elections. In summary, these minimum standards require that elections will be held under universal and equal suffrage at reasonable intervals, as established by law, for, at a minimum, all seats in one chamber of the legislature; the executive must be accountable either directly to the electorate or to elected legislators; there must be a clear separation between parties and state; individuals have the right to stand for office, organize themselves in political parties, obtain information and access to the media unimpeded by intimidation or administrative obstacles on a basis of equal treatment before the law and by the authorities, and to serve out their terms of office, once elected; and votes are to be cast by secret ballot, or equivalent, and honestly counted, reported, and made public.

The Copenhagen Document did not limit itself to speaking for one particular region but rather declared "that the will of the people, freely and fairly expressed through periodic and genuine elections, is the basis for the authority and legitimacy of all government." One scholar of international law, New York University Professor Thomas Franck, has suggested that the Copenhagen Document is detailed "to an unprecedented degree, establishing a standard which might profitably be emulated by a resolution of the General Assembly of the UN."[5]

The Copenhagen minimum standards have been the chief tool for the proliferating teams of international elections observers, not only in the OSCE region but wherever the international or regional organizations have accepted the task of advising governments on electoral processes, observing elections, or evaluating the results of elections. Some nongovernmental organizations evaluating elections have put stress on elements not strictly covered in the relevant international documents, such as the degree of acceptance of election results by losing parties and the level of participation in the election. Some of these added standards, such as the requirement for an independent elections monitoring body or functional equivalent, are close to acceptance as core standards.

The growing global acceptance of these core standards was reflected in the willingness of Secretary of State Colin Powell to urge Uganda's leadership on his May 2001 Africa trip to move to multiparty democracy. It was suggestive of an increasingly direct appeal to international standards, where once fudging would have been reflexive. Uganda, with its popularity with the International Monetary Fund (IMF) for successful economic stabilization, has never been held to task for its "no-party movement," relatively benign political system. Now Powell not only made the lack of free and fair elections in Zimbabwe his main message to that country on the same trip but, in a friendly manner, told Ugandan President Museveni that "to have a democracy, you really do have to have opposition, you have to have people who are free to speak out."[6]

The increasing confidence in appealing to core standards that the Powell statements represent symbolizes one trend in organizing the chaotic field of global democratization, with its real and phony advances and setbacks. Elections offer the international community and internal parties a specific line of action to pursue in postconflict or other transitional situations. Because Copenhagen standards are concrete enough to be operationalized with the development of discrete indicators, the trend has been to harden these standards to make them even more useful in response to a wave of demands. As a result, OSCE and other monitoring missions and organizations have moved a long way from the days of the 1990s, when meeting international standards meant running a clean election day and nothing more. Standards for the pre- and postelectoral period—press freedom, separation of state and party, neutral use of state resources, avenues for effective challenges of results, and freedom of association and expression—are now routinely assessed by both international and domestic monitors.

Because core standards are increasingly concrete and accepted as universally applicable, it is feasible to use them as criteria for recognition and as membership requirements. The determination of Slovakia to run a "good" election in 1998 was overwhelmingly caused by its desire to become a member of North Atlantic Treaty Organization (NATO). The European Community (EU) has a democracy membership requirement, as will the Free Trade Area of the Americas when it comes into force. As minimum standards harden, their violation becomes an increasingly functional trigger for actions in the collective defense of democracy, such as the "anticoup" 1991 Organization of American States (OAS) Santiago Declaration (AG/Res. 1080), which obligates member states take certain, if limited, actions in the event of a coup against a democratically elected member government. Secretary Powell received word of the September 11 attack at a meeting of the General Assembly of the OAS in Lima, Peru. The Assembly agreed to the Inter-American Democratic Charter. The provisions of the charter expanded on Resolution 1080. Under Article 19 of the charter, an "unconstitutional interruption" of the democratic order or "an unconstitutional alteration of the constitutional regime that seriously impairs the democratic order" will trigger an immediate, provisional suspension of a member state. Resolution 1080 had not been invoked in the crisis precipitated by presidential runoff elections in Peru in May 2000, when the prospect of fraud had caused the withdrawal of the chief opposition candidate, Alejandro Toledo, and of OAS election monitors. There was not, therefore, a threat of suspension from OAS membership. However, there is little doubt that the active and eventually successful interjection of the OAS into the crisis created a precedent for considering fraudulent elections a trigger for suspension or withholding of membership and that fear of suspension was an important factor motivating the political actors in the crisis.

In Lome, Togo, in July 2000, African heads of state moved in the same direction, agreeing to a Declaration on the Framework for an Organization of African Unity (OAU) Response to Unconstitutional Changes of Government (AHG/Decl. 5 (XXXVI)). Under the declaration, members agreed on nine democratic principles and values and on situations that would constitute an unconstitutional change in government. Such a change would trigger condemnation by members and provisional suspension from OAU policy bodies. If no restoration of constitutional order occurs, a range of other sanctions may be added.

The U.S. government may have been uncomfortable at the prospect of having to declare the ouster of Ecuador's President Mahuad in 2000 a "coup" or divided on whether to stick with Peru's President Fujimori, but the fact that both crises were handled without jettisoning the OAS democracy commitments is evidence of the power of international standards as an independent driver of democratization. Especially in the post–September 11 environment, it has become less likely that interested outside powers will take the "let-the-dust-settle" line of inaction, even without the Bosnia worst-case precedent to galvanize them. Rules are now available to guide action.

Toughening standards should be seen chiefly as a process of elaborating existing core standards, although the problems of newly democratizing countries have opened up areas where new minimum core standards may be added to those that exist and modifications proposed to existing standards. Both processes were in evidence at the May 2001 OSCE's Office of Democratic Institutions and Human Rights (ODIHR) Conference on Election Processes. The main purpose of the conference was to debate recommendations for the sharpening or clarification of Copenhagen requirements. Among these proposals were standards requiring a well-defined legal framework for conducting campaign rallies, standards prohibiting the requirement of an excessive numbers of signatures for the registration of parties, and proposals for studying electoral district delimitation standards for their impact on the right to equal and universal suffrage. Another proposal with wide support would add to core standards (instead of developing new concrete indicators for existing ones) by making Article 8 of the Copenhagen Document a required standard instead of a recommendation. Article 8 deals with election observation by foreign and domestic observers, which "enhances the electoral process for States in which elections are taking place." There is a consensus developing that any government that bans election observation by domestic observers should be considered to have violated required minimum standards.

Also important were recommendations that OSCE look at actions to be taken when a participating state repeatedly fails to meet required standards, starting with a cautious proposal that in, such cases, reports on implementation of the OSCE recommendations to that government would be taken up at the political level of OSCE for debate. Recommendations stopped well short of threats to expel members. Another recommendation, in a document tabled at the conference by the National Democratic Institute (NDI), suggested that the OSCE consult with OAS on its experience with the operation of the Santiago Declaration.

If we look ahead for new areas where minimum standards for acceptable practice may be developed, the possibilities are quite numerous. For example, should it be acceptable for constitutional amendments on lifting term limits for a chief of state to benefit the incumbent, as has happened in Namibia and elsewhere? What should be the standards governing the use of libel laws to repress political opponents in an election campaign? What about the area of campaign finance?

The flood of "democracy events" drives a process of hardening of international standards from precedent to precedent. However, at the same time, in the same rush of events, other precedents are established. Failure to meet international standards by democratizing countries is overlooked, and countries gain legitimacy as "democracies" without meeting core standards.

In the spring of 1999, the U.S. government welcomed Nigeria into the community of democracies following presidential elections that no observers found met international standards. In November 2000, NDI characterized parliamentary elections in Azerbaijan as failing to meet "even minimum international standards." Nevertheless, Azerbaijan was admitted to the Council on Europe (COE) shortly after the elections, the COE claiming that Azerbaijan "was willing to comply with COE standards."[7] The desire of European governments for the integration of Azerbaijan into European institutions and a political decision to link Azerbaijan's and Armenia's COE membership applications almost certainly explained the weak OSCE/COE report on the elections. In the case of Nigeria, policymakers quite correctly judged the change over to civilian rule as an unequivocal move toward democracy and pocketed the flawed elections as a step in the right direction. In effect, both Azerbaijan and Nigeria have promised to do better. But is that enough? Even when the elections themselves go well and amply warrant positive international support, there are questions relating to international standards. Indonesia's democratic elections, for example, took place under an undemocratic constitution that reserves seats in Parliament for the army. While retaining this constitutional provision may be necessary under present circumstances, that does not mean that it is not a limitation on the democratic rights of Indonesians.

Is the lesson to take from these and other cases that international standards are not the driving force in international democratization? Governments will always have conflicting interests in their relations with other governments, and certainly that is the case with the goal of promoting democracy. Even within the goal of supporting global democratization, there is a built-in tension between "encouraging" democratic progress by overlooking failure to meet international standards and holding governments to standards. However, even with a maximum incentive to fudge standards or engage in double standards, the logic of democracy events, especially the fact that they are coming in a flood tide, is working to strengthen international standards, not to dilute them.

International standards play a paradoxical role. On the one hand, they float in timeless formulations above the battlefield of abrupt and often violent regime change. On the other hand, they provide the machinery, in the form of minimum electoral standards, for managing and stabilizing regime changes, something that uncertain publics, nascent political parties, and nervous external observers can hang onto as the only available action plan. Open and competitive elections are the nexus where the external forces and the internal forces meet like a magnet organizing a force field. Given almost daily reports from the democracy front, in this context, fudging international standards is proving to be a subset of highlighting them. Democracy events are likely to grow in number. The emphasis on elections is inevitable given the consensus that open competitive elections are an essential characteristic of democracy and given the nature of democratic transitions. The only way to stop the emphasis is to stop the transitions.

This hardening of core standards that has resulted from this dynamic has reinforced what some analysts and policymakers deplore as an overemphasis on elections at the expense of more amorphous standards and indicators of long-range democratic development and consolidation. This area, to which we now turn, is subject to trends that are driven by a different dynamic but that interact significantly with the development of international core standards.

TREND II: EXPANDING DEMOCRATIC NORMS

There is confusion on what core or minimum standards are (i.e., are the Copenhagen standards the definition or something more or less?), but there seems to be general agreement that meeting those standards is not enough to become a genuine democracy or, rather, that it is only enough to become an "electoral democracy." Electoral democracy is always contrasted unfavorably with "consolidated" or "liberal" democracy and hence meeting universal minimum standards with their focus on electoral processes takes on the connotation of meeting a lowest common denominator. If consolidated democracy is the goal, then there would appear to be no reason not to expand standards beyond the minimum, with no expectation that all electoral democracies could meet these standards. Such a division of democracies into electoral or consolidated sets up a two (at least)-class, two (at least)-step system of democratization.

Consolidating democracy is likely to be a long-term process, on any definition of what constitutes a high-quality democracy. Some definitions, however, are so expansive as to make any formulation of concrete norms and standards difficult indeed. Democracies, for example, are said by a foremost democracy theorist, Larry Diamond, to be consolidated when all significant political actors "believe that the democratic regime is the most right and appropriate for their society, better than any realistic alternative they can imagine."[8] Depending on one's definition of which political actors are "significant," this is a test that even long-established democracies would have difficulty passing. Worse, in Diamond's view, if nascent democracies stall on the path to the goal of consolidated democracy, they risk falling off the democratization bandwagon altogether. Just as democracy itself is characterized by change, so is the constellation of significant political actors. The major events in democratic development occur when "significant political actors" disappear or arise, not when they convert to democratic values.

Taking the focus off core standards and onto the characteristics of consolidated democracy has many practical consequences for policymakers and practitioners. Standards for consolidated democracy can be debated on their own terms, but it is clear that devising concrete indicators that could serve as standards for meeting membership democracy requirements or aid conditionalities will be difficult to devise or justify. Focusing on requirements for a "high-quality" consolidated democracy locates democracy firmly in the future. Devaluing core standards, which countries can achieve in the short term, also devalues the urgent issues of timing that the OSCE is seeking to address as it looks at questions of how many "transitional" elections can be flawed before a country loses its democratizing "status."[9]

Pressures to broaden the field of international democracy norms and standards, on the policy side, are linked to pressure for gradualism, long-range development, and a preconditions approach toward international activism in support of democratization, that is, assessing economic and social thresholds as requirements for moving to full democracy. Here the movement is clearly toward ever-greater comprehensiveness. Partly this is the result of governments and development agencies' desire to maintain a maximum degree of flexibility in their diplomatic and development assistance policies. Multiplying the targets of engagement is also useful from the point of view of public presentation, for example, avoiding a "Somalia syndrome" effect, whereby high-profile investments in elections in Cambodia or Indonesia give elections a "bad name"—as Somalia did "nation building"—because they appear to have failed to produce either real democracy or stability. Even without discouraging case histories, the trend is to move beyond core standards. EU foreign affairs commissioner Chris Patten recently suggested that in dealing with democratization in non-EU countries, it might make sense, precisely in the areas of memberships and assistance conditionality, to move beyond the current focus on electoral processes to "broader and deeper measures of democratic health."[10]

A maximum comprehensiveness covering democratic standards, norms, and ideas is an ideal framework for development agencies, which have their own historical and bureaucratic reasons for "depoliticizing" democracy and emphasizing the broad social, cultural, and economic characteristics of mature democracies that—it is constantly reiterated—take "generations" to produce. The political institutions side of democracy is usually defined by the term "governance." Since its introduction into the World Bank lexicon over a decade ago, the term has generally translated into anticorruption programs and public service reform measures, partly because of bank charter prohibitions against political assistance.[11] Perhaps because of the dominance of the bank in development assistance, national development agencies such as the U.S. Agency for International Development (USAID) adopted a similar conception of governance, which also includes long-range programs targeted at the more amorphous areas of democratic development such as the strengthening of civil society, the rule of law, the media, women's participation in politics, parliaments, and decentralization. Electoral assistance is also encompassed in democracy and governance programs of USAID but not embraced enthusiastically, as it is felt to be "political" as opposed to desirably nonpartisan and neutral development assistance.

Long-range and comprehensive development frameworks act in synergy with dominant theories of democratic transition that stress continuities and pacts between old and new regimes as largely effective transition modes. Such frameworks have the bureaucratic virtue of allowing for the development of the same type of program in both authoritarian and democratic transition contexts. It is a strategy of gradualism, liberalization, and reform, rather than a strategy of democracy assistance supported by a theory of sharp breaks and discontinuities. Elections—whether postconflict or postauthoritarian—create the most discomfort (even while eliciting assistance, seen to be driven by high politics), precisely because they mark change and discontinuity.

An everything-is-important framework for democratization is actually more closely related to the minimum standards approach than might be apparent; clearly, for example, women's participation in politics or media and judicial independence is part of the hard Copenhagen requirements, with their growing acceptance as universally valid. Long-range development approaches also frequently circle back to an emphasis on elections as one of the few areas of assistance to democratization that have proven effective. It is also being recognized that electoral assistance has the potential for contributing beyond entrenching the practice of free and fair elections toward other components of a "high-quality" democracy, such as a vital civil society. Domestic election monitors, for example, have been used in Slovakia as the nucleus of organizations that monitor parliamentary performance. This concept is spreading. The trend to greater comprehensiveness is also extremely valuable if it is used to open up debate in new democracies—as well as old—on the nature of democratic institutions and values.

Emphasizing long-range democratization has the unintended effect of devaluing the importance of the trend to global democratization, both because so many new democratizers can be categorized as "mere" electoral democracies instead of consolidated liberal democracies and also because the policy driver of long-term consolidating democracy is assistance. Democracy and governance assistance does not get high marks from policy analysts and scholars for effectiveness. One of the few studies of democracy assistance, *Aiding Democracy Abroad* by Thomas Carothers, reaches the conclusion that

in transitions gone wrong, just as in good transitions democracy aid does not have a major influence on the factors that are at the root of the situation. . . . In countries that are under non-democratic rule and have not experienced a democratic opening, the effects of democracy aid are similarly minor in most cases.[12]

The tendency to expand areas for democracy support dilutes the impact on actual democracy events, the transitions from conflict-ridden or repressive regimes to democratic transitions. Multiplying ideas about democracy and opening them up for debate have intrinsic value, but only if a careful separation is kept between core standards of universal acceptance and areas where movement will be linked with the specific socioeconomic environment. A program of assistance to "civil society," for example, might typically target support for professional associations, chambers of commerce, lobbying groups, and the like, all of which function differently in different cultural contexts. The contribution of such programs to the development of democratic values also varies. The same development agency or organization may support both these civil society programs and electoral assistance, but they are very far from each other conceptually. Even in programs exclusively focused on political institutions, there is a danger in confusing core standards with long-term democratic development ideas. For example, decentralization was for some years a criterion that Freedom House used to rank countries on the degree of political freedoms enjoyed by their citizens. Decentralization has been dropped as a criterion because Freedom House decided that it was not a necessary requirement for democracy. Similarly, "power-sharing" is often a Western prescription for avoiding violent transitions and is so often urged that it is beginning to take on the character of a core standard—inappropriately. Power-sharing arrangements are best thought of as neither core criteria nor a good beginning on long-term democratic development but as a pragmatic and possibly short-term political decision to solve certain political problems, taken in the context of an overall decision to move to democracy.

TREND III: SOLVING PROBLEMS

The trend to reach ever further in defining and assisting democratic development is welcome—with three qualifications. First, it must be recognized that international standards drive democratization largely to the degree that they are universal core standards. These standards will continue to focus on elections. Second, while in some sense all aspects of human life are relevant to the success, failure, and character of democracy, not all aspects are equal.[13] Not only is there agreement on some core standards that are essential to democracy, but also that some areas of democratic development may be more important than others for kicking off democratic transitions. Speculatively, for example, research might target freedom of the press as a priority in that sense. Third, gradualistic approaches should not detract from attention to the characteristics of the abrupt discontinuities that characterize many, if not most, democratizations. Certainly, post-1989 democratization has been characterized by sharp breaks; all of the former Soviet Union and Warsaw Pact transitions (and most recently Indonesia and Nigeria's) were kicked off by the death or ouster of the dictator.

Following breaks into democratic transition, many kinds of often very innovative measures have been taken almost as "bridging measures" to get across the fragile democratic beginnings. Election monitoring, both international and domestic, truth and reconciliation commissions, and national conventions or "dialogues" are all innovations that have been grassroots responses to problems in many very different national contexts. These responses can be looked at as "grassroots" in the sense that most were not launched or even supported by international organizations and major donor governments. The United States, for example, was very much a Johnny-come-lately to support for truth commissions. These problem-solving measures deal with human rights abuses from past authoritarian regimes, with massive distrust of political institutions, and with the necessity for quickly creating public confidence and participation. Other bridging institutions and practices will undoubtedly be put in place in response to other problems. For example, the greatest threat to democratization in cases of sharp discontinuity is often ethnic conflict. Recently, research coming out of the World Bank has narrowed the threat to a certain defined class of ethnic profile and suggested very concrete measures that could be taken to reduce the risk of violence in such cases, specifically, quotas for public sector employment in situations of ethnic dominance. Power-sharing arrangements, including governments of national unity, can be useful as a solution to the particular problems in the early stages of a transition, or they can be desirable political structures for the long term. This will depend on factors specific to a given country and should not, as noted above, be understood as a requirement for democratic transitions.

Some of these problem-solving measures may create new "hard" standards, such as those, already noted, on the electoral process. Innovations should be expected and encouraged in the area of constitutional development, with norms and "transition protocols" devised that allow for stages and amendments when the early phase of democratization has passed. Transition norms should be developed for relations between development agencies and democratizing countries. Most such problem solving will remain short-term and in the area of "best practices." Such fast-launching legitimating measures, although short-term, may be of the highest priority looked at from the point of view of what the key determinants of success and failure will be in a particular democratization.[14]

CONCLUSION

International influence will be more effective if all three trends sketched out here are anchored in a framework that emphasizes the "new/old" dichotomy that marks so many democratic transitions and can powerfully fix a new direction, both via institutions and psychological orientations. We know that the goal of democratic forces in predemocratic contexts is to change the regime or force change on the old regime. There are methods that have been developed to reach this objective that can almost be called cookie cutters: from within, the tools of passive resistance, boycotts, creating "alternative structures"; from without, orchestrating pariah status in the international arena, through appeals to international human rights and democratic standards. Because the goals are simple, the strategies of external friends to help democratic forces—assuming that they want to help, for whatever reasons—can also be straightforward. There are fewer models for working with authoritarian governments to reform in a democratic direction that have been proven effective. In fact, it is very nearly a general rule that we can never understand the nature of an authoritarian regime until it is over.

By contrast with helping pro-democracy movements—Poland's Solidarity, South Africa's African National Congress (ANC), or Burma's National League for Democracy (NLD)—in the pretransition period, there are few cookie cutters, except for electoral assistance, to support the early phases of transition, and those that might be developed—in the security area, for example—face formidable political obstacles. This stage appears to be maximally determined by forces unique to the particular state or would-be state, as new and old actors jockey for position. The power calculations and goals of all sides, the available resources, the quality of leadership, the background political culture, including specific historical memories, the external environment, including ideological factors, and class, regional, and ethnic configurations all come into play in unique combinations. Paradoxically, at the same time, there is a maximum receptivity to external pressure (often unacknowledged) because of the international spotlight and the interest of key actors in outside support. The most effective international intervention is often assistance to elections precisely because there is maximum international consensus on standards. Assistance in that context is not therefore easily seen as a threat to what may be quite fragile sovereignty and legitimacy. Once an interim transition period has been passed, the development and influence of international standards for democratization become rather fractionalized, as they are applied to tracks of slow or fast progress on long-range democratic development targets, elections still serving a key function as snapshots of democratic progress.

Given the rich event field of global democratization, the safe conclusion is that all trends having an impact on international standards will continue; core standards will be increasingly hardened, democracy assistance will aim broadly at the goal of democratic consolidation, and the repertoire of solutions to typical problems of democratic transitions will grow. Taking stock of this extraordinary decade of global democratization has hardly been done to death. Governmental, quasi-governmental, and intergovernmental agencies and organizations will continue to set—or fail to set—the pace. It will often suit their purposes to obscure the nature of trends in global democratization. It would be helpful if there were more nongovernment-supported democracy organizations and think tanks to make independent assessments. There are no elections or democracy "watchdog" groups strictly comparable to Human Rights Watch or Transparency International, for example.[15] Global trends are more likely to open the field for effective action strategies and shape events in a positive direction if they are clearly understood and distinguished. It is one thing to require certain minimum standards as a price for conferral of international benefits and quite another to debate and nurture various concepts of the good society or to develop and deploy specialized solutions keyed to problems characterizing critical moments in democratic development.

NOTES

1. Paula Dobriansky, Report of the Institute for the Study of Diplomacy, "Sustaining Global Democratization: Priority Task Now More than Ever," October 10, 2001, Georgetown University.

2. Rudolph W. Giuliani, Remarks to the United Nations General Assembly Special Session on Terrorism, October 1, 2001, New York City.

3. Fareed Zakaria, "Next: 'Nation-Building Lite,'" *Newsweek* (18 October 2001): 53.

4. UNGA Res 45/150 (1991).

5. Thomas M. Franck, *Fairness in International Law and Institutions* (New York: Oxford University Press, 1995), 114.

6. *International Herald Tribune*, 28 May 2001.

7. Svante E. Cornell, "Democratization Falters in Azerbaijan," *Journal of Democracy* (April 2001): 118–131.

8. Larry Diamond, *Developing Democracy: Toward Consolidation* (Baltimore: Johns Hopkins University Press, 1999), 65.

9. The word "consolidation," in my view, carries with it the unfortunate connotation of closure. Laurence Whitehead, in an article "Bolivia and the Viability of Democracy" in the April 2001 issue of the *Journal of Democracy*, makes the useful point that "it may be necessary to consider a more open-ended vocabulary, one that allows for cyclical

patterns and that directs attention to the viability rather than the immutability, of democratic processes."

10. *Financial Times*, 23 May 2001.

11. These prohibitions are eroding as bank studies directly link economic growth to core democratic standards.

12. Thomas Carothers, *Aiding Democracy Abroad: The Learning Curve* (Washington, DC: Carnegie Endowment for International Peace, 1999), 307.

13. A recent project of the mixed intergovernmental/NGO organization International IDEA is an indication of how broadly an inventory of democracy can be cast. IDEA has developed a questionnaire on democratic practices that national groups can use for purposes of evaluating the status of democracy in their countries. The seventy-seven questions cover virtually every aspect of "democracy." Some of the concepts of democracy implicit in the questions would be widely accepted; others are controversial or based on one particular democratic model. Since all elements are accorded equal weight, the effect is to imply that all elements must be equally present to delineate a high-quality, consolidated democracy.

14. The author is indebted to Sasha Lezhnev for the idea of "stopgap" democracy assistance in an unpublished paper, "Can Democracy Successfully Manage Ethnic Conflict? A Proposed Three Step Process Using Nigeria as a Case Study" (April 2001).

15. See Elizabeth Spiro Clark, "Why Elections Matter," *The Washington Quarterly* (Summer 2000): 27–40.

Chapter 9

Elections to End Conflict: War Termination, Democratization, and International Policy

Terrence Lyons

Elections form a critical component of democracy, serving as the necessary mechanism for citizens to participate, realize their choices, and enforce accountability. They are designed as a process of competition for government positions and public office and as a mechanism to bestow legitimacy and authority on the winners.[1] Electoral democracy can provide institutional structures to manage conflicts through nonviolent competition—ballots, rather than bullets. For specific types of elections following civil war, however, additional goals relate to conflict resolution and peace-building. In recent years, elections have become a standard component of peace agreements negotiated to end civil wars.[2] In the 1990s, peace accords called for elections to serve as the mechanism to mark the end of a transition from war to peace in Angola (1992), Cambodia (1993), Mozambique (1994), El Salvador (1994), Bosnia-Herzegovina (1996), Liberia (1997), and Tajikistan (1999/2000).[3] Postconflict elections therefore represent a key, culminating event in peace implementation processes, and such elections must be analyzed and assessed with relation to the primary goal of war termination.

An examination of recent cases suggests that elections sometimes have succeeded in providing a mechanism for selecting new political leadership and institutions capable of preserving the peace and beginning a process of democratization. This was the result in El Salvador and Mozambique. In Cambodia, the election marked the closure of the war and a partial transition of the government, but democracy remained weak and vulnerable.[4] In other cases, postconflict elections precipitated renewed conflict, most tragically in Angola. Finally, in cases such as Bosnia-Herzegovina, Liberia, and Tajikistan, elections served more as a mechanism of war termination with only a limited and perhaps damaging relationship to democratization. Even war termination was ambiguous, given the continued presence of peacekeeping forces in Bosnia-Herzegovina, the escalating violence in Liberia in 2001, and continued tensions in Tajikistan.

The record is mixed, in part, because postconflict elections relate to multiple, often contradictory goals. They are designated in the peace agreement as a primary instrument of implementation and therefore inherently play critical goals with relation to war termination. At the same time, they are designed to promote a process of democratization and to serve as "breakthrough" elections that initiate a new set of rules and institutions for competitive, multiparty politics.[5] In addition, postconflict elections are critical to international goals such as peacekeeping and foreign assistance for reconstruction.

The topic of violence and elections is broader than the focus of this chapter on postconflict elections in the context of a negotiated peace agreement. Elections have served as a means to legitimate new political authority in the absence of a comprehensive peace agreement, as in Nicaragua (1990) and Sierra Leone (1996). In other cases, elections consolidated the military victory of one party, as in Ethiopia, Uganda, and Rwanda.[6] In Algeria (1991), Burundi (1993), and Côte d'Ivoire (2000), elections sparked or reignited conflict as the military intervened to prevent the elected government from taking office. In yet other cases, elections have served as a conflict management mechanism where conflict did not reach the threshold of civil war, as in South Africa (1994) and Haiti (1995).[7] Electoral campaigns often have served as the context for heightened communal violence and political assassinations, as in Sri Lanka, Bangladesh, India, Colombia, Jamaica, Kenya, Zimbabwe, and the United States (as evidenced by the assassination of Robert Kennedy and attempted assassination of George Wallace).[8] Violence and election processes are related in a wide variety of ways, and the literature on democracy and conflict is wide and growing.[9] The focus of this chapter on the specific use of elections to implement peace agreements most clearly raises the issue of the relationships between (1) the dual goals of war termination and democratization and (2) the implications for assessing postconflict elections.

Much of international policy toward peace has been based on liberal internationalism that posits that peace, both between and within states, is based on market democracy—that is, a policy of "pacification through political and economic liberalization."[10] The 1990s represented the merging of democratization and negotiated settlements to civil war, leading to the large number of postconflict elections to implement peace agreements.[11] While established democracy may reduce violence, the process of democratization often polarizes and generates conflict.[12] Rapoport and Weinberg suggest that "turbulence is an inevitable by-product of democratic principles and processes" and note that bullets and ballots are intimately related rather than opposites.[13] Indeed, democracy (and capitalism) not only encourages conflict but thrives on it.

WAR TERMINATION

War termination—to end the fighting—is the primary purpose of postconflict elections because such polls are organized as an integral part of a peace process and because war termination is a requirement for sustainable democracy. Democratization is a critical requirement of long-term, sustainable peace-building, but war termination must be the priority in the short term. Some postconflict elections have succeeded in ending armed conflict, most notably, Mozambique, El Salvador, and Cambodia. Others perhaps have succeeded to mark war termination in the short term but with less clear results with regard to long-term peace-building, such as Bosnia-Herzegovina, Liberia, and Tajikistan. In Angola, the 1994 elections sparked a renewal of conflict and failed to succeed even with respect to the limited objective of war termination.

Elections are but a small part of whether a peace process succeeds or fails to end a conflict. Other dimensions, particularly those related to such issues as overcoming the security dilemmas, marginalizing potential "spoilers," demobilization, and effective international peacekeeping or peace enforcement missions, are critical.[14] During peace implementation, processes to build security will take place in the context of preparations for elections, and the two processes will interact. Institutions and norms that encourage effective elections may reinforce the incentives to end the war, as in Mozambique and El Salvador, and a weak or flawed electoral process may encourage defection from the agreement and a return to fighting, as in Angola. By the same token, successful management of the security provisions of a peace agreement may strengthen the prospects for a successful election. If armed forces are successfully demobilized and the security sector effectively reformed and if militias are transformed into credible political parties, then the processes of war termination and democratization can reinforce each other.[15] To the extent that these security elements are managed in a manner that encourages the "demilitarization of politics," the prospects for elections that serve both war termination and democratization goals are increased.[16]

DEMOCRATIZATION

Another set of goals for postconflict elections relates to the process of democratization. As has been analyzed in cases of breakthrough or founding elections following authoritarian rule, multiparty elections may mark the beginning of a new pattern of contesting politics. Postconflict elections, like any transitional elections, have the purpose of serving as the first step in and a new foundation for a much longer-term process of democratic consolidation through which new rules of the political game are institutionalized and made routine. While consolidation is a complex and lengthy process, at least some postconflict elections have put in place the basis for sustainable democratic practice, most notably, in El Salvador and Mozambique, where competitive (if imperfect) elections have continued to take place after the first postconflict election. In other cases, subsequent elections have had an ambiguous relationship to democratization, as in Bosnia-Herzegovina and Cambodia. (Subsequent elections have not been held to date in Angola, Liberia, and Tajikistan.) In all cases, analysts will have to wait until several rounds of elections and leadership transition have taken place over a period of decades before reaching reliable conclusions regarding the vitality and sustainability of the democratization process.

Voters still traumatized by war and fearful of its return often select the candidates who either most credibly promise to protect them from their rivals (as in Bosnia-Herzegovina) or use their vote to appease the faction that threatens to return to war if it loses (as in Liberia). Elections under these circumstances therefore risk increasing the power of nondemocratic forces. This was the result in Bosnia-Herzegovina, Liberia, Tajikistan, and to an extent in Cambodia. In Angola, postconflict elections did even more damage, creating a sense of cynicism about the democratic process and making it much more difficult to implement democratic institutions in the future.

In Liberia, memories of the brutal conflict clearly shaped how many voters viewed the July 1997 election and the choices available to them.[17] As one observer put it, the voters "were intimidated not by thugs at the polling stations but by the trauma of the last seven years of war."[18] Many Liberians believed— with good reason—that if the powerful factional leader Charles Taylor lost the election, then the country would return to war. Taylor's rivals pointed to his violent past during the campaign but could not propose credible actions to contain him if he refused to accept the results.[19] Liberian voters made a calculated choice that they hoped would more likely promote peace and stability and used their vote to appease the powerful ex-militia leader. During the campaign young Taylor supporters frightened voters by chanting, "He killed my Pa, he killed my Ma, I'll vote for him."[20] In the end the elections ratified and institutionalized the political topography and imbalance of power created by seven years of war. The nature and ending of the war and the lack of a successful process to demilitarize politics—not the election itself—created this result. An organization and leader that amassed great power during the conflict through violence and intimidation converted that influence into positions of constitutional authority through elections. This result, understandable in the fearful context of Liberia in 1997, did little to advance democratization and raises considerable concerns regarding long-term stability and peace-building and of the ability of the electorate to constrain their ruler.

Similar patterns of voters in postconflict elections supporting the party that offered security in a context distorted by fear are evident in other cases. Nationalist parties in Bosnia-Herzegovina campaigned in 1996 on the basis of chauvinistic pledges and threats. The Croat Democratic Party (HDZ) issued advertisements warning that the "survival of their nation" depended on the vote, while Republika Srpska television warned that a vote against the Serb Democratic Party (SDS) would constitute a vote "against the Serb people."[21] Bosnian

Muslims made the same sort of appeals: "A vote for the SDA (Party of Democratic Action) is a vote for the survival of the Muslim nation" went the slogan in 1996.[22] Fear of other nationalist factions still powerful under the Dayton peace agreement led voters to rally to the nationalist faction that could most credibly promise security for their group. Small, multiethnic parties such as Joint List '97 that could not promise security won few votes.[23] In Ethiopia, fear and memories of the authoritarian rule of the old regime of Mengistu Haile Mariam led many voters to acquiesce to the ruling Ethiopian People's Revolutionary Democratic Front's power. As one Oromo farmer explained his 1995 vote for the ruling party, "I was afraid. The Government said I should vote so I voted. What could I do?"[24]

In Angola, many observers expected Jonas Savimbi's *União Nacional para a Independencia Total de Angola* (UNITA) party to do well in the elections. UNITA had successfully used force to compel the ruling *Movimento Popular de Libertação de Angola* (MPLA) party to hold elections, had a strong ethnic base among the Ovimbundu people, and was led by the charismatic (if demagogic) Jonas Savimbi. The period of the MPLA's rule under Eduardo dos Santos had seen unrelenting conflict, economic hardship, and corruption. During the campaign, however, Savimbi used threatening language that heightened fears and persuaded many that continuing to live with the MPLA was better than the uncertain and potentially violent future promised by UNITA. Unlike in Liberia, Savimbi's threats backfired and lost him support. The election results were quite close, with the MPLA's winning a thin majority in the Parliament, and dos Santos held just below 50 percent in the presidential race. In a context in which both parties had fought to a stalemate prior to the peace agreement, Angolan voters split in their perceptions of which party could best deliver peace and security to their communities.[25]

In Tajikistan, a prolonged conflict ended in a settlement between the government and the United Tajik Opposition in June 1997. The agreement created a cease-fire and allowed the government to develop its administrative presence in some parts of the country. The agreement, however, failed to settle the contentious issue relating to the place of Islamic parties in the secular state and its power-sharing provisions were not implemented. Elections were held for the president (November 1999) and Parliament (February and March 2000), but international observers regarded the exercise as flawed. State-controlled media and candidate registration favored the ruling People's Democratic Party, and observers questioned the vote-counting procedures.[26] Incumbent President Imomali Rahmanov ran unopposed and was reelected with 97 percent of the votes.[27] The process of elections did little to increase the popular mandate for the regime, and power in Tajikistan remained divided among rival warlords. As one report concluded, "[T]he formal structures of the country have proven almost irrelevant to the daily political processes."[28]

The danger with regard to long-term democratization is that postconflict elections will serve to entrench and provide electoral legitimacy to parties that are not democratic and continue to rely upon fear and force to remain in power. Leaders and political organizations that derive their power from the structures of war—whether insurgent militias and so-called warlords or a militarized government—often remain powerful at the time of the elections and therefore win the vote. Such leaders, after winning the first postconflict election, often then use the power of incumbency to prevent rivals from organizing and to circumvent future elections that may challenge their hold on power. In Cambodia, the Cambodian Communist Party forced the newly elected National Union Front for an Independent, Neutral, Peaceful, and Cooperative Cambodia (FUNCINPEC) party to share power after the postconflict election. This tense power-sharing arrangement broke down in violence in July 1997, and the 1998 elections were held amid charges of fraud and intimidation. In Liberia, Charles Taylor has used his power as elected president to systematically attack his political opponents.

It is important to recognize, however, that even in these cases the election did not "cause" these unfortunate results but rather reflected either a conflict that had not been resolved during negotiations or a poorly designed or poorly implemented process that failed to demilitarize politics prior to the vote. Charles Taylor became president of Liberia not because of a flawed electoral process but because he emerged from the war as the most powerful political actor, and the elections confirmed that fact. Nationalist parties did well in Bosnia-Herzegovina because they remained powerful in the context of the Dayton agreement, not because of the implementation of the agreement's voting provisions.

Even when long-term consolidation of democracy remains questionable, a postconflict election may at least represent a return to constitutional rule, an important step in the most difficult cases where the old state structures had collapsed. Constitutional restraints on power by no means are sufficient to prevent authoritarian rule, but they represent a set of norms against which rulers may be judged. In some cases an election that puts in place a constitutional government, despite questionable democratic credentials, may at least begin to create stability and serve as a first step in a longer-term process of democratization. While war termination does not by itself generate democracy, it is extremely difficult even to begin democratization until the war has ended. There are more models of transition from authoritarian rule to democracy than there are examples of transitions directly from war to democracy.

While the issue of peace dominates the agenda in postconflict elections, voters do not always choose the most militant parties. In Cambodia, the FUNCINPEC coalition won the election over both the ruling Cambodian People's Party (CPP), which controlled the state's security forces, and the Khmer Rouge, which retained a significant military capacity. Many voters regarded FUNCINPEC as the party best positioned to come to a settlement with the Khmer Rouge and rejected the brutal and violent behavior of the ruling CPP during the election campaign. The CPP campaign suggested that FUNCINPEC was in league with the Khmer Rouge, and since many Cambodians believed that a deal with the Khmer Rouge was necessary for peace, they voted for FUNCINPEC.[29] The deputy leader of FUNCINPEC took advantage of the desire for peace by highlighting his party's links to the Khmer Rouge:

> Some parties (for example, the CPP) promise that if they win they won't let the Khmer Rouge come back. But will they make war in order that the Khmer Rouge don't return? We have had fourteen years of war already, and Khmer killing Khmer. . . . We are sick of war which we have had since 1970. We won't take your children to go to war. . . . Do you want war, or peace? If FUNCINPEC wins, we will make an invitation to the Khmer Rouge. . . . So vote for FUNCINPEC so it can solve the problems of Cambodia.[30]

In Cambodia many voters believed that a vote for FUNCINPEC would lead to an accommodation with the Khmer Rouge and an end to the armed conflict, thereby making a vote for FUNCINPEC a vote for peace.

In El Salvador and Mozambique, more successful processes to demilitarize politics reduced the legacy of fear and put in place institutions that could better sustain peace and democracy. Relatively strong interim regimes, consultative processes to manage the challenges of implementation and electoral administration, and successful processes to transform militias into political parties established a new institutional context that served to bridge the conditions of war to those of peace and democratization. In Mozambique, some voters engaged in tactical voting to balance the two powerful parties by selecting the ruling *Frente de Libertação de Moçambique* (Frelimo) candidate as president while choosing the opposition *Resistência Nacional Moçambicana* (Renamo) candidates for the parliament.[31] Salvadoran voters made their selection on the basis of policy preferences with less concern that the outcome would reignite conflict, although some voters reportedly voted against the *Frente Farabundo Martí para la Liberación Nacional* (FMLN) due to their involvement in the war.[32] In both cases the ruling party won the elections, but the opposition won significant representation and completed the transition from insurgency to loyal opposition operating within a rough but reasonably effective democratic system.

The results in these recent cases suggest that postconflict elections may best be characterized as referendums on peace in contexts where legacies of fear and violence dominate voters' concerns unless politics has been demilitarized. For elections to be fully meaningful, however, they must give voters a significant choice. In many of these cases, voters understood their choice to be war or peace in the hands of a nationalistic, military leader, an unenviable range of options. If the transitional period of peace implementation prior to the elections can demilitarize politics and build security, as in El Salvador and Mozambique, then a greater range of choice and more effective elections are possible.

INTERNATIONAL PEACEKEEPING AND RECONSTRUCTION ASSISTANCE

Postconflict elections further relate to an additional set of goals for the international community. In some cases, the inclusion of postconflict elections in a peace agreement was critical to convincing international peacekeeping forces to intervene. The United States would have been extremely reluctant to commit to involvement in Bosnia-Herzegovina without elections serving as a convenient point to structure an (eventually unused) "exit strategy." In Tajikistan, the UN operation pressed for rapid elections. In Liberia, the Economic Community of West African States Cease-fire Monitoring Group (ECOMOG) peacekeeping force insisted that elections take place in 1997 so that it could withdraw. The costs of a large peace implementation force are tremendous, as was seen in Cambodia, and the dangers are considerable, as was seen in Somalia, the former Yugoslavia, Rwanda, and Sierra Leone. Without some event to mark the end of the transition and allay concerns regarding open-ended commitments, international peacekeeping forces are unlikely to get involved. In the most difficult cases, prospects for either peace or democracy are minimal without such support.

Postconflict elections have also provided the context for great powers to disengage from support to insurgent groups or regimes that no longer served the great powers' interests. Disentangling external powers from local conflicts may be a critical step in resolving an internal war. The peace processes and elections in Cambodia and Nicaragua served this purpose. The elections in Liberia provided Nigeria with a mechanism to get out of its conflict with Charles Taylor and to end its support for other insurgent groups.

International financial institutions such as the World Bank, International Monetary Fund, and important bilateral donors have great difficulty in designing projects for desperately needed reconstruction with an interim regime that lacks a clear mandate. Lending institutions require a recognized government to serve as their partner in making large sums of capital available. The reluctance of international donors to find creative ways to provide desperately needed resources to the self-proclaimed Republic of Somaliland illustrates these constraints. The daunting tasks of postconflict reconstruction and the imperatives to provide jobs to consolidate the peace often remain on hold until constitutional rule returns and the transition is "over," at least in a formal sense. Postconflict elections provide that end point and serve as a signal to lenders that they may begin to make binding loan commitments.[33]

MULTIPLE GOALS, PRIORITIES, AND TRADE-OFFS

Postconflict elections, therefore, must be assessed in relation to multiple goals relating to war termination, democratization, and international peacekeeping and assistance. These multiple goals operate on different timelines and sequences, and they require different preconditions. In some cases priorities among these important objectives must be established, at least in the short term. For a postconflict election to serve the purposes of democratization, for example, a long transition that provides sufficient time and appropriate institutions to encourage the creation of peacetime political and civil structures prior to voting may be necessary.[34] In some cases, however, the nature of the conflict and the peace agreement required quick elections in an atmosphere in which leaders continued to derive power from their control over fighters, and the structures of war remained effectively in place. With the important exceptions of Cambodia and Mozambique, the international community generally has been unwilling to provide the resources and peacekeeping troops necessary to support a relatively long transition. Waiting until conditions are more propitious relative to the democratization goals may put the peace process at risk, discourage international peacekeepers, and delay needed support from international lenders for reconstruction. Under such difficult circumstances, the "least bad" policy outcome may be to have an election that serves important goals with relation to war termination or international policy but makes less progress (at least in the short run) in promoting democratization. Such war termination elections may provide limited but nonetheless important opportunities for a new political order that may be a prerequisite to advance the longer-term policy goals of furthering democratization and rule of law and strengthening civil society.

It is important, therefore, to recognize that while elections inherently and appropriately should be associated with democratization, they also may serve other important roles. The international community should not cynically accept meaningless "demonstration elections" that legitimate authoritarian regimes without providing real scope for voter choice.[35] But neither should it insist that democratization is the only criterion by which to judge the value of postconflict elections. Other goals, most notably, war termination and, in many cases, a desire by the international community to have a clear exit strategy for peacekeeping, are also important and legitimate. The opportunity of a given election to serve as a tool of war termination may be greater than its potential with regard to democratization. It may also be that in a number of the most difficult cases, ending the conflict is the only goal that can be met in the short run.

In addition, the value of a postconflict election should be judged relative to the most likely alternatives available. If the transitional period can be prolonged to provide the time, space, and security for civil society and political parties to organize, such a transition is more likely to result in meeting both war termination and democratization goals. If, however, postponing an election until democratization goals are more likely to be met risks derailing the peace process and returning the country to war, it may be necessary to hold the election, implement the peace agreement, and focus policies to promote democratization on the postconflict government.

Finally, if holding quick but flawed elections is more likely to ignite a new round of conflict resulting in neither war termination nor democratization goals being advanced, then supporting the election is clearly dangerous and counterproductive. Judging whether supporting a postconflict election in a specific transition is more likely to promote both, one, or neither of the twin goals of war termination and democratization requires careful analysis and is inevitably easier to judge in hindsight. That, however, is inherently the nature of the policy challenges facing the international community in trying to assist peace-building following civil war.

NOTES

Support for this research was provided in part by the U.S. Institute of Peace.

1. Seymour Martin Lipset, "Introduction," in *Encyclopedia of Democracy*, ed. Seymour Martin Lipset (Washington, DC: Congressional Quarterly Press, 1995), lv; Philippe C. Schmitter and Terry Lynn Karl, "What Democracy Is . . . and Is Not," in *The Global Resurgence of Democracy*, 2nd ed., ed. Larry Diamond and Marc F. Plattner (Baltimore: Johns Hopkins University Press, 1996), 50.

2. Christopher Clapham, "Rwanda: The Perils of Peacemaking," *Journal of Peace Research* 35, no. 2 (1998): 195. See also the comments by Larry Garber, senior policy adviser for democracy and human rights, U.S. Agency for International Development, cited in Timothy D. Sisk, "Elections and Conflict Management in Africa: Conclusions and Recommendations," in *Elections and Conflict Management in Africa*, ed. Timothy D. Sisk and Andrew Reynolds (Washington, DC: U.S. Institute of Peace Press, 1998), 146.

3. These seven represent all of the cases in the 1990s in which a peace agreement used elections as an instrument of implementation following a period of civil war. In other cases the peace process failed prior to elections, as in Rwanda and earlier efforts in Liberia; elections were held in the context of civil war but without a comprehensive peace agreement, as in Nicaragua and Sierra Leone (1996); the conflict did not reach the level of civil war, as in South Africa and Haiti; the conflict ended in national liberation and withdrawal of one of the warring parties, as in Namibia, East Timor, and Eritrea; or elections were held to consolidate the power of the winning party in a conflict that ended with unilateral victory, as in Ethiopia, Uganda, and Rwanda.

4. The antidemocratic moves by Second Prime Minister Hun Sen against First Prime Minister Prince Norodom Ranariddh in 1997 make the 1993 Cambodian election a difficult case to assess. A successful election is not a guarantee against subsequent backsliding, but, to the extent that the 1997 crisis had its basis in the failure of the 1993 elections to result in sustainable institutions, the elections failed to promote democratization.

5. Guillermo O'Donnell and Philippe C. Schmitter, *Transitions from Authoritarian Rule: Tentative Conclusions about Uncertain Democracies* (Baltimore: Johns Hopkins University Press, 1986), 57.

6. Terrence Lyons, "Closing the Transition: The May 1995 Elections in Ethiopia," *Journal of Modern African Studies* 34 (1996): 121–142; Martin Doornbos, "African Multipartyism and the Quest for Democratic Alternatives: Ugandan Elections, Past and Present," in *Chasing a Mirage? Observing Elections and Democratization in Africa*, ed. Jan Abbink and Gerti Hesseling (New York: St. Martin's Press, 1999); International Crisis Group, "Consensual Democracy in Post-Genocide Rwanda: Evaluating the March 2001 District Elections," *International Crisis Group, Africa Report* 34 (9 October 2001).

7. On defining civil war, see Roy Licklider, ed., *Stopping the Killing: How Civil Wars End* (New York: New York University Press, 1993), 9–10. Many analysts, however, count South Africa as a civil war.

8. Dennis Austin, *Democracy and Violence in India and Sri Lanka* (New York:

Council on Foreign Relations Press, 1995); Tony Payne, "Multi-Party Politics in Jamaica," in *Political Parties in the Third World*, ed. Vicky Randal (London: Sage, 1988), 137–154; Todd Eisenstadt and Daniel Garcia, "Colombia: Negotiations in a Shifting Pattern of Insurgency," in *Elusive Peace: Negotiating an End to Civil Wars*, ed. I. William Zartman (Washington, DC: Brookings Institution, 1995); Human Rights Watch, *Divide and Rule: State-Sponsored Ethnic Violence in Kenya* (New York: Human Rights Watch, 1993); Robert I. Rotberg, "Africa's Mess, Mugabe's Mayhem," *Foreign Affairs* 79, no. 5 (September–October 2000): 47–61.

9. David C. Rapoport and Leonard Weinberg, eds., *The Democratic Experience and Political Violence* (London: Frank Cass, 2001); Jakub Zileinski, "Transitions from Authoritarian Rule and the Problem of Violence," *Journal of Conflict Resolution* 43, no. 2 (April 1999): 213; Jack Snyder, *From Voting to Violence: Democratization and Nationalist Conflict* (New York: W. W. Norton, 2000).

10. Roland Paris, "Peacebuilding and the Limits of Liberal Internationalism," *International Security* 22, no. 2 (Fall 1997): 56.

11. David W. Roberts, *Political Transition in Cambodia, 1991–99: Power, Elitism, and Democracy* (New York: St. Martin's Press, 2001), xi.

12. Edward Mansfield and Jack Snyder, "Democratization and War," *International Security* 20, no. 1 (Summer 1995): 5–38.

13. Rapoport and Weinberg, *The Democratic Experience*, 3, 5.

14. Stephen John Stedman, "Spoiler Problems in Peace Processes," *International Security* 22, no. 5 (Fall 1997): 5–53; Barry R. Posen, "The Security Dilemma and Ethnic Conflict," in *Ethnic Conflict and International Security*, ed. Michael E. Brown (Princeton, NJ: Princeton University Press, 1993), 103–124; Jack Snyder and Robert Jervis, "Civil War and the Security Dilemma," in *Civil Wars, Insecurity, and Intervention*, ed. Barbara F. Walter and Jack Snyder (New York: Columbia University Press, 1999); David A. Lake and Donald Rothchild, "Containing Fear: The Origins and Management of Ethnic Conflict," *International Security* 21, no. 2 (Fall 1996): 41–75; Stephen John Stedman, Donald Rothchild, and Elizabeth Cousens, eds., *Ending Civil Wars: The Implementation of Peace Agreement* (Boulder, CO: Lynne Rienner, 2002).

15. On demobilization, see Nat J. Colletta, Markus Kostner, and Ingo Wiederhofer, "Disarmament, Demobilization, and the Social and Economic Reintegration of Ex-Combatants: Lessons and Liabilities in State Transition," paper presented at the "Conference on Reinvigorating and Resuscitating Weak, Vulnerable, and Collapsing States," World Peace Foundation, Cambridge, MA, June 2001. On transforming militias into political parties, see the excellent study by Carrie Manning, "Constructing Opposition in Mozambique: Renamo as Political Party," *Journal of Southern African Studies* 24, no. 1 (March 1998): 161–190.

16. For more on "demilitarizing politics," see Terrence Lyons, "The Role of Postsettlement Elections," in *Ending Civil Wars*, ed. Stedman, Cousens, and Rothchild.

17. Terrence Lyons, *Voting for Peace: Postconflict Elections in Liberia* (Washington, DC: Brookings Institution, 1999).

18. Victor Tanner, "Liberia: Railroading Peace," *Review of African Political Economy* 25 (1998): 140.

19. For example, anti-Taylor posters with pictures of the brutalities of the war and the caption "Chucky [Charles Taylor] did it" served to increase the levels of fear and raise anew concerns that the civilian candidates would not be able to prevent him from doing it again.

20. Stephen Ellis, *The Mask of Anarchy: The Destruction of Liberia and the Religious Dimensions of an African Civil War* (New York: New York University Press, 1999), 109. Such characterizations were featured in a number of press reports on the election. A Liberian was quoted as saying, "He [Taylor] killed my father but I'll vote for him. He started all this and he's going to fix it." John Chiahemen, "Liberians Vote in Peace against War," *Reuters*, 19 July 1997. Another voter is quoted as saying, "Charles Taylor spoiled this country, so he's the best man to fix it." Donald G. McNeil Jr., "Under Scrutiny, Postwar Liberia Goes to Polls," *New York Times*, 20 July 1997. A leading human rights leader in Liberia said that "the only thing Liberians wanted was an end to the war." "Interview with Samuel Kofi Woods of Liberia," *African Affairs* 99 (2000): 107.

21. International Crisis Group, *Elections in Bosnia and Herzegovina, ICG Report 16* (New York: International Crisis Group, 22 September 1996).

22. Cited in Susan L. Woodward, "Bosnia and Herzegovina: How Not to End Civil War," in *Civil Wars, Insecurity, and Intervention*, ed. Walter and Snyder, 96.

23. Joint List '97 did better in the local elections of September 1997. In Tuzla, Bosnia's second largest city, where multiethnic institutions protected minorities during the war, Mayor Selim Beslagic of the Joint List '97 defeated the SDA. See Bill Egbert, "A Noble Act of Harmony in the Balkans," *Christian Science Monitor*, 9 October 1997. Vesna Bojičić and Mary Kaldor, "The 'Abnormal' Economy of Bosnia-Herzegovina," in *Scramble for the Balkans: Nationalism, Globalism, and the Political Economy of Reconstruction*, ed. Carl-Ulrik Schierup (New York: St. Martin's Press in association with the Centre for Research in Ethnic Relations, University of Warwick, 1999), 98–108, contrast Tuzla with Mostar.

24. Quoted in Stephen Buckley, "Ethiopia Takes New Ethnic Tack: Deliberately Divisive," *Washington Post*, 18 June 1995, A21.

25. Marina Ottaway, "Angola's Failed Elections," in *Postconflict Elections, Democratization, and International Assistance*, ed. Krishna Kumar (Boulder, CO: Lynne Rienner, 1998). For an insider's view, see the account by the United Nations special representative Margaret Joan Anstee, *Orphan of the Cold War: The Inside Story of the Collapse of the Angolan Peace Process, 1992–3* (New York: St. Martin's Press, 1996).

26. *The Republic of Tajikistan Elections to the Parliament, 27 February 2000: Final Report* (Warsaw: Organization for Security and Cooperation in Europe, Office for Democratic Institutions and Human Rights, 17 May 2000).

27. Nasrin Dadmehr, "Tajikistan: A Vulnerable State in a Post-War Society," paper presented at the "Conference on Reinvigorating and Resuscitating Weak, Vulnerable, and Collapsing States," World Peace Foundation, Cambridge, MA, June 2001.

28. International Crisis Group, *Central Asia: Crisis Conditions in Three States, ICG Asia Report 7* (New York: International Crisis Group, 7 August 2000).

29. Judy Ledgerwood, "Patterns of CPP Political Repression and Violence during the UNTAC Period," in *Propaganda, Politics, and Violence in Cambodia: Democratic Transition under United Nations Peace-keeping*, ed. Steve Heder and Judy Ledgerwood (Armonk, NY: M. E. Sharpe, 1996), 117, 130.

30. Cited in Kate Frieson, "The Politics of Getting the Vote in Cambodia," in Ledgerwood, *Propaganda, Politics, and Violence in Cambodia*, ed. Heder and Ledgerwood, 200. Lizée argues that many Cambodians voted on the basis of a logic that "a FUNCINPEC victory would mean that Prince Sihanouk would return to power and that he would then bring peace to Cambodia by initiating a rapprochement between the four Cambodian

factions." Pierre P. Lizée, *Peace, Power, and Resistance in Cambodia: Global Governance and the Failure of International Conflict Resolution* (New York: St. Martin's Press, 2000), 125.

31. Alex Vines, *Renamo: From Terrorism to Democracy in Mozambique?* (London: James Currey, 1996), 159.

32. Tommie Sue Montgomery, *Revolution in El Salvador: From Civil Strife to Civil Peace* (Boulder, CO: Westview Press, 1995), 266.

33. See James K. Boyce and Manuel Pastor Jr., "Aid for Peace: Can International Financial Institutions Help Prevent Conflict?" *World Policy Journal* 15 (1998): 42–50.

34. Krishna Kumar and Marina Ottaway, "General Conclusions and Priorities for Policy Research," in *Postconflict Elections*, ed. Kumar, 231–237.

35. Edward S. Herman and Frank Brodhead, *Demonstration Elections: U.S.-Staged Elections in the Dominican Republic, Vietnam, and El Salvador* (Boston: South End Press, 1984). See also Terry Karl, "Imposing Consent? Electoralism vs. Democratization in El Salvador," in *Elections and Democratization in Latin America, 1980–85*, ed. Paul Drake and Eduardo Silva (San Diego: CLAS/Center for US-Mexican Studies, 1986), 9–36.

Chapter 10

The Impact of Democratization and Economic Globalization on Workers' Rights: A Comparative Analysis

David L. Cingranelli

This chapter reports the results of a large-scale, comparative research project examining the effects of democratization and the increasing economic globalization of international economic transactions on changes in government protections of workers' rights. Previous research has consistently demonstrated that democratization leads to greater respect for other types of human rights. It has also generally argued that democratic governments are more likely to produce policies that protect workers, though there are some important caveats to this argument that are discussed below. The literature on economic globalization is much more varied in its predictions about how globalization will affect workers. Concerns about the effects of unregulated globalization on workers have even prompted violent mass demonstrations in recent years. Events such as the "battle of Seattle" in 1999 demonstrated that substantial opposition to U.S.-led economic globalization exists. Much of that opposition is fueled by speculation that economic globalization hurts workers everywhere.

Are democratization and economic globalization both encouraging governments to increase protections of workers' rights, or are the two processes exerting opposite effects? If the effects are opposing, which effects are stronger? Before answering these questions, some central concepts—workers' rights, economic globalization, and democratization—are defined. Then, to illustrate the variety of predictions concerning the effects of democratization and globalization on workers' rights, arguments are derived from applicable theories. Finally, evidence is presented concerning the trends in worldwide government respect for workers' rights between 1981 and 1999, the relationship between how globalized a country's economy is and how democratic its government is, and the degree of protection that its government provides for workers.

The evidence shows that there has been a gradual but statistically significant improvement in worldwide government respect for workers' rights. This improvement has been greater in those countries whose economies have become more integrated into the global economy. The most remarkable advance in government protections of workers' rights has occurred in the formerly communist and socialist, now democratic and capitalist, countries of Central Europe and the former Soviet Union. Among less-developed, less-globalized countries, workers' rights still have advanced, and they improved the most under democratic rather than authoritarian governments. This evidence provides strong support for the arguments derived from conventional economic theory. One of the most heated current policy debates focuses on whether the World Trade Organization (WTO) should make rules that prohibit trade with states whose governments refuse to adopt internal rules safeguarding workers' rights and the environment. In the conclusion of the chapter, the relevance of these findings to that debate is discussed.

WORKERS' RIGHTS

Many workers' rights are recognized in international human rights agreements such as the Universal Declaration of Human Rights, the International Covenant on Economic, Social, and Cultural Rights, and the International Covenant on Civil and Political Rights. They are elaborated in more detail in the 181 Conventions and 188 Recommendations of the oldest international governmental human rights organization in the world—the International Labor Organization (ILO), the United Nations agency that is focused on labor issues.[1]

The Declaration of Fundamental Principles and Rights at Work requires all ILO members "to respect, to promote, and to realize in good faith" five core rights that are considered fundamental human rights: freedom of association, the effective recognition of the right to collective bargaining, the elimination of all forms of forced or compulsory labor, the effective abolition of child labor, and the elimination of discrimination in respect of employment or occupation.

The level of government respect for workers' rights in a country is particularly important for several reasons. As Leary[2] argues, the status of workers in a country is a bellwether for the status of human rights in general. It is rare that a government will respect other human rights if workers' rights are not respected also. When workers possess rights such as freedom of association at the workplace, they are empowered to challenge a political and economic regime if they choose. Thus, it is not surprising that labor organizers and leaders are among the most frequent victims of human rights abuses. According to Weisband and Colvin,[3] who analyzed data contained in the International Confederation of Free Trade Unions annual survey, suppression of trade unions is a common form of human rights violation that regularly occurs in both democratic and authoritarian political systems. Leary also provides several examples of repressive regimes trying to control or destroy trade unions in recent history.[4]

Most commonly, government policies affect, protect, or violate workers' rights indirectly by regulating the relationship between employers and employees. Those regulations may *guarantee* that employers provide a minimum wage, safe and healthy working conditions, or paid vacations. Governments also can *prohibit* employers from discriminating in hiring and treatment at the workplace, requiring mandatory overtime work, or from arbitrarily terminating employment. Another way that government policies can affect workers' rights is through legislation that helps workers directly such as national unemployment insurance.

ECONOMIC GLOBALIZATION

The term "economic globalization" is used here to refer to the substantial increase in the volume of international economic activity since 1990. A particular country is more or less "economically globalized" to the degree that it participates in these worldwide economic interactions beyond some minimum threshold level. Economic globalization is not new. Nations have been involved in economic transactions for thousands of years. However, the rapid increase in economic interconnectedness is new. Separating the effects of economic globalization on workers' rights from the effects of other forms of globalization is difficult—perhaps even impossible. We return to this point later. For now, it suffices to remind the reader that, for some, globalization refers to far more general phenomena. For example, as defined by Held et al., it is a "widening, deepening, and speeding up of world interconnectedness in all aspects of contemporary social life, from the cultural to the criminal, the financial to the spiritual."[5]

The extent to which different countries participate in global economic transactions is not uniform. Some countries are deeply involved in transnational economic activities of many kinds. Others are hardly involved at all. Thus, if globalization has an impact on workers' rights, its impact should be greatest in countries that have the greatest involvement in or experience the greatest increase in transnational economic activities. The richer countries of Europe and North America, along with Japan, Australia, and New Zealand, have long been major exporters of industrial products and services. They have been major participants in the world economy for a long time. They now are able to extend their economic relations in a more vigorous way to more states. Workers in these countries have experienced the consequences of both the highest level of involvement in international economic activities and the greatest amount of increase in those activities since 1990. Most of the economic interactions of the richer countries are with each other.

Among the poorer nations are five categories of states whose workers may have been affected in different ways by the increased rate of globalization at the world system level. First there are the big emerging markets. These states have become large-scale industrial producers of a broad range of products. They also have substantial populations with enough affluence to provide markets for goods produced elsewhere. There is some consensus that the big emerging markets today are China, India, Indonesia, South Korea, Taiwan, Thailand, Argentina, Brazil, Mexico, South Africa, and Turkey.[6] Since the economies of these countries have changed the most over the past decade, the workers within them may have been affected the most by systemic changes in the world economy.

A second category of countries might be called simply "emerging markets." These have moved beyond simple assembly of clothing and electronics into a few more diversified industrial and service sectors. However, the range of products and services is less than what is produced by the big emerging markets, and the ability of the citizens of these states to be consumers of products and services produced elsewhere is more limited. The countries considered to be emerging markets in this analysis are Malaysia, the Philippines, Singapore, Pakistan, Saudi Arabia, Chile, Colombia, Peru, Venezuela, Egypt, Israel, the Czech Republic, Hungary, Poland, and Russia.

An important third category of poorer states is represented by the former communist and socialist economies that have become more or less democratic and capitalist but have not yet "emerged" as major players in the globalized economic system. These countries have achieved a relatively high degree of industrialization but are handicapped by the need to make a rapid shift from socialism to deregulated market economies. Workers in these states are faced with increased demands for productivity and a less substantial safety net if they fail to meet those demands. Examples of former communist and socialist economies include Albania, Azerbaijan, Kazakhstan, Latvia, Romania, Slovakia, and Ukraine.

There is also a large category of states not yet affected very much by globalization. At most, they have been indirectly affected by the major changes that have taken place in the global economy since the end of the Cold War. These states have little industry. Many depend upon the export of raw materials that they have exported for fifty years or more. Most are so poor that their economic connections to the rest of the world are very limited. This fairly large group of Third World states includes such countries as Benin, Bolivia, El Salvador, Ghana, Haiti, Liberia, Nepal, Nigeria, Yemen, and Zimbabwe.

Finally, five countries in the world have remained communist and socialist for at least the last twenty years—China, Cuba, Laos, North Korea, and Vietnam. Workers in these countries have been the most isolated from the effects of economic globalization on their rights. In the analysis that follows, China is treated as part of this last group rather than as one of the big emerging markets.

WHY DEMOCRATIZATION AFFECTS WORKERS' RIGHTS

Democratization refers to the process of moving from a more closed political system to one where rulers can be held accountable for their actions in the public realm by citizens.[7] Democratization is expected to improve government protections for workers because democracy empowers the masses. The masses are expected to use that power to improve their well-being in society, including their ability to recognize basic rights such as workers' rights.

Still, new democratic governments do not always favor workers over employers. Huang argues that if workers are not an important part of the movement to create democracy in an authoritarian state, the policies of the newly democratic state may not be favorable to workers.[8] He contends that South Korea and Taiwan both achieved democratic transitions a decade ago without the strong support of organized labor. As a consequence, the democratic governments of both countries are viewed as hostile by organized labor. For example, in 1997, the South Korean government made revisions in the Labor Standard Law giving employers greater flexibility in terminating workers and in assigning working hours. Similarly, according to Huang, workers protesting changes in Taiwan's constitutional framework were ignored by the ruling and opposition parties.

Even the long-established democratic governments of Europe and North America suppressed the trade union movements in their countries in the first fifty years or so of trade unionism. According to Jacobs, "[O]ne may say that before 1850 labor relations in European countries were characterized by repression. In all these countries trade unions were at first illegal, as were the industrial struggles conducted by workers."[9] In the United States, repression of trade unions continued well into the early part of the twentieth century.[10]

Previous research examining the effects of democracy on workers' rights has focused almost exclusively on how democratic movements in modern, industrialized economies affected workers. They conclude that, in those countries, democratization led to greater protections of workers' rights. The effects of democratization on workers' rights in less-developed countries has not been the subject of large-scale comparative analysis. However, in many less-developed countries, unions have posed a real or imagined threat to the ruling elite. In countries with political instability, unions are often viewed as potential alternatives to the ruling party. Thus, in many less-developed countries, there has been a pattern of repression of trade union leaders and organizers that is either conducted by or condoned by the government. Also, prior to democratization in the Third World, there were many more experiments with socialized economies. In these cases, governments were the main employers, and employee rights were very limited.

The direction of the causal relationship between democracy and government respect for workers' rights could be disputed. It is possible that the development of some basic government protections of workers' rights might be an important, even necessary precondition for the development of a stable democracy. Adams[11] argues that democracies provide workers with more rights than authoritarian systems do. The implication is that having a democratic system empowers workers. Empowered workers, in turn, lobby governments to produce public policies that protect workers' rights. However, among less-developed countries (LDCs), the causal relationship may be reversed or, more accurately, circular.

One enduring characteristic of LDCs is the absence of a large middle class. Much of the democratization literature stresses the importance of a middle class to the development of democracy. Protecting workers' rights is the most important way to ensure that the masses have a fair share of the wealth and well-being in any society. Rights like freedom of association and collective bargaining are likely to produce higher wages for workers and a more equitable distribution of income. This more equitable distribution of income, in turn, may pave the way for a successful transition from an authoritarian to a democratic system and from an unstable to a stable democracy. One well-known example of workers' leading the fight for democracy in an authoritarian regime was Poland's Solidarity movement in the 1980s. Students and workers are often in the forefront of social movements pressing for progressive political reforms in many parts of the world in both authoritarian and in recently democratized regimes.

WHY ECONOMIC GLOBALIZATION AFFECTS WORKERS' RIGHTS

Theories of the effects of economic globalization suggest that changes at the highest level of aggregation, in this case the operations of the world economic system, affect the behaviors of all of the constituent parts of the system, in this case nation-states and the workers within them. At the world economic system's level, there has been a sharp increase in the amount of economic activity in the world that takes place between people who live in different countries relative to the amount of economic activity among people who live in the same country.[12]

There are two schools of thought on the nature of the relationship between globalization and workers' rights. One is conventional economic theory, which posits that a more globalized economy creates more aggregate wealth and that workers directly benefit from the trickle-down effects of that wealth. The more that a particular country participates, the greater the benefits to its workers. Workers in LDCs are likely to gain the most from participation in the global economy because there tends to be more investment where pay, benefits, and working conditions are low. Once capital investments have been made in a low-workers'-rights country, workers gain more leverage to improve their rights relative to employers. This might lead to a "leveling up" effect as workers' rights in LDCs catch up with workers' rights in the more advanced economies. On the other hand, it might lead to a convergence of respect for workers' rights in all countries whose national economies significantly participate in the global economy. The convergence hypothesis suggests that workers in the more advanced economies will lose some rights and that workers in the less advanced economies will gain some. The convergence will take place somewhere in the middle.

Neo-Marxist theorists emphasize the class conflict elements of the world economy. They see the interests of multinational corporations (MNCs) as completely at odds with the interests of workers.[13] Globalization, in their view, primarily benefits MNCs to the detriment of workers. The more that a particular country participates in the global economy, the greater the suffering of its workers.[14] Since capital can move easily in the more global economy, but workers cannot, capital always seeks the lowest cost labor, and capitalists move their factories whenever workers seek greater protections for their rights.[15] This inevitably leads to what some Neo-Marxists refer to as a "race to the bottom."

According to Neo-Marxists, the least economically developed capitalist countries are likely to have the dubious distinction of being the winners of this race to the bottom partly because of their dependence on foreign assistance. Neo-Marxist theorists note that Western bilateral foreign aid and multilateral official development assistance are often conditioned upon the recipient's adopting certain free market initiatives. Deeply indebted developing countries seeking International Monetary Fund (IMF) and/or World Bank loans are required to accept structural economic adjustment policies as loan requirements.[16] The general result of these austerity programs has been the slashing of government spending, including a decrease in welfare programs.

In many developing countries, labor unions strongly oppose these measures. Therefore, it is possible that one of the measures that the governments of LDCs take to weaken the opposition to structural adjustment policies is to weaken their protections of workers' rights. Clashes between South Korean unions and authorities have centered on such issues. Frundt[17] describes how a Texas-based Coca-Cola franchisee used the Guatemalan government to violate the physical integrity rights of Guatemalan bottling company employees in response to their initiative to unionize. McLaren[18] finds some empirical evidence that IMF austerity programs may actually worsen human rights conditions in developing countries. However, few systematic, scientific studies of the relationship have yielded strong evidence of negative effects of IMF austerity programs.

WHY GOVERNMENTS RESPECT OR VIOLATE HUMAN RIGHTS

As argued above, workers' rights are a subcategory of human rights. Therefore, research results explaining why some governments respect human rights while others do not should be relevant to the present inquiry. Government abuse of physical integrity rights has, thus far, been the phenomenon of chief theoretical interest in almost all empirical studies of the determinants and consequences of government abuse of human rights.[19] Physical integrity rights are rights against such government behaviors as political killing and imprisonment, torture, and disappearance. The leading theoretical perspective guiding this stream of research suggests that governments respect these rights the least when they are authoritarian or threatened by either domestic or international conflict or both.[20]

Several studies have examined the relationship between foreign economic investment and the level of government respect for human rights in developing countries.[21] However, the results have been mixed, and no previous study has focused on the impact of a foreign economic investment on workers' rights in particular. Richards et al. come closest to measuring the impact of economic globalization on workers' rights, because they focus on foreign economic penetration rather than a single item such as foreign direct investment or trade. Moreover, they use the term "foreign economic penetration" (FEP) to describe the broader array of ways in which foreign capital can penetrate the economy of a developing nation, including foreign direct investment, portfolio investment, foreign aid, and long-term debt. Finally they assess the impact of FEP on an index of political rights and civil liberties. This index includes the rights to travel, join unions, and participate in the political system and freedom of religion. They found evidence that one aspect of FEP, foreign direct investment, is significantly associated with *increases in government respect* for political rights and civil liberties.

Some believe that there is a trend toward greater government respect for human rights, a trend that accelerated with the end of the Cold War, an acceleration that coincides with the period of rapid economic globalization. However, there is little evidence of major improvements in the average level of government respect for human rights around the world since 1990. Cingranelli and Richards[22] examined a random sample of seventy-nine countries from 1981 to 1996 to see how average government respect for physical integrity rights had changed from the Cold War period (1981–1990) to the post–Cold War period (1991–1996). They found no significant change in mean government respect for three of the four rights considered—the rights not to be tortured, extrajudicially killed, or made to disappear. However, they did find evidence of substantial improvement in government respect for the right not to be politically imprisoned in the post–Cold War period. Cingranelli and Richards then examined some alternative explanations for improvements in the treatment of political prisoners around the world. They concluded that the more that a country participated in the global economy and the more democratic that it was, the more that the government had improved its respect for the right not to be politically imprisoned in the 1981–1996 period.

HYPOTHESES

The first step in the analysis to follow is to see how average government respect for workers' rights has changed for the six different groups of countries with differentially globalized economies described above. For those countries that were fully globalized throughout the 1981–1999 period, conventional economic theory would lead one to expect that workers' rights would be fully protected for the entire period. Neo-Marxist theory would expect that those rights would deteriorate after 1990, as the governments in all countries, including the most fully economically developed, took part in the race to the bottom.

For countries that once were socialist and then became capitalist, conventional economics would lead us to expect a major improvement in government protection of workers' rights. Neo-Marxists would predict a decline in the protection of workers in a capitalist system. For the big emerging markets and emerging markets, conventional economics would predict improved protections of workers' rights, with the big emerging markets experiencing the greatest improvement. Neo-Marxists would expect worsened protections of workers' rights, with the greatest decline occurring in the big emerging markets whose governments are winning the race to the bottom. Neither theory would predict any change for those countries that remained more or less outside the global economy— eighty-five less-developed countries and the five remaining communist societies.

The second step was to examine the effects of democratization. This was done by dividing the eighty-five nonglobalized, less-developed countries into those that were democratic throughout the period, those that became more democratic, those that became less democratic, and those that remained authoritarian. The expectation was that workers' rights would improve the most in those countries that had become more democratic and would decline in those countries that had become less democratic. The level of protection of workers' rights was expected to stay the same for those that had been at about the same level of democracy or authoritarianism throughout the period.

METHODS

The six groups of countries with the numbers of countries in each group are the advanced economies (N = 21), the big emerging markets (N = 10 excluding China), the emerging markets (N = 15), the former communist countries (N = 37), the nonglobalized LDCs (N = 85), and the "communist/socialist countries" (N = 5 including China). Particular attention is paid to changes in government respect for workers' rights from the period before the beginning of accelerated democratization and economic globalization (1981–1990) to the period during which rapid democratization and economic globalization occurred (1990–1999). This part of the analysis is performed using a cross-sectional time-series data set comprising of 170 countries for the years 1981, 1984, 1987, 1990, 1993, 1996, and 1999. Countries were included in the study if they had a population of 500,000 or more in 1981. The time period is lower-bound at 1981 due to problems with the quality and availability of workers' rights data before 1981.

China is one of the most interesting cases. China could have been placed in the "big emerging market" category. It is the most populous country in the world. By some estimates its economy also is the fastest growing in the world. Moreover, despite the communist ideology of its government, China rapidly expanded its trade relations with the rest of the world over the past decade. By these criteria, China is the biggest of the big emerging markets. Despite these facts, it was put it into the "communist" category because China's almost total lack of respect for workers' rights is much more similar to government policy in the other four communist countries than it is to the policies of the other countries in the "big emerging markets" category.

The poor treatment of workers in communist countries apparently has little to do with the level of economic globalization of those countries. Two of the countries that remained communist from 1981 to 1999, China and Vietnam, have vigorously pursued stronger and varied economic relationships with other countries around the world. The other three have not. Though it is difficult to generalize on the basis of so few cases, the China and Vietnam cases indicate that communism is a stronger predictor of government policy toward workers than is the degree of economic globalization.

Information about the level of respect that governments around the world provided for important workers' rights was taken from the U.S. State Department's annual *Country Reports on Human Rights Practices*. This report, published since 1974, includes analyses of workers' rights in each country's report. The workers' rights reported on are those that are defined in Section 502(a) of the Trade Act of 1974. These are freedom of association, the effective recognition of the right to collective bargaining, the elimination of all forms of forced or compulsory labor, the effective abolition of child labor, and acceptable conditions of work with respect to minimum wages, hours of work, and occupational safety and health. This list is much the same as the ILO's list of five core labor rights. However, the last element on the list, "acceptable conditions of work," is not among the core rights recognized by the ILO. In addition, one of the core rights recognized by the ILO, the elimination of discrimination in respect of employment or occupation, is not included in the U.S. State Department analysis.

The coding for each country-year is based on a three-point scale as follows:

Workers' rights are:

(0) Not protected by the government

(1) Somewhat protected by the government

(2) Protected by the government

(3) Not mentioned

Coders were instructed to code a particular country for a particular year as zero if that government did not allow workers to form trade unions or prohibited strikes. If a government allowed workers to form trade unions and to use strikes against employers, but the State Department Report mentioned other problems with government respect for workers' rights (the use of forced or compulsory labor, the abuse of child labor, or unacceptable conditions of work with respect to minimum wages, hours of work, and occupational safety and health), then the country was to be coded as a 1. If a government ensured that workers had the freedom to form unions and collectively bargain, and there was no mention of other problems with government practices toward workers, the country was to be coded as a 2.

Many governments prevent the police, military, emergency medical personnel, and firefighters from forming unions. If other workers can form unions and strike, and there are no other problems with government treatment of workers, then the country was coded as 2. If the police, military, emergency medical personnel, and firefighters were allowed to form unions but were not allowed to strike, this fact also was not be used as evidence of lack of respect for workers' rights. This is because international labor law recognizes the right of governments to prohibit strikes of employees whose work is essential to the public's safety.

The application of these rules is best illustrated using some examples. In 1981, the Congo received a score of zero largely based on the following language in the *Country Reports*: "The Congolese Confederation of Trade Unionists (CSC) represents workers but, as an appendage of the state, is restricted in its right to strike, bargain collectively, and lobby."[23]

Another example of a country that did not respect the rights of its workers in 1981 and therefore received a score of zero for that year was Angola. According to the *Country Reports*: "There is a government-sponsored trade movement, the National Union of Angolan Workers (UNTA). Traditionally labor union activities and rights are tightly restricted by government. Strikes are prohibited by law as a crime against the security of the state."[24]

The amount of information about workers' rights included in the *Country Reports* has grown dramatically over time. Until the mid-1980s, the rights of freedom of association, collective bargaining, and freedom of trade unions from government control or serious interference and the right to strike were discussed consistently. Other workers' rights were discussed less consistently. They were mentioned only when the U.S. State Department wished to emphasize workers' rights problems. Now there is a section discussing the situation in all six areas of workers' rights.

Some would argue that the *Country Reports* are a potentially biased source of information about workers' rights. According to this point of view, governments allied to the United States would be likely to receive better treatment in the reports than neutral countries or those allied with adversaries.[25] The reports prior to 1981 are not used in this analysis largely because of such criticisms. However, there is widespread agreement that the reports since that date are objective and accurate. Poe, Vazquez, and Carey[26] compared the *Country Reports* with the annual reports produced by Amnesty International and found few discrepancies in the evaluations of government human rights practices made by the two sources. As an illustration of the lack of bias in the *Country Reports*, Angola was communist in 1981. According to the "bias" argument, the negative evaluation of workers' rights in Angola that year may have been influenced by that fact. However, in 1992, Angola held democratic elections and has been relatively democratic since. Despite this fact, the U.S. State Department's review of the level of government respect for workers' rights in Angola continues to be very negative.

It is true, though, that almost all communist countries received the lowest possible score (0) for their protection of workers' rights. Yugoslavia was one of the few communist countries described by the *Country Reports* as having some government protections (1) of workers' rights. While there were and are trade unions in most communist countries, they were closely allied to the government. Workers are not allowed to form new trade unions, and the degree to which the unions are allowed to challenge state-run enterprises is very limited. On the basis of these constraints, the communist countries were almost always coded as having no workers' rights. Workers may have received many benefits from the state, consistent with Marxist ideology, but, if they did, it was not because of the independent exercise of their rights at the workplace or in the political system.

The *Country Reports* were used as the source of information about government protection of workers' rights because it is the only source that covers a long period of time, reports on almost all countries in the world, and reports on government practices protecting or violating a fairly wide range of workers' rights. The Amnesty International reports do not discuss workers' rights. The International Confederation of Free Trade Unions (ICFTU) has produced some reports on freedom of association at the workplace and the right to collective bargaining, but other rights are largely ignored. There are no reports available for many countries, the kind of information included for different countries is not consistent, and the ICFTU reports have been produced only since 1995.

The *Country Reports* were also the source of information used to code the level of democracy in each country. To what extent do citizens have freedom of political choice and have the legal right and ability in practice to change the laws and officials that govern them? This right is sometimes known as the right to self-determination, and "by virtue of this right [citizens] freely determine their own political status."[27]

Coders evaluated the situation in each country as follows:

Political participation is:

(0) Very limited

(1) Moderately free and open

(2) Very free and open

(9) Not mentioned

FINDINGS: ECONOMIC GLOBALIZATION

The evidence concerning changes in government respect for workers' rights due to economic globalization is presented in Table 10.1. It strongly supports the conventional economic theoretical perspective concerning globalization and

Table 10.1
The Relationship between Degree of Economic Globalization and Mean Levels of Government Respect for Workers' Rights from 1981 to 1999

Globalization	Year							
	1981	1984	1987	1990	1993	1996	1999	N
Fully Globalized throughout Period	2.0	2.0	2.0	2.0	2.0	2.0	2.0	21
Communist; Then Capitalist	.20	.20	.20	1.0	1.37	1.30	1.40	37
Emerging Markets	.79	.71	.93	1.14	1.07	1.07	1.33	15
Big Emerging Markets	.40	.60	.90	.70	.90	1.20	1.20	10
Not Globalized	.55	.53	.64	.67	.80	.85	1.06	85
Socialist throughout Period	0.0	0.0	0.0	0.0	0.0	0.0	0.0	5

Key: a score of 2 = Full Government Protection of Worker's Rights; a score of 1 = Some Government Protection of Workers' Rights; a score of 0 = No Government Protection of Workers' Rights.

workers' rights. The top row of Table 10.1 show that the twenty-one countries classified as having advanced industrial economies were coded at the highest level (2) throughout the period. There was no evidence of reduced protections of workers to compete with the levels of protections of workers in LDCs. The bottom row of Table 10.1 shows that the five countries that remained socialist were coded at 0 throughout the period. As of 1999, the country groups were ordered in terms of their protection of workers' rights fairly close to the way that conventional economic theory would lead us to expect. The advanced economies offered the greatest protections for workers. The "socialist, then capitalist" countries ranked second. The emerging and big emerging market countries ranked third and fourth, respectively. The countries "not globalized" ranked fifth, and the countries that were "socialist throughout the period" ranked last.

In all four country groupings where some change in the level of protection of workers' rights did occur, workers' rights became more protected between 1981 and 1999. For all four country groupings the amount of this change is statistically significant. There is no evidence of a decline in the level of protection of workers' rights around the world, let alone a race to the bottom. The rapid improvement of workers' rights in the former communist countries after the fall of communism is evidence of the strong negative effect of communism on government respect for workers' rights. The sharpest increase in government protection of workers' rights for the formerly communist countries occurred between 1987, when all of these countries were still socialist, and 1990, when almost all of them had adopted some form of capitalism. However, the advance in workers' rights continued after 1990. This group of countries was rated lowest of all the groups between 1981 and 1987 but was highest of all the groups between 1993 and 1999.

From a conventional economic theory perspective, there are only two surprises in Table 10.1. First, the emerging markets had a slightly higher level of protection of workers' rights than the big emerging markets. Conventional economics would lead us to expect that a greater participation in world economy would be associated with greater benefits for workers. There is some support for this view when one compares the amount of change in protections of workers' rights for these two groups of countries over time. Whether one compares the amount of change from 1981 or from 1990, the big emerging markets have made greater *advances* in protections of workers' rights.

Second, neither theory predicted any change for those countries that remained outside the global economy, but even those countries not yet involved very much in the global economy experienced significant improvements in respect for workers' rights. Between 1981 and 1999, the average level of respect improved from .55 (about halfway between "no respect" and "some respect") to 1.06 ("some respect"). This means that, by 1999, in the average less-developed country, the government protected the right of workers to form trade unions and to strike against their employers if they wished. However, some problem(s) still remained with the use of forced or compulsory labor, the abuse of child labor, or unacceptable conditions of work with respect to minimum wages, hours of work, or occupational safety and health.

There are two possible reasons for improvement in the treatment of workers in less-developed countries that remain outside the global economy. One possibility is that, since the ratification of the UN Universal Declaration of Human Rights in 1948, there has been an increased acceptance of global human rights norms by governments around the world. These norms include consensus concerning the appropriate protections of workers by governments. Governments, international governmental organizations such as the United Nations and the ILO, and nongovernmental organizations such as Human Rights Watch have all played a role in reinforcing these norms. The second possibility is that the improvement in treatment of workers is due to democratization in many less-developed countries. Evidence concerning this argument is presented below.

FINDINGS: DEMOCRACY AND DEMOCRATIZATION

As shown by the results presented in Table 10.2, in thirty-three (39 percent) of the eighty-five less-developed countries not yet integrated into the global economy, the level of democracy increased between 1981 and 1999. As shown

Table 10.2
The Relationship between Democratization and Mean Levels of Government Respect for Workers' Rights from 1981 to 1999 in Eighty-five Nonglobalized LDCs

Democratization	Year							
	1981	1984	1987	1990	1993	1996	1999	N
Democracy Is Strong throughout Period	1.5	1.67	1.5	1.33	1.5	1.33	1.5	6
Democracy Increased	.58	.50	.75	.88	.97	1.12	1.42	33
Some Democracy throughout Period	.58	.53	.68	.63	.84	.63	.94	18
Democracy Decreased	.50	.50	.50	.58	.58	.58	.46	13
Authoritarian throughout Period	.07	.13	.13	.07	.31	.56	.75	15

Key: a score of 2 = Full Government Protection of Worker's Rights; a score of 1 = Some Government Protection of Worker's Rights; a score of 0 = No Government Protection of Worker's Rights.

by the information in the first row of Table 10.2, workers' rights were protected the most in those six countries that were most democratic throughout the period covered in the analysis. By 1999, they were also protected strongly in those LDCs that had become more democratic since 1981. Protections for workers were the weakest where there was no democracy or where it had declined over the period. Thus, Table 10.2 provides strong support for both the idea that democracies tend to provide greater protections for workers and the idea that democratization does the same.

The evidence presented in the bottom row of Table 10.2 also suggests that one or more causal forces other than economic globalization and democratization are having an effect on the level of government protection of workers' rights around the world. This row shows that there has been significant improvement in government protection of workers' rights even in the fifteen countries that remained authoritarian throughout the period from 1981 to 1999. The level of protection increased from .07 (virtually none) in 1981 to .75 in 1999 (three-quarters of the way to "some protection").

DISCUSSION AND CONCLUSION

Some critics of economic globalization contend that globalization without regulations protecting workers' rights and the environment is hurting workers all over the world. The results of this research project do not support this critique. Instead, this research supports the idea that democracy and democratization have been good for workers' rights and that economic globalization has not been an obstacle to stronger government protection of workers where democratization has occurred. The more that a country participates in the international economy and the more democratic that it is, the better the level of government protection of workers' rights.

Moreover, governments of the most advanced economies had not reduced their high level of protection of workers' rights in the 1990–1999 period. The governments of the big emerging markets and the emerging markets were shown to have experienced increased respect for workers' rights during this same period, and the rate of improvement of workers' rights in these groups of countries was higher than the rate of improvement of workers' rights in the group of countries still not very involved in worldwide economic transactions—countries still on the periphery of the world economy. Moreover, the governments of the five countries that have remained communist throughout the 1981–1999 period have had and still have the worst record of government respect for workers' rights.

This evidence further suggests that democratization and economic globalization are causing a "leveling up" of workers' rights over time, such that the workers in the most advanced economies have not suffered, but the rights of workers in the LDCs are approaching those enjoyed by workers in the most advanced economies. The alternative specification predicting a convergence of the rights of workers worldwide, with workers in the most advanced economies losing some rights, while the workers in the LDCs gain some, is not supported by the evidence presented here.

There is no support for the "race-to-the-bottom" hypothesis suggesting that the more that a less-developed country participated in the international economy, the worse the level of government protection of workers' rights. The governments of the big emerging markets and the emerging markets were shown to have increased their protections of workers' rights even faster than the governments of LDCs that have been largely left out of the economic globalization process. This is the opposite of what one would expect based on Neo-Marxist theory.

Thus, these results provide no support for critics of economic globalization. They suggest that government protections for labor are improving worldwide even without the incorporation of labor standards in international trade agreements as advocated by most trade union activists. On the other hand, the results suggest that incorporation of such standards in trade agreements would not constitute an especially onerous burden on most LDCs, because, on average, rapid improvement in government protections of workers is occurring anyway.

These findings are clear but not the last word about the debate concerning the effects of globalization on workers' rights. Without a more sophisticated multivariate analysis, one cannot be sure about the relative importance of democratization and globalization in the process that is causing improved government protections of workers. In many countries, both processes are taking place more or less simultaneously. A multivariate analysis examining the effects of one of these phenomena while controlling for the effects of the other is a necessary follow-up to the findings presented here. Moreover, as Richards and Gelleny[28] suggest, more refined and differentiated measures of economic globalization should be employed to see if different types of global economic transactions produce different types of impacts on workers' rights. It is possible that the results of future research will show that most of the improvement in government practices protecting workers can be attributed mainly to democratization. Economic globalization may contribute relatively little, but it is unlikely that further research will show that having a globalized economy actually impedes improvements in government respect for the types of workers' rights considered here.

More important, future research should examine the impact of economic globalization on other outcomes that are as important, or even more important, to workers than those examined here. These outcomes include wages, benefits, production quotas, and changes in the use of contingent labor. Such analyses may uncover negative impacts of economic globalization that are not considered in the present analysis. Finally, it is important to keep in mind that the full effects of economic globalization may take some time to develop. The rapid gains made in the former communist countries may eventually erode. Workers in the advanced economies may yet experience pressures leading to a reduction in their workplace rights.

NOTES

1. International Labor Organization (ILO), *International Labor Standards* (Geneva: ILO, 1998).

2. Virginia A. Leary, "The Paradox of Workers' Rights as Human Rights," in *Human Rights, Labor Rights, and International Trade*, ed. Lance A. Compa and Stephen F. Diamond (Philadelphia: University of Pennsylvania Press, 1996).

3. Edward Weisband and Christopher J. Colvin, "An Empirical Analysis of International Confederation of Free Trade Unions (ICFTU) Annual Surveys," *Human Rights Quarterly* 22, no. 1 (2000): 167–186.

4. Leary, "The Paradox of Workers' Rights," 23.

5. David Held et al., *Global Transformations: Politics, Economics and Culture* (Stanford, CA: Stanford University Press, 1999), 2.

6. Sarah Anderson and John Cavanagh with Thea Lee, *Field Guide to the Global Economy* (New York: New Press, 2000), 9.

7. Phillipe C. Schmitter and Terry Lynn Karl, "What Democracy Is . . . and Is Not," in *The Global Resurgence of Democracy*, 2nd ed., ed. Larry Diamond and Marc F. Plattner (Baltimore: Johns Hopkins University Press, 1996), 40.

8. Chang-Ling Huang, "Learning the New Game: Labor Politics in the Newly Democratized South Korea and Taiwan," paper presented at the 2000 annual meeting of the American Political Science Association, Washington, DC.

9. Antoine Jacobs, "Collective Self-Regulation," in *Making of Labor Law in Europe: A Comparative Study of Nine Countries up to 1945*, ed. Bob Hepple (New York: Continuum International, 1986), 195.

10. Melvyn Dubofsky, *The State and Labor in Modern America* (Chapel Hill: University of North Carolina Press, 1994).

11. Roy J. Adams, "Regulating Unions and Collective Bargaining: A Global, Historical Analysis of Determinants and Consequences," *Comparative Labor Law Journal* 14 (1993): 272–301.

12. Held et al., *Global Transformations*.

13. Michael Parenti, *The Sword and the Dollar* (New York: St. Martin's Press, 1989).

14. David Carleton, "The New International Division of Labor, Export-Oriented Growth and State Repression in Latin America," in *Dependence, Development, and State Repression*, ed. George Lopez and Michael Stohl (Westport, CT: Greenwood, 1989), 211–236.

15. Jonathan W. Moses, "Love It or Leave It: Exit, Voice and Loyalty with Global Labor Mobility," paper presented at the 2000 annual meeting of the American Political Science Association, Washington, DC.

16. William H. Meyer, "Human Rights and MNCs: Theory versus Quantitative Analysis," *Human Rights Quarterly* 18, no. 2 (1996): 368–397.

17. Henry J. Frundt, *Refreshing Pauses* (New York: Praeger, 1987).

18. L. M. McLaren, "The Effect of IMF Austerity Programs on Human Rights Violations: An Exploratory Analysis of Peru, Argentina, and Brazil," paper presented at the 1998 annual meeting of the Midwest Political Science Association, Chicago.

19. See, for example, Lars Schoultz, "U.S. Foreign Policy and Human Rights," *Comparative Politics* 13 (1981): 149–170; Michael Stohl, David Carleton, and Steven E. Johnson, "Human Rights and U.S. Foreign Assistance: From Nixon to Carter," *Journal of Peace Research* 21 (1984): 215–226; David L. Cingranelli and Thomas Pasquerello, "Human Rights Practices and the U.S. Distribution of Foreign Aid to Latin American Countries," *American Journal of Political Science* 29 (1985): 539–563; Neil J. Mitchell and James M. McCormick, "Economic and Political Explanations of Human Rights Violations," *World Politics* 40 (1988): 476–498; Steven C. Poe, "Human Rights and the Allocation of U.S. Military Assistance," *Journal of Peace Research* 28 (1991): 205–216; Steven C. Poe, "Human Rights and Economic Aid under Ronald Reagan and Jimmy Carter," *American Journal of Political Science* 36 (1992): 147–167; Conway Henderson, "Conditions Affecting the Use of Political Repression," *Journal of Conflict Resolution* 35 (1991): 120–142; Conway Henderson, "Population Pressures and Political Repression," *Social Science Quarterly* 74 (1993): 322–333; Steven C. Poe and C. Neal Tate, "Repression of Rights to Personal Integrity in the 1980s: A Global Analysis," *American Political Science Review* 88 (1994): 853–872; Patrick M. Regan, "U.S. Economic Aid and Political Repression: An Empirical Evaluation of U.S. Foreign Policy," *Political Research Quarterly* 48, no. 3 (1995): 613–628; Mark Gibney and Matthew Dalton, "The Political Terror Scale," in *Human Rights and Developing Countries*, ed. David L. Cingranelli (Greenwich, CT: JAI Press, 1996); David L. Richards, "Perilous Proxy: Human Rights and the Presence of National Elections," *Social Science Quarterly* 80 (1999): 648–665; David L. Cingranelli and David L. Richards, "Measuring the Level, Pattern, and Sequence of Government Respect for Physical Integrity Rights," *International Studies Quarterly* 43 (1999): 407–417; David L. Cingranelli and David L. Richards, "Respect

for Human Rights after the End of the Cold War," *Journal of Peace Research* 36, no. 5 (1999): 511–534.

20. Steven C. Poe, C. Neal Tate, and Linda Camp Keith, "Repression of the Human Right to Personal Integrity Revisited: A Global Cross-National Study Covering the Years 1976–1993," *International Studies Quarterly* 43, no. 2 (1999): 297–313.

21. Conway Henderson, "Dependency and Political Repression: A Caveat on Research Expectations," in *Human Rights in Developing Countries*, ed. David Louis Cingranelli (Greenwich, CT: JAI Press, 1996), 101–114; William H. Meyer, *Human Rights and International Political Economy in Third World Nations* (Westport, CT: Praeger, 1998); Christian Davenport and Kathy Barbieri, "Pacific Inducement or Terroristic Impulse: Investigating the Relationship between Trade-Dependency and the Violation of Human Rights," paper presented at the 1997 annual meeting of the American Political Science Association, Washington, DC; Richard Burkhart, "The Capitalist Political Economy and Human Rights: Cross-National Evidence," paper presented at the "Hinman Symposium on Democratization and Human Rights," Binghamton University, State University of New York, 1998; McLaren, "The Effect of IMF Austerity Programs on Human Rights Violations"; David L. Richards, Ronald D. Gelleny, and David H. Sacko, "Money with a Mean Streak? Foreign Economic Penetration and Government Respect for Human Rights in Developing Countries," *International Studies Quarterly* 45, no. 2 (2001): 219–239; David L. Richards and Ronald D. Gelleny, "Is It a Small World After All? Economic Globalization and Human Rights in Developing Countries," in *Coping with Globalization*, ed. Steven Chan and James Scarritt (Essex: Frank Cass, 2002).

22. Cingranelli and Richards, "Respect for Human Rights," 511–534.

23. U.S. Department of State, *Country Reports on Human Rights Practices* (Washington, DC: Government Printing Office, February 1982).

24. Ibid.

25. Mitchell and McCormick, "Economic and Political Explanations," 476–498.

26. Steven C. Poe, Tanya Vazquez, and Sabine Carey, "How Are These Pictures Different? A Quantitative Comparison of the U.S. State Department and Amnesty International Human Rights Reports, 1976–1995," *Human Rights Quarterly* 23, no. 3 (2001): 650–677.

27. United Nations International Covenant on Economic, Social and Cultural Rights, Part I, Article 1.

28. Richards and Gelleny, "Is It a Small World After All?"

Chapter 11

Globalization and Democratic Performance in Low-Income Nations

Nicolas van de Walle

INTRODUCTION

In the last decade or so, a large and quite varied literature has documented the growing integration of national economies and has speculated about its impact.[1] Most striking has been the sharp growth in the volume of international capital movements and trade. Overall, total net capital inflows to the developing world in 1995 totaled $193.7 billion, according to the International Monetary Fund (IMF), up from $43.5 billion as recently as 1990 and including some $37 billion in portfolio investments.[2] In addition, the recent growth of international trade has been particularly rapid, increasing on average at one and a half times the rate of growth of world gross domestic product (GDP) between 1965 and 1990. The World Bank[3] predicts that world trade will continue to grow at this rapid rate, with a forecast of over 6 percent annual growth for the 1995–2005 period. It predicts especially fast growth in the developing countries, with East Asia leading the way with growth of over 10 percent a year.

In some respects, this period of economic globalization is not as new as some observers would argue. Critics of the globalization literature have pointed out that, in many respects, the nineteenth century of free trade achieved even higher levels of international integration.[4] Others have pointed out that the current trends in globalization have focused primarily on the developed countries and a handful of middle-income countries but have not included many low-income countries.[5] Thus, the extent or novelty of the current trends toward international economic integration should not be exaggerated. Nonetheless, there is no denying the trend, nor the important policy debates that it is engendering.

This chapter examines the impact of this surge of international economic integration on politics in the low-income economies and in particular its impact on the practice of democratic politics. Current globalization processes have unfolded at the same time that a wave of democratization hit the Third World. Today, several dozen fledgling democracies are trying to consolidate multiparty electoral politics. To what extent are these two processes compatible? Will democratic consolidation be undermined by economic globalization? Will globalization favor certain types of national institutions rather than others? The literature suggests several mechanisms by which globalization affects political stability and the long-term prospects for democracy, in particular, it is argued, to promote economic volatility, while undermining state sovereignty. The primary purpose of this chapter is to assess these claims.

The chapter is divided into four sections. The next section examines the claim of the critics of globalization that it threatens democratic politics by increasing economic volatility. Following is an examination of the parallel claim that globalization undermines the sovereignty of national governments and takes away the ability of elected governments to act upon the policy preference of their voters. Next is identification of three other sets of issues that are likely to prove more troublesome to the proper functioning of democratic institutions in low-income countries.

GLOBALIZATION AND ECONOMIC VOLATILITY

An important set of arguments about the negative political impact of globalization posits that international economic integration fuels instability because it speeds up the pace of economic change, placing extra stress on already vulnerable social systems. International economic integration, it is argued, is increasing the *volatility* of the international economy and the *speed* at which low-income national economies are forced to evolve. Given the pressure to maintain international competitiveness, governments have less time to adjust to changes in the international environment. They cannot deviate even briefly from an economic policy orthodoxy that is dictated by Western financiers, even when it implies austerity-inducing stabilization policies that are clearly against the expressed wishes of their electorate. Here, too, the changes are alleged to have a disturbing impact on public opinion. The need to maintain competitiveness increases the pace of change and disrupts people's lives; job tenures are less secure and many social benefits apparently threatened; even if incomes continue to rise and objective measures of welfare continue to improve, the pace of change leaves people with a deep sense of insecurity, which may lead to various political grievances and eventual instability.

This increased pace and uncertainty of economic activity are particularly dangerous for democratic polities, it is argued, because the increase in political participation and competition that is inherent to pluralist systems necessarily slows down decision making. Giving different segments of the population a voice takes time. Democracy requires more persuasion and fewer faits accomplis. Horizontal accountability in government is similarly time-consuming, as the executive branch no longer dictates policy but is now accountable to legislative oversight and judicial review.

There can be little doubt that the highly volatile nature of international finance complicates economic management, particularly in the smaller, more vulnerable countries of the developing world. In the *short run*, markets are volatile; they overreact to certain signals, can be slow to respond to imbalances, and then overshoot equilibrium prices when they do respond. Even virtuous governments can find themselves destabilized by international speculation, as happened in a number of middle-income countries in the wake of the East Asian crisis in 1997 and 1998. At the time, speculative attacks on national currencies appeared to occur regardless of the prevailing macroeconomic fundamentals. Countries found themselves under threat, even if they appeared to be following completely orthodox monetary and fiscal policies. In the *medium to long run*, however, steady and sustainable macroeconomic management is consistently rewarded by financial markets, as indeed was demonstrated by many of these same economies. By 1999, South Korea had returned to close to double-digit growth. Indeed, in countries with much weaker policy environments—for example, like Indonesia or Russia—the effect of the 1997 crisis seemed to have more lasting negative consequences.[6]

Much of the literature on the breakup of the Soviet Union or on the conflict in the Balkans during the 1990s argued that the policy reforms that these countries undertook to rejoin the world market economy had socioeconomic effects that led directly to political instability. A typical example of this line of argument is offered by Woodward in *Balkan Tragedy*,[7] who argues that policies of economic liberalization in Yugoslavia led to economic austerity, unemployment, and growing income inequalities, all of which "led to conditions that could not easily foster a political culture of tolerance and compromise. Instead, the social bases for stable government and democratization were being radically narrowed."[8] For observers like Wooodward, in other words, the transition from socialism in these countries has fueled instability by dramatically undermining social structures and changing popular attitudes. Other scholars have linked the rise of conflict in the Third World to World Bank- and IMF-led programs of economic liberalization and privatization.[9] For instance, a number of observers have argued that the rise of ethnic conflict in Rwanda and Burundi in the 1990s was directly related to their economic crises and donor-led reform attempts.[10]

Several points can be made about such arguments: First, there can be little doubt that economic policy reform is politically difficult. As Woodward argues, economic reform "fundamentally alters the existing distribution of rights and power."[11] In many cases, reform entails austerity and sharp cuts in consumption levels. Insofar as policy reform creates winners and losers, governments must find ways to weaken or isolate certain classes of often well organized and powerful interests linked to the old policy regime while also shaping a coalition on behalf of the interests that will benefit from the new policies. This is particularly difficult to achieve when reform is dominated by an agenda of economic liberalization, privatization, and deregulation, as recent policy reforms have been. These reforms take away government's discretion to accommodate winners and losers with skillful dispensing of state resources in the form of patronage or subsidies, particularly when they take place in a climate of economic austerity and resource scarcity. Moreover, significant policy reform rarely yields quick results. Even in middle-income countries with established business communities and substantial infrastructure, governments may have to sustain politically thankless austerity policies for several years before investors respond to the new policies and growth resumes. In low-income countries, where fewer of the prerequisites for rapid growth are present, this wait may stretch out even longer, as is suggested by the recent experience in Africa.[12]

Is rapid policy reform harder for democracies? Insofar as political participation slows down decision making, one might think that democratic governments would be less nimble on their feet. In fact, empirical studies do not suggest a democratic disadvantage.[13] This may be because democratic executives are less likely to pursue incautious economic policies, in part because they are more accountable to other branches of government, the media, and the citizenry. The evidence thus suggests that democracies run lower budget deficits than do authoritarian governments. It may be because, as a practical matter, many of the key economic decision-making institutions are not all that participatory in nature. The Central Banks in the Organization for Economic Cooperation and Development (OECD) countries respond quickly to exogenous shocks because they do not have their decisions vetted by the public. Most democracies accept the necessity of nondemocratic "agencies of restraint" in the economic realm as advantageous in the long run. In fact, it is more likely that an authoritarian government chooses to interfere in the setting of interest rates for short-term political gain, precisely because it faces fewer constraints on its ability to do so.

Second, it is important to make a distinction between marketization and globalization. Transitions from socialism are first and foremost processes of marketization, which can be defined as the process by which domestic public institutions and state intervention are replaced with market-based allocation mechanisms. Insofar as marketization does take place and is linked to a need to enhance international competitiveness, it is accompanied by international economic integration and is thus relevant to our discussion. But, marketization of the local economy does not necessarily result in greater integration, and vice versa. Oil exporters may be quite highly integrated in the world economy, for example, but highly "statist" in their internal policy regimes, while a big, low-income country like India has advanced far in the marketization of its economy in the last decade, while remaining relatively isolated from the world economy.[14] In short, marketization and globalization do not necessarily coincide.

Although the ultimate objective of the policy reforms undertaken in Yugoslavia in the early 1990s may have been to increase the country's international competitiveness, the reforms were still in their infancy and had not yet had much impact on the country's relationship with the world economy. Moreover, it is clearly the *process of change*, undertaken in a hurried and chaotic manner, that is destabilizing, rather than the liberal economy that was to emerge at the end of the process of reform. There certainly is no empirical evidence to suggest that political stability is positively correlated with the degree of state regulation of the economy. In other words, it is the reform period of marketization that is argued to be destabilizing, rather than the open policy regime to emerge at the end of the reform process.

Third, these arguments about the destabilizing effect of policy reform are not always based on a convincing *counterfactual* argument. Countries like Yugoslavia or Rwanda typically undertake economic reform to overcome substantial fiscal and monetary crises. The maintenance of the status quo was simply not an option, as economic policies had brought about some combination of international debt, balance of payments crises, fiscal deficits, and hyperinflation. Whatever its merits, leaders undertake policy reform often only after a dreadful crisis has convinced them that a leap into the unknown cannot be any less favorable to their interests than the status quo.[15] Moving from a set of closed economic policies to a policy regime that actively seeks integration with the world economy typically represents a calculated gamble that the local economy will benefit enough from the capital and technology available on world markets to overcome whatever increase in volatility is occasioned by closer integration. That gamble may not be attractive to the leaders of the handful of remaining closed economies that, like North Korea, have managed to avoid fiscal or balance of payments crises. But the previously closed economies that underwent economic liberalization in the 1990s are invariably countries whose previous policies had brought them to the brink of disaster and could no longer be sustained. For the leaders of essentially bankrupt and illegitimate regimes of countries like Yugoslavia in the early 1990s, reaching out to the West was viewed as the least dangerous option.

Fourth, to be convincing, the attempt to link globalization and domestic politics must ultimately specify the precise mechanisms by which economic factors come to impact political systems. By themselves, economic forces probably have an indeterminate impact on politics. At best, they provide the context or background in which social and political institutions interact with individual agents in the political arena. Even if it could be demonstrated that integration into the world economy had doubled the probability of political violence in a well-defined sample of countries, to understand how and when violence had actually broken out or why violence had not broken out in the other half of the sample, it would remain necessary to examine the country's political culture and its institutions of political accommodation and conflict mediation, as well as the actions of its politicians. For this reason arguments about the impact of globalization are most convincing when they examine its impact on domestic political institutions.

GLOBALIZATION AND STATE SOVEREIGNTY

For many observers, economic globalization's strongest political impact lies in the way in which it undermines national sovereignty and weakens states by lessening the degree of policy discretion available to governments that want to maintain sustainable policies. Even as globalization exacerbates inequality and economic volatility, its critics assert, it undermines the ability of governments to adequately address these problems, which only adds to the possibility of instability.[16] There are thus two claims worth assessing: that globalization strips states in the developing world of decision-making power in the economic realm and that this leads to political instability. Let us examine each in turn.

What does it mean to say that economic globalization undermines sovereignty? In the overblown language of the business guru, Ohmae exclaims that as a result of "fundamental changes" in the world economy, "nation states have *already* lost their role as meaningful units of participation in the global economy of today's borderless world."[17] For Ohmae, the critical variable is the modern international conglomerate and its increasingly global strategies and production processes. The largest firms, with billions of dollars worth of assets and operations all over the globe, obviously can rival the power of the weaker states in the international community and have considerable discretionary power even vis-à-vis the most powerful states.

Most observers suggest nonetheless that the international mobility of capital is more significant than the emergence of multinational conglomerates in the weakening of state sovereignty. Capital mobility weakens the ability of government to pursue independent monetary and fiscal policy. In particular, in a world of fully mobile capital, national policy loses control of either the exchange rate or the national interest rate. Governments can no longer set both. In a flexible exchange rate system, any policy that has a negative effect on the real, risk-adjusted return to holders of financial assets results in an outflow of capital to other markets holding the promise of higher returns and eventually results in currency depreciation. In sum, changes in monetary policy affect only the value of the national currency.

Governments that try to implement alternative economic policies at odds with those of the most powerful economies in the West see themselves eventually punished by the market. An example often given of this phenomenon is the dramatic failure of France's go-it-alone reflation of the early 1980s under the first socialist government led by François Mitterrand. Although growth was briefly spurred, these policies resulted in a dramatic capital outflow that required three devaluations between 1981 and 1983 and eventually convinced the socialists to adopt the policy of the "Franc Fort" and convergence on the much more conservative policies set by the German Bundesbank.[18] The power of international capital markets vis-à-vis sovereign governments is not new but has grown exponentially in recent years; as *The Economist*[19] has pointed out, the Wilson government in Great Britain was able to stave off devaluation of sterling for three years in the 1960s with the judicious intervention by the Bank of England, whereas in 1992, financial speculators forced sterling's delinkage from the European monetary system despite the Major government's expressed intentions in a matter of days. With much less active financial markets in the past, governments could sustain situations of macroeconomic disequilibria for much longer periods than they can today.

Powerful OECD economies like France and Great Britain, nonetheless, retain more leverage than the smaller economies of the developing world. For many observers, the Mexican bond crisis of 1994 and the speed with which it spread to other Latin American countries provided a good example of the capricious power of international finance vis-à-vis developing country governments; overnight, not only did financial speculation punish Mexico for its large current account deficit, but it also hit other Latin American economies with much better macroeconomic fundamentals. As Thomas Friedman has put, "[Y]ou could almost say that we live again in a two-superpower world. There is the U.S. and there is Moody's. The U.S. can destroy a country by leveling it with bombs; Moody's can destroy a country by downgrading its bonds."[20] For many observers, the international bond market is proving a lot more arbitrary and unpredictable than American foreign policy.

Third World governments, it has been concluded, are powerless to fight the diktat of international finance, or, as Mkandawire puts it, developing countries have been left "choiceless" by international economic forces.[21] At the present time, this remains an exaggeration. To understand exactly how globalization circumscribes policy choices, it is useful to distinguish the short and long run. In the long run, I would argue that globalization is serving to lessen the number of *good choices*. Developing countries can still choose to adopt policies of economic isolation and autarchy—witness countries like Libya, North Korea, or Cuba. Such policies have always led to slower growth and endemic balance of payments crises; today, in addition, the growing availability of international capital dramatically increases the opportunity cost of not engaging the world economy. Closed economies forgo not only access to international capital but also the access to technology transfers, commercial expertise, and skilled labor that comes with it.[22]

That does not mean that all countries are forced into a single, "neoliberal" policy mold, as is sometimes argued. The sharp differences that remain among the highly integrated economies of the OECD suggest that governments retain important degrees of policy initiative and discretion, at least at present levels of global integration.[23] After all, Scandinavian and Northern European social democracy, with its higher levels of taxation, public expenditures, and various corporatist arrangements between the state, business, and labor, appears to be as sustainable as the more laissez-faire regime in the United States.[24] Even within the European Union, where policy convergence has been actively promoted for several decades, there remain sharp differences in the position of the state, with the proportion of central government expenditures in total GDP varying between some 30 and 50 percent.[25]

Attracting and retaining capital in the globalized economy thus appear to be compatible with several distinct political economies. Maintaining long-term competitiveness does seem to require focusing government efforts on various types of physical and human capital investments. Countries with public policies that improve education and infrastructure, facilitate labor flexibility, and support growth industries are rewarded with sustainable economic growth. Far from a race to the bottom, competition entails a no less difficult race to provide an array of public goods that promote economic adaptation and innovation. The great difficulty for the states of the future concerns how to limit taxation so as to not antagonize capital holders, while at the same time providing the expensive public goods that ensure long-term competitiveness.

In the short run, on the other hand, states that choose to engage the world economy for the promise of access to much greater capital pay the price of having to accept greater volatility and less policy discretion. Having come to rely on international capital to finance their economic growth, governments must accommodate it with more conservative management of the macroeconomy. To attract and maintain investment, they must keep taxes on business low. Economic management appears to be a thankless task, in which governments can never rest on their laurels and must ever maintain discipline. Comparing North Korea and South Korea is instructive in this respect. With periodic labor and student unrest, in addition to a sharp macroeconomic shock in 1997, South Korea appears paradoxically less stable. Despite an average annual GDP growth rate of 7.7 percent during the 1990s, there is today much talk of the end of the "Korean miracle" as the record of rapid growth is threatened by rising wages and competition from poorer economies in Southeast Asia, and the economy is struggling to move into new product cycles.[26] At least from a distance, on the other hand, North Korea appears to be a haven of stability. Having never attracted any foreign investors, the government need not worry about disappointing them, and decision makers do not lose sleep over the reaction of Wall Street to their every policy pronouncement. In the short run, the North Korean government probably has more latitude in its fiscal and monetary policies than its southern counterpart, at least in the sense that no policy initiative that it takes could result in an instantaneous run on its currency. Of course, after half a century of closed economy policies, North Korea finds itself with a per capita GDP that is but a fraction of South Korea's.

What about the second claim that globalization complicates the state's ability to manage conflict and change? Even if it is true that globalization weakens central states, this does not necessarily imply that it brings about political instability, as some claim. As Bardhan puts it, the "global integration of commodity and capital markets severely reduces the policy options of the nation-state, disrupts the process of building the institutions that govern the incipient national economy and weakens the state's capacity to mediate in ethnic disputes."[27] The argument is probably founded in the short run. The state's political management is particularly weakened if and when economic globalization is accompanied by marketization. In other words, the emphasis on liberalization, privatization, and deregulation strips governments of traditional political instruments such as patronage or the selective distribution of monopoly rents, licenses, import duty exemptions, and subsidies. Without these resources, it is harder for governments to "grease the squeaky wheel" or co-opt opposition and consolidate support with state favors. To retain this discretion while at the same time gaining the growth advantages of globalization, developing country governments seek to maximize integration into the world economy while minimizing marketization. While they recognize and worry about the power of multinational corporations, they are likely to promote foreign direct investment much more assiduously than trade liberalization or privatization. They are most ambivalent about the policy areas for which globalization and marketization overlap, for example, the liberalization of foreign exchange markets, where they face a direct trade-off between economic benefit and loss of sovereignty.

A major caveat, however, is the practical reality that for the foreseeable future, governments will retain considerable policy discretion. The state apparatus in developing countries is typically smaller, in relative terms, than the state in OECD countries. Despite the rhetoric of the World Bank and the IMF, low-income state expenditures rarely represent the equivalent of more than a quarter of GDP, whereas states in the OECD countries routinely spend the equivalent of half of GDP. It is thus hard to argue that low-income states are prohibitively too big in the new era of globalization. Instead, insofar as there is a need for state reform, it must concern *the quality of state expenditures and the nature of the institutions that link state and citizen.* Most states in the developing world can probably even increase their economic role, which is today at quite a low relative level, if they find ways to improve the state's effectiveness and the efficiency of public expenditures. Thus, for example, it is wrong to suggest that globalization undermines the viability of public social expenditures in the low- and middle-income countries, even if it is true that it puts pressures on governments to improve policy design and implementation, to get "more bang for the buck," as it were.

It is useful here to distinguish small and large low-income countries. Large economies have a much larger margin of error. Their economies are less likely to be particularly globalized. In other words, a smaller share of their national production is likely to be exported, and their capital markets are more likely to be developed and be able to finance a significant share of domestic investment. In countries like India or Brazil, many efficiency gains can be achieved through further marketization. Globalization pressures are likely to be relatively minor, as foreign investors are less likely to demand greater economic integration into the world economy and more likely to support import substitution economic strategies. Large countries have other problems, of course, which complicate decision making.[28] Regional disparities may weigh on democratic governance while national unity is more likely to be an issue. Federal institutions create another level of government and have complex implications for regulation. Nonetheless, the larger the country, the more that it engages the world economy on its own terms.

In small countries, on the other hand, resisting integration into the world economy is not really an option for governments that wish to promote economic growth and the welfare of their population. The smaller the economy, the less that it can sustain manufacturing industries that are not internationally competitive and the less it is likely to have adequate domestic financial markets to finance industrialization. On the other hand, the lesson from Western Europe is that these small economies may actually have an advantage in dealing with the world economy.[29] Katzenstein shows that the relatively small economies of Western Europe were able to build corporatist political arrangements that allowed these countries to adjust effectively to external shocks to the economy. These countries combine an expansive and redistributive role for the government with international capital mobility and an open trade regime. This success depends on stable and broad social alliances in the political system between different economic interests. These are almost certainly easier to forge in a small political system, which is more likely to be homogeneous and in which there is more chance of personal contact and less delegation. The evidence also suggests that small countries are more likely to be democratic, and Larry Diamond[30] and others have noted the preponderance of small countries among the democracies of the Third Wave. The model small democracy that engages the world economy may well be Mauritius. Bräutigam[31] shows that the country's success may well be the result of the same institutional features found in the small social democracies in Western Europe. Economic policy flexibility is part of a political deal that has cemented a broad political alliance in support of a relatively progressive state committed to social welfare.

NEW PRESSURES, NEW RESOURCES

This chapter has so far argued that policy discretion is lessened by integration into the world economy and that this serves to undermine the participatory dimension of democratic politics, albeit in a much less dramatic manner than is usually argued. Moreover, I have shown that in a number of respects, democratic politics may provide certain advantages to deal with economic globalization. I would, however, like to add two sets of factors that result from globalization and introduce somewhat different dynamics not yet featured adequately in debates about globalization.

First, it should be pointed out that, in at least one respect, states are strengthened by their international links; states can borrow capital on international markets. The dramatic rise in the international indebtedness of governments all over the world suggests that the international arena actually offers a way for governments to expand their budget constraint. Developing country debt rose from around $55 billion in 1970 to $916 billion in 1985 and a little over $2 trillion in 1997. During this period the growth of international capital markets allowed governments to sustain bigger budget and current account deficits than they otherwise would have been able to. In the long run, the market disciplines highly indebted governments, but in the short run, it allows them an extra margin, which can be used for the purpose of political management. Thus, complaints during the Mexican collapse of 1994 that international financial markets could have dramatic consequences for political stability were losing sight of the fact that those same markets had allowed the government to run huge current account deficits during the run-up to the presidential elections, securing the victory of the Partido Revolucionario Institucional (PRI).

It has long been an adage of international politics that governments derive certain advantages by standing between national politics and the international community. It would be wrong to think that globalization undermines those advantages. This points to the irony that most observers suggest that globalization will undermine democracy by weakening the state, yet in this case, globalization serves to provide additional resources to incumbents and protects them from domestic accountability. In this sense, at least, international capital mobility does not promote democracy.

Second, the impact of globalization on the democratic consolidation of Third World political systems is likely to be in large part determined by the quality of international and regional institutions that exist to regulate the international economy. Regional institutions can play a significant role in mediating relations between individual economies and the world economy. For example, a customs union among small economies will make each of its members more attractive to international investors while simultaneously strengthening the hand of member governments. Indeed, some observers have argued that the present evolution of the world economy is not toward globalization but rather toward economic regionalization as a small number of massive regional trade blocs compete with each other. The weakness of the world's low-income countries in Asia or Africa is that they do not belong to the core group of any of these blocs. A solution is clearly greater regional economic integration.

Globalization increases the demand for new and stronger mechanisms of international governance. In the West, the agenda concerns the "deepening" of integration with the harmonization of domestic regulation and mechanisms for policy conflict resolution. The more that two economies are integrated, the more that populations in one country will demand the right to have a voice in the decisions made in the other economy that concern them. The more that two economies are integrated, the more that positive and negative externalities legitimate this demand. This will play itself out in international forums. It is not at all clear how much domestic sovereignty populations and their governments will be willing to give up in the name of integration. Recent events in Western Europe show how strong the pull of national sovereignty remains. Nonetheless, it is clear that globalization will increase the demand for shared sovereignty. In the poor and relatively weak countries of the Third World, this is bound to conflict directly with principles of democratic sovereignty, and many of these countries will lack the resources to resist international pressures. International organizations have increased the scope of their conditionality toward low-income countries in an evolution that is bound to continue. Narrow macroeconomic conditionality is now supplanted by political conditionality, as well as conditionality over everything from the environment to gender and foreign policy issues. Whatever justification one finds for such conditionality, it clearly has the potential to undermine the results of democratic elections. Indebted governments that live off international assistance will find it exceedingly difficult to disregard international conditionality, even when it contradicts the explicit electoral intentions of their citizens.

Even more important than the role of international organizations is the potential role of international civil society in this respect in the coming years. Economic globalization has brought in its wake an explosion in international civil society. The last couple years has witnessed the ability of nonstate actors to flex their muscles, whether at the World Trade Organization (WTO) meetings in Seattle or in protests at other meetings of international organizations. The more that economies are integrated, the more that these groups can affect both political and economic governance within individual countries. In some cases, these groups will strengthen democratically elected governments in the Third World. But it is naive to think that this will always be the case. During the WTO negotiations in Seattle, for example, at least some democratically elected Third World governments were openly resentful that their agenda at the negotiating table was usurped by the chorus of Western NGOs protesting around the meeting.

CONCLUSION

Over thirty years ago, Huntington[32] argued that the capacity of political institutions to manage rapid change was the central conundrum of politics in the developing world. The preceding discussion suggests that economic globalization both accelerates the pace of change faced by developing country governments and weakens their discretionary power to manage change. This only confirms a key theme of this chapter, that far from making states irrelevant, ironically, the continued growth of economic globalization will place an ever greater premium on state capacity and legitimacy to ensure stability and economic prosperity. It will become increasingly easy to distinguish states according to whether or not they possess these qualities in adequate supply.

A small number of governments in the developing world that are disciplined and benefit from capable state institutions will continue to be integrated into the global economy without too much difficulty. They will weather the episodes of short-run volatility from international financial markets and will enjoy faster growth, thanks to access to foreign capital and technology. At the other extreme are the smallest low-income countries, primarily based in sub-Saharan Africa, which have so far failed to take advantage of global integration and which are facing a progressive delinkage from the world economy. Deficiencies in the quality of their labor force, infrastructure, and governance will continue to militate against their integration. Economic globalization holds relatively few dangers for them because they have never interested private global finance. The public policy challenge for these countries and their donors will be to find ways to relink them with the world economy. The danger is that they will be attempting this transition at a time when "aid fatigue" is overtaking the traditional donor countries.

In between these two extremes are most states in the developing world. Globalization holds opportunities and risks for them. The promise of faster growth and employment for their rapidly increasing labor force will be counterbalanced by the danger that they will not be able to maintain macroeconomic discipline in the short term and provide the necessary public goods in the long run. As the pace of change increases, the managerial and political capacity of these states will sorely be tested. They need to increase the effectiveness of their policies. Will their governments avoid the sirens of debt to manage the more volatile business cycle? Will they find the discipline to invest in a more productive labor force, with investments in education and health that hold no immediate tangible return? Will their citizens be tempted by populist and ethnic entrepreneurs who offer temptingly easy solutions to their difficulties? The answers that countries find to these questions will in no small part determine the extent to which the twenty-first century is peaceful and prosperous.

NOTES

1. David Held et al., *Global Transformations: Politics, Economics and Culture* (Stanford, CA: Stanford University Press, 1999); Peter Dicken, *Global Shift: Transforming the World Economy*, 3rd ed. (New York: Guilford Press, 1998); Barbara Stallings, ed., *Global Change, Regional Response: The New International Context of Development* (New York: Cambridge University Press, 1995); Anthony G. McGrew and Paul Lewis, eds., *Global Politics: Globalization and the Nation-State* (Oxford: Polity Press, 1992); Vivien A. Schmidt, "The New World Order, Incorporated: The Rise of Business and the Decline of the Nation-State," *Daedalus* 124, no. 2 (Spring 1995): 75–106; Charles Oman, *Globalisation and Regionalism: The Challenge for Developing Countries* (Paris: OECD, 1994); Kenichi Ohmae, *The End of the Nation State* (New York: Free Press, 1995); World Bank, *Global Economic Prospects and the Developing Countries, 1996* (Washington, DC: World Bank, 1996).

2. International Monetary Fund (IMF), *International Capital Markets: Developments, Prospects and Key Policy Issues. World Economic and Financial Surveys* (Washington, DC: IMF, 1996).

3. World Bank, *Global Economic Prospects*.

4. Angus Maddison, *The World Economy in the 20th Century* (Paris: OECD Development Center, 1989); The Economist, "The World Economy: The Hitchhiker's Guide to Cybernomics," *The Economist*, 28 September 1996.

5. Robert Wade, "Globalization and Its Limits: Reports of the Death of the National Economy Are Greatly Exaggerated," in *National Diversity and Global Capitalism*, ed. Suzanne Berger and Ronald Dore (Ithaca, NY: Cornell University Press, 1996), 60–88.

6. Stephan Haggard, "The Political Economy of the East Asian Financial Crisis." Manuscript, 1 March 2000.

7. Susan Woodward, *Balkan Tragedy: Chaos and Dissolution after the Cold War* (Washington, DC: Brookings Institution, 1995).

8. Ibid., 383.

9. For example, John Walton and David Seddon, *Free Markets and Food Riots: The Politics of Global Adjustment* (Oxford: Blackwell, 1994).

10. Catherine Newbury. "Rwanda: Recent Debates over Governance and Rural Development," in *Governance and Politics in Africa*, ed. Goran Hyden and Michael Bratton (Boulder, CO: Lynne Rienner, 1992); Timothy Longman, "State, Civil Society and Genocide in Rwanda," in *State, Conflict and Democracy in Africa*, ed. Richard Joseph (Boulder, CO: Lynne Rienner, 1998), 359–376.

11. Woodward, *Balkan Tragedy*, 384; also see Dani Rodrik, "Understanding Economic Policy Reform," *Journal of Economic Literature* 34 (March 1996): 9–41.

12. Janine Aron, "The Institutional Foundations of Growth," in *Africa Now: People, Policies and Institutions*, ed. Stephen Ellis (London: James Currey, 1995), 93–118; Nicolas Van de Walle, *African Economies and the Politics of Permanent Crisis* (New York: Cambridge University Press, 2001).

13. For example, Adam Przeworski et al., *Democracy and Development* (New York: Cambridge University Press, 1998).

14. Rob Jenkins, *Democratic Politics and Economic Reform in India* (New York: Cambridge University Press, 1999).

15. Joan Nelson, "The Political Economy of Stabilization: Commitment, Capacity, and Public Response," *World Development* 12, no. 10 (1984): 983–1006; Rodrik, "Understanding Economic Policy Reform," 9–41.

16. Jeffrey Frieden, "Invested Interests: The Politics of National Economic Policies in a World of Global Finance," *International Organizations* 45 (1991): 425–451; Benjamin Cohen, "Phoenix Risen: The Resurrection of Global Finance," *World Politics* 48, no. 2 (January 1996); Stephan Haggard and Sylvia Maxfield, "The Political Economy of Financial Internationalization in the Developing World," *International Organization* 50, no. 1 (1996): 35–68; Don D. Marshall, "Understanding Late-Twentieth Century Capitalism: Reassessing the Globalization Theme," *Government and Opposition* 31, no. 2 (1996): 193–215; Susan Strange, "The Defective State," *Daedalus* 124, no. 2 (Spring 1995): 55–74.

17. Ohmae, *The End of the Nation State*, 11.

18. Peter A. Hall, *Governing the Economy: The Politics of State Intervention in Britain and France* (New York: Oxford University Press, 1986).

19. The Economist, "The World Economy."

20. Cohen, "Phoenix Risen," 282.

21. Thandike Mkandawire, "Economic Policy-Making and the Consolidation of Democratic Institutions in Africa," in *Domination or Dialogue? Experiences and Prospects for African Development Cooperation*, ed. Kjell Havnevik and Brian Van Arkadie (Uppsala, Sweden: Nordic Institute for African Studies, 1966), 24–47; see also Claude Ake, "Globalization, Multilateralism and the Shrinking Democratic Space," unpublished manuscript, James Madison College, Michigan State University, 1996.

22. Rodrik, "Understanding Economic Policy Reform."

23. Geoffrey Garrett, *Partisan Politics in the Global Economy* (New York: Cambridge University Press, 1998); Linda Weiss, *The Myth of the Powerless State* (Ithaca, NY: Cornell University Press, 1998).

24. Stallings, *Global Change*; Berger and Dore, eds., *National Diversity and Global Capitalism.*

25. Vito Tanzi and Ludger Schuknecht, *The Growth of Government and the Reform of the State in Industrial Countries, IMF Working Paper* (Washington, DC: International Monetary Fund, December 1995).

26. Haggard, "The Political Economy of the East Asian Financial Crisis."

27. Pranab Bardhan, "Method in the Madness? A Political-Economy Analysis of Ethnic Conflicts in Less Developed Countries," *World Development* 25, no. 9 (September 1997): 1381–1398.

28. Larry Diamond, *Developing Democracy: Towards Consolidation* (Baltimore: Johns Hopkins University Press, 1999), 117–160; John P. Lewis, "Some Consequences of Giantism: The Case of India," *World Politics* 34, no. 3 (April 1991): 367–399.

29. Peter Katzenstein, *Small States in World Markets: Industrial Policy in Western Europe* (Ithaca, NY: Cornell University Press, 1985).

30. Diamond, *Developing Democracy.*

31. Deborah Bräutigam, "Institutions, Economic Reform, and Democratic Consolidation in Mauritius," *Comparative Politics* 30, no. 1 (October 1997): 45–62.

32. Samuel P. Huntington, *Political Order in Changing Societies* (New Haven, CT: Yale University Press, 1968).

Chapter 12

Research and Practice in Democratization: Cross-Fertilization or Cross-Purposes?

Harry Blair

The importance of combining theory and practice has been a prominent item on civilization's agenda at least since Aristotle's insistence in the fourth century B.C. that thought in action constituted humanity's highest form of activity. Despite continuous exhortations, however, the two have always had a hard time getting together. The challenge remains with us in the twenty-first century A.D., not least in the area of democratization, where academic understanding and practitioner realities tend to slip past one another rather than informing each other. This chapter takes up this old separation, focusing on avenues along which theory and research can inform practice in the U.S. Agency for International Development's (USAID's) Democracy and Governance (DG) sector. The first topic is to delineate the kinds of questions and issues that characterize academic inquiry into democratization, then those that practitioners ask. Next comes a look at the scale of the research problem and how it has grown in the last decade or so. The third theme analyzes the key research issues in the assessment area that have occupied practitioners over that time and how they have changed, arguably in a positive direction. Concluding observations attempt to tie this practical research agenda back to academic democratic theory.[1]

THE QUESTIONS WE ASK

Democratization may be most simply defined as a process whereby a polity becomes more democratic. What we think is important about that process not surprisingly stems from what aspects of it we are engaged in. If academics study democratization while practitioners "do" it, the questions that the two communities find critical are necessarily going to differ. Academic inquiry centers primarily on the *context* and *consequences* of democratization. The questions tend to look like this:

• What good is democracy? What does it do relative to other political arrangements?
• What makes democracy come about? How does it emerge? What are the conditions under which it flourishes or fails?
• Should donors promote democracy? Why?
• If donors do support democratization, what are the consequences for the countries assisted?

Practitioners generally assume that supporting democratization is an appropriate task and then ask a rather different set of questions, concentrating on what might be called *text* rather than context and *results* rather than consequences. Their questions go like this:

• When and where should democratization be supported?
• How should it be promoted programmatically?
• How can one tell when democratization assistance has accomplished something significant?

A second-order difference concerns not so much the questions themselves but *how* they are asked. The academic thinks of others as doing the work of democratization, while the practitioner thinks of himself or herself and his or her organization as doing the work. The operative pronoun for the former is *they*; for the latter, *we*. The implications of this distinction are significant. Academics can attain a broad perspective in their analyses but lack a feel for what it's like to actually be promoting democracy, while for practitioners, the reverse tends to be the case.

There is also a third-order difference between the two approaches, stemming from the first- and second-order contrasts. The academic approach tends inherently to be more critical, focusing on why ideas fail, how plans misfire, and what causes bad things to happen. The urge to uncover and explain, to show how things are not what they seem, is also the urge to find that they are not as good as might have initially appeared. Indeed, an academic career often hinges on one's skills as a social critic. The distancing of analyst from activity being analyzed—symbolized by the use of the third-person *they*—reinforces these tendencies. Practitioners, on the other hand, tend to resemble salesmen in their desire (and career need) to show how a program will work or has worked. In a world of increasingly intense competition for steadily diminishing donor funding, the practitioner finds it necessary to oversell a program to gain funding for it, reinforcing the urge to be positive. If it is true that a good salesman believes in the product being pushed, it is most fitting that the preferred pronoun is the first-person *we*.

These differences on the democracy front parallel similar divisions elsewhere. Within the academic realm itself, there is the long-standing divide between political science with its more theoretical orientation and public administration with its practical focus. The former is long on theory; the latter, on distilled experience. Economics and business management form a similar pair. Academics do cross the line into practice (e.g., Larry Diamond in political science), as do practitioners into theorizing (e.g., Thomas Carothers in democracy), but these examples form more the exception than the rule.

There is, to be sure, widespread feeling that more crossing over is needed, that cross-fertilization would result, that each side would be better off knowing more about what the other has been doing. Most academics researching democratization readily admit that they should spend time on the ground involving themselves with democracy support efforts to see what really goes on, while it would be hard to find a USAID officer taking issue with the notion that more theoretical understanding of the whole democratization enterprise would be highly worthwhile. But these feelings do not get translated into behavior. Professors at good institutions do not generally get tenure and promotion for their consulting activities—if anything, such work tends to count against career advancement.[2] Academic culture in essence frowns on applied work, holding theory to be its true calling. On the other side, USAID officers have little time to gain an academic perspective, and in recent years—as the agency has steadily downsized, and the bureaucratic workload has correspondingly increased—they have had even less.[3] By force of circumstance, if not design, there is scant time for theory.[4] In sum, then, on neither side does one find much serious incentive for cross-fertilization from the other.

We should entertain the counterfactual as well. What if there were more academic interest in application and more practical interest in theory? How would those from either side fare in understanding what goes on in the other? To deal with such a question means determining just how much there is to be understood. Some rough outlines can be penciled in easily enough and show that developments on both sides during the 1990s give considerable reason for pause. An academic interested in tracking USAID's work in the democracy sector would find that funding levels had grown from about $165 million in fiscal year (FY) 1991 by more than threefold to just over $538 million by the end of the decade, as shown in Figure 12.1—representing far more activity than any individual scholar or even team could explore in any detail. One specializing in the single subsector of civil society would find less to deal with overall but a much greater rate of expansion over the 1990s, from around $30 million in FY 1991 to almost $200 million at decade's end in 2000, as indicated in Figure 12.2.[5]

The perspective from the practitioner side is even more daunting, as we see in Figures 12.3 and 12.4, which depict the number of journal articles and books published over the past fifteen years that can be elicited from several databases using the phrase "civil society" as a keyword in the search.[6] The burden of

Figure 12.1
USAID Support for Democracy, FY 1991–2000 (new obligating authority)

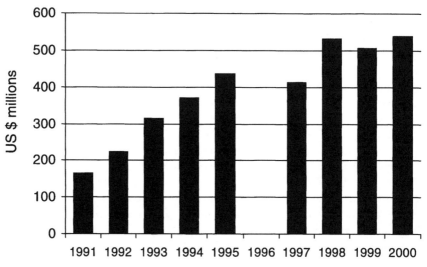

Note: Data for FY 1996 are not available.

Source: Data provided by the Management Bureau of the U.S. Agency for International Development, 2001.

Figure 12.2
USAID Support for Civil Society, FY 1991–2000 (new obligating authority)

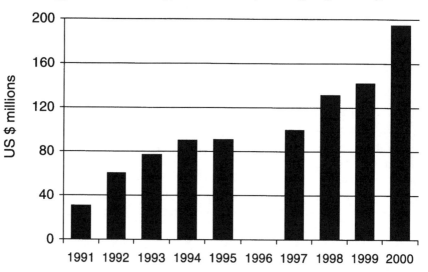

Note: Data exclude funding for civic education programs; data for FY 1996 are not available.

Source: Data provided by the Management Bureau of the U.S. Agency for International Development, 2001.

Figure 12.3
Journal Articles on "Civil Society" from Three Databases by Year of Publication, 1986–2000

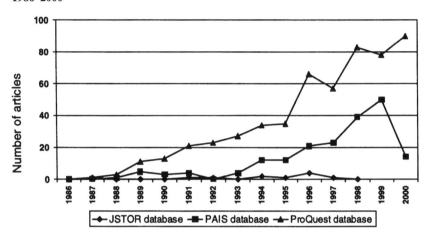

Source: Author.

Figure 12.4
Books on "Civil Society" by Year of Publication at Two Major Research Libraries, 1986–2000

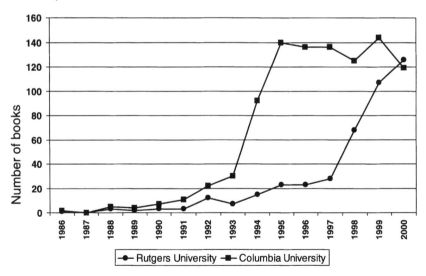

Source: Author.

tracking the most theoretical dimensions of political science is not so great, as is evident in Figure 12.3's Journal Storage ("JSTOR") citations, which track the more recondite journals like the *American Political Science Review* and the *Journal of Politics*. The rather less arcane articles tracked by the Public Affairs Information Service (PAIS) database, however, show a significant increase across the mid- and later 1990s, and those included in ProQuest have mushroomed even faster from one or two a year in the late 1980s to about ninety in 2000.[7]

Even more intimidating is the number of books published, which are tracked for the library collections at two major research universities in Figure 12.3. At Columbia University, books on civil society exploded in the mid-1990s from around 20 a year to about 140. At Rutgers University, perhaps initially constrained by a more modest library acquisitions budget, new books on civil society totaled only in the low 20s until near the end of the decade but then quickly reached the same level as at Columbia.

In sum, academics who might want to ground their theorizing in practice face a rapidly growing universe of real-world experience in civil society, while practitioners interested in keeping up with the field confront an even more rapidly escalating mountain of literature to comprehend. The challenge to both sides has become increasingly daunting. Fortunately, there are some possibilities for combining theory and practice without having to digest the entirety of either side's output. It took the whole of the 1990s to work out such a hope, however, as we see in the next section.

THE KEY ASSESSMENT RESEARCH QUESTION AT USAID

The challenge of linking theory and practice can be found in all the substantive aspects of development assistance, from grand strategy to specific program elements like monitoring and assessment. The following discussion looks at assessment as illustrative of the theory–practice relationship as a whole, with USAID programs in the Philippines serving as an example.

Any donor in the foreign assistance field needs some method of assessing its program effectiveness, if only to assure its benefactors—whether governmental or philanthropic—that it is spending their money wisely. But there has also been a strong internal motivation to determine what works and what doesn't so as to do a better job in a field so inherently full of uncertainties. Accordingly, USAID has used various measures over the years to evaluate its work. Beginning with the Carter administration and on through the succeeding Reagan and Bush years, the "logical framework" or "logframe" served as the standard model for this purpose. With its insistence on establishing measures for project outputs, short-term results ("purpose" in the logframe discourse), and outcomes or higher-level results ("goal"), the logframe approach sought to capture what the work was accomplishing in ways that could be assessed and reported. The evaluational focus, however, tended to center on what a given project did in terms of outputs—how many people trained, how many cooperative loans granted or repaid, how many pilot schemes begun, and so on. In addition, most projects were subjected to midterm reviews and many to final evaluations, which provided qualitative assessments of accomplishment.

The Clinton administration sought to change the basic approach with its "managing for results" philosophy that began philosophically with Osborne and Gaebler's influential book *Reinventing Government*[8] and continued through Vice President Al Gore's National Performance Review exercise,[9] attaining bureaucratic reality in the Government Performance and Results Act (GPRA) of 1993. As interpreted at USAID, GPRA meant exchanging the old emphasis on outputs for one emphasizing specific outcomes. Rather than asking what an assistance initiative did, now the query would ask how an initiative effect changed in behavior or performance as a result of what it accomplished. Instead of looking at how many individuals were trained, for example, one would analyze how an institution changed its behavior as a result of the training. In place of projects, USAID field missions would now have "programs" and "strategic objectives" (SOs) that would be achieved through programs attaining "intermediate results" (IRs).

USAID enthusiastically embraced the managing-for-results philosophy and incorporated it into all its reporting systems at field mission, regional, and global levels. In place of Annual Budget Submissions, USAID field missions were to produce annual Results Review and Resource Request documents (known as R4s) that would chart progress toward both SOs and IRs in terms of specific indicators.[10] By the end of the decade, the agency's annual report portrayed its achievements largely in terms of targets met or exceeded at these various levels.[11] As the GPRA approach waxed, the older evaluational orientation declined, as is indicated in Figure 12.5, which shows the number of all types of evaluations coming into the agency's central collection agency over the 1990s. In the earlier 1990s, interest in evaluations increased—the Center for Development, Information, and Evaluation (CDIE) as the agency's evaluational arm grew several-fold in personnel during that time—but then with the advent of GRPA, the number of reports dropped off rapidly until by 2000 their number appeared to be less than a fourth of what had been their high point in mid-decade.[12] Qualitative assessment had largely—if not completely—given way to quantitative measures.

The Philippines illustrates the GPRA approach in the civil society subsector. In the late 1990s, the USAID mission had in place two DG activities, one of which was its Governance and Local Development (GOLD) Project (the old term was still being used in this case), which had a substantial civil society component. Figure 12.6 illustrates one of the indicators reported by the Manila mission in its R4 for the years 1996–1999: the number of non-governmental organization (NGO) representatives actively participating in the "local special bodies" (e.g., school boards, municipal development councils, law enforcement boards), which were mandated by the Local Government Code of 1991 and

Figure 12.5
USAID Evaluations, FY 1990–2000 (as collected at USAID/Washington)

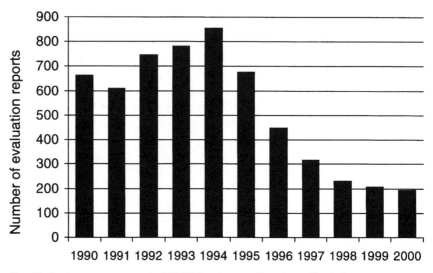

Note: Evaluation reports sent to the USAID Development Experience Clearinghouse.

Source: Development Experience Clearinghouse (DEC) online database, U.S. Agency for International Development, 2001.

Figure 12.6
NGO Representatives Actively Participating in Local Special Bodies in the Philippines, 1996–1999

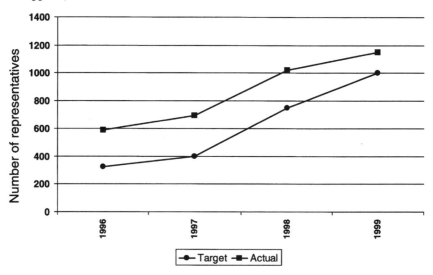

Source: U.S. Agency for International Development, *Results Review and Resource Request (R4)* (Manila: USAID, 2000), 87.

Figure 12.7
Target Local Government Units Implementing Environmental Plans with Effective Citizen Participation in the Philippines, 1996–1999

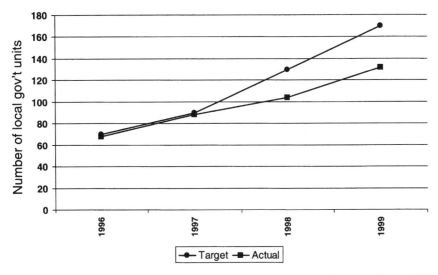

Source: U.S. Agency for International Development, *Results Review and Resource Request (R4)* (Manila: USAID, 1998).

became a special focus of the GOLD initiative. A fairly rigorous definition of "actively participating" was employed, including such specific queries as whether the NGO community itself had chosen the representative for the board rather than the mayor and whether the board in question had been active for at least a year. For the four-year period shown, performance exceeded target comfortably each time, counting as a success for the mission's democracy effort. The measure employed in Figure 12.6 is a reasonably good one, but an even better one appears in Figure 12.7, which shows the number of GOLD local government units employing active citizen participation in implementing their environmental plans—arguably as good a measure of local civil society activism as one might get.[13] Here the performance, though steadily improving in the last two years shown, still did not meet the target, which was rising even faster.

While the measures employed in Figures 12.6 and 12.7 are perhaps not perfect, they would seem to give good indications of program impact and implications for local civil society, at least in the short and perhaps even intermediate term. Other indicators appeared to hold considerably less promise in this regard. To take the same local development program in the Philippines, for example, Figure 12.8 portrays another indicator—revenues raised by local government units participating in the USAID program. One wonders why the targets were set so far below performance. Why not more? Other program indicators elsewhere evoke even more questions. In Nicaragua, for instance, the indicator used to measure progress against the IR labeled "strengthened civil society" was the

Figure 12.8
Net Self-Generated Revenues Generated by Target Local Government Units in the Philippines, 1996–1999

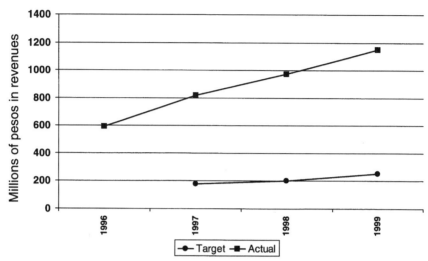

Source: U.S. Agency for International Development, *Results Review and Resource Request (R4)* (Manila: USAID, 2000), 85.

number of municipal meetings held with public participation, a target comfortably exceeded. Just what might have occurred at the meetings or what "public participation" meant was much less clear.

Probing only slightly further raises a whole host of issues.[14] For one thing, the data on achievement were generally collected by program implementors themselves (contractors and grantees) rather than an outside agency, and so were susceptible to bias and taint. After initial mission complaints that they had been overly taxed with excessive reporting requirements in GPRA's early years, missions were encouraged to select each year just a few indicators for sending to Washington—an opening that could be interpreted as incentive to report only their successes while suppressing their failures.[15] At its worst, it can encourage missions to build their initiatives around easily achievable targets as opposed to worthwhile objectives, rather as overemphasis on school testing can motivate instructors to "teach to the test" instead of teaching to educate their students.

Even so, the managing-for-results approach did bring some advantages. For one thing, it was now possible for the first time to obtain an overall picture of what missions were engaged in by region and globally and by sectoral activity as well as subsectors or even greater levels of specificity. For example, FY 1998 found USAID missions undertaking sixty-four program efforts in democratic decentralization, of which eleven focused on improving the enabling environment (laws, regulations, etc.), thirty-two on capacity-building (improving local ability to respond to democratic demands), and twenty-one on participation/ accountability (actual citizen involvement in the whole decentralization enterprise). Geographically, exactly half the sixty-four initiatives were situated in the Europe and Eurasia region. Missions were asked to gauge their own accomplishment in meeting the GPRA targets that they had set and for FY 1998 collectively reported that they had "met or exceeded" twenty-three of fifty-seven targets, mainly in the capacity-building area. Thus, it became possible to see at a regional or global level what aspects of their work field missions saw themselves succeeding at. In short, data to inform strategy and policy were now at hand in ways that had not been the case earlier.[16]

AN UNEASE WITH QUANTITATIVE MEASURES

The managing-for-results approach, then, did offer some scope for facilitating strategic thinking at USAID, but there is little evidence that it actually did so. One agency report did present a complete overview of USAID work in all sectors on the basis of strategic objective indicators exceeded/met/not met in the aggregate, as shown in Figure 12.9, but this was more in the nature of recounting an overall achievement than presenting any serious strategic analysis.[17] Basically, however, the approach that generated SOs, IRs, and indicators had virtually no relation to strategic analysis in the DG sphere. The reason is not far to seek: these measures simply could not show any connection between programs' meeting targets and a country's progress in democratizing. In the end, knowing whether a target was met on holding town meetings in Nicaragua or devolving additional functions to local government units in Kazakhstan would not give much idea about the overall progress of democratization in either country. There was, in short, a serious disconnect between the measurement of USAID efforts and the ability to discern whether any actual progress was being attained in any given country, to say nothing of regional or global aggregates of countries.

To be sure, other measures exist that attempt to gauge overall democratic progress at the country level, most notably, the annual rankings issued by Freedom House.[18] But while these indices offer an excellent diagnostic of a country's state of democratic health and its changes over time—the rankings began in 1972–1973 and ran through 2000–2001 as of this writing—they capture that health at so gross a level that it would be exceedingly difficult to link USAID programming activity to movement on the Freedom House scales.

Nonetheless, in the absence of better measures that could be used on a national, regional, or global basis, the Freedom House rankings were indeed employed in USAID's *Annual Performance Report* as global measures of the agency's performance for several years in the late 1990s.[19] This use of clearly unsuitable measures gave rise to considerable uneasiness within USAID—a conceptual problem often referred to as "the missing middle," that is, the analytical construct that could link USAID democracy support activity on the ground to

Figure 12.9
USAID Self-Assessment Scores, FY 1999

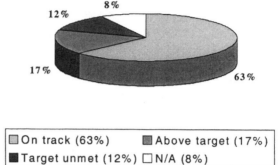

| On track (63%) | Above target (17%) |
| Target unmet (12%) | N/A (8%) |

Source: U.S. Agency for International Development, *FY 2000 Performance Review* (Washington, DC: USAID, 2001).

some measurable outcome(s) that would be understandable and legitimate both inside the agency and to external constituencies, particularly Congress. By 1999, the discomfort level had become sufficiently acute that the agency pledged in its *Annual Performance Report* that in future, "We plan to show our program impact through case studies, with examples from each region."[20]

A RETURN TO THE QUALITATIVE

Against this backdrop USAID's Democracy and Governance Center in 2000 launched a quite different attempt to connect program activity to overall democratic progress, one that, unlike the more crudely empirical GPRA-inspired efforts, sought to incorporate democratic theory into the assessment of democratic outcomes. The center picked three countries—Bolivia, Bulgaria, and South Africa—in which to conduct across-the-board assessments of all DG subsectors, tracing back over the previous five years, with the goal of finding the links between program impact and system change, that is, the very "missing middle" causal connections that had thus far eluded previous attempts to connect agency activity with results in the field. The countries selected all had DG programs in a number of subsectors—four in one case and five in the two others. All had initiatives in rule of law, political parties/processes, and local governance, while two had legislative efforts. Civil society, media, and conflict prevention were each represented by one country program.

Early on in its work, the study team found that it had to go back further than five years, in essence a decade, that is, to the beginning of concerted USAID democratic assistance. This longer look allowed it to assess impact at three distinct levels—individual citizens, institutions, and system. To take one example, USAID work with Bolivian political processes (a sector that had fallen into serious disrepute by the late 1980s) helped at the *individual level* to increase registered voters from 1.7 to 3.5 million citizens (or more than 70 percent of the voting-age population) over the 1990s, while also improving counting procedures. Opinion surveys indicated that citizens had come to feel that elections were more likely to reflect their views than earlier. At the *institutional level*, an independent National Election Court established in 1991 has managed to run free and fair elections since then, a distinct improvement over earlier practice that was widely perceived as corrupt. In terms of the political *system*, electoral competition between parties has improved with a more honest vote-counting system, the contorted process that used to characterize presidential elections (in which the candidate with the most votes customarily failed to win) became much more transparent, and losers became more likely to accept election results.

There were problems, to be sure. The National Election Court proved itself incapable of dealing fully with a new law requiring 30 percent of seats to go to women in the 1999 municipal elections, for one thing, and then a software procurement scandal tarnished its image somewhat. But on the whole, it succeeded in improving the electoral climate in Bolivia and, by inference, the general democratic climate as well. Other Bolivian DG subsectors did not fare quite as well, but there was significant improvement in most of them. For example, the USAID model developed in its pilot local government initiative had been adopted for replication throughout the entire country.[21]

The team's final report (one assumes the first of several to come in future years) begins to address some of the fundamental questions about democracy assistance, in particular, what might be called the "value-added" issue. Given that democratization is necessarily a function primarily of factors beyond donor control such as the strength of pro-democratic forces, prior experience with pluralism, and internal political will, just what is it that foreign democracy assistance can provide? Is its "value-added" sufficient to justify the donor effort? The answer in all three cases was that assistance contributed materially to enlarging and bolstering political will beyond its initial impetus. That is, the political will to bring the polity through the democratic transition had to emerge internally, but the need for political will did not stop at that point. New obstacles continued to emerge, such as erupting political cleavages, sagging economic performance, bureaucratic infighting—and donor reinforcement proved of material benefit in steering past them. A second value-added contribution was to introduce new ideas that otherwise would likely never have surfaced, such as a human rights ombudsman or criminal procedure code revisions in Bolivia. These judgments are qualitative, it should be noted, not the quantitative indicators of the 1990s. Thus, they are imprecise, but they do extend over all the cases at hand and allow comparison of each with the others in ways that the GPRA-based quantitative indicators could not do.[22]

The case studies also provided some linkages from application to theory, for instance, in connection with the long-standing academic query about the relationship between democracy, economic growth, and income inequality. One tantalizing indication is that local government reform holds the promise of attenuating some of the downside effects of income inequality by increasing citizen satisfaction with democracy. This relationship could prove critical in cases like Bulgaria where democratization has been accompanied by increasing income inequalities.[23]

This initial round of country case studies whets the appetite for ways to connect theory and practice on a grander scale—to ask such questions as, *What can democracy assistance do to promote actual systemic improvement?* The answers would seem to lie somewhere in the issue of what constitutes the term "democratic consolidation" and how does one get there. If, with Linz and Stepan,[24] we define democratic consolidation as the point at which democracy becomes agreed upon by all significant players (both real and potential) as the "only game in town," the italicized question above becomes the critical one. Most USAID DG programs work in countries like those chosen for the DG exercise discussed above—beyond the initial democratic transition but somewhere short of consolidation. How, then, do we help move them toward this latter stage? For the still considerable number of countries assisted by USAID but as yet not past that initial transition, the obvious track for analysis points to what can be done to promote it.

There are many issues to explore here. Taking the Bolivian example again, we know from recent events there that consolidation has not yet been attained. The political disturbances of spring and fall 2000 over utility rates and coca production clearly demonstrated that, for significant numbers of Bolivians, democratic processes were not "the only game in town"—other cards were available to be played, and large numbers of citizens began to play them. Could some initiatives be launched along one or more of the four DG fronts being pursued by the USAID mission that might bring those discontented players firmly into the democratic fold? More responsive local governance, perhaps, or better linkages between parliamentarians and their constituents?

Political changes in Bolivia during the 1990s opened real possibilities along both these avenues. A 1994 Popular Participation Law brought real representative governance to the entire country for the first time ever, along with a built-in mechanism to assure some (if perhaps not enough) civil society oversight of the process. In a break with the old proportional representation setup, half the parliamentarians were for the first time elected from single-member districts (average size around 110,000) in 1997, thereby allowing for the possibility of real linkage between *diputado* and citizen.[25] The kind of holistic analysis being pioneered in the new USAID country-level assessments should facilitate realistic analysis of how improvements in these two structures might bring those dissident elements to accept democracy as the only game worth playing.

The country-level approach is certainly not without a few problems. Pulling all the DG subsectors together to form a judgment about the polity as a whole will likely prove difficult. Will the sum of the DG parts add up to a convincing whole? How much, if any, discernible change can really be attributed to USAID interventions as opposed to internal system evolution, charismatic leadership, or exogenous factors—all of which were certainly present in Bolivia? Assuming that the methodology for such holistic assessments does get operationalized, how many can be conducted in a given year? Each study involves money and staff time, and these efforts cannot be conducted in the fashion of the GPRA-inspired reporting that operated as a kind of hidden levy on the contractors and grantees who were saddled with collecting the data for the GPRA indicators. Moreover, most countries with USAID democracy initiatives have only a couple of DG subsectors in play, making it impossible to conduct the kind of broad-gauge DG sectorwide assessment done in the three pilot countries used for 2000.

Nonetheless, the new approach does bring at last a real promise of seriously combining theory and practice, of comparing how democratization works with what we think theoretically should be going on, and what role USAID played in linking the two. Academic research in democratization and donor investment in it both increased greatly in the 1990s. It is surely high time that these two growth industries grew together. The synergistic possibilities awaiting academics and practitioners are exciting.

POSTSCRIPT

USAID's annual performance report for 2000, published in the spring of 2001,[26] indicates that while the agency has moved toward using this new approach, it has thus far hedged its bets. The report includes all three approaches presented in this paper: the Freedom House measures of earlier reports; the GPRA-related mission self-assessments on indicators; and the country-level qualitative analysis just discussed. The only one that even begins to make a convincing case in connecting USAID activity with systemic impact is the country-level presentation, partial though it admittedly is. Present indications are that the DG Center will undertake three more country-level assessments in 2002. One hopes that the agency will continue them in future years.

NOTES

1. In the spirit of full disclosure, the author should admit to having worked both sides of the democratic street, as an academic political science professor for most of his career, combining this with extensive sojourns in USAID's DG Center and its Center for Development Information, and Evaluation (CDIE). The experience has hopefully facilitated insight and acumen from both sides, but at the same time, it has doubtless also insinuated prejudice and bias from both sides into his outlook. To the extent that it becomes appropriate in this chapter to illustrate the argument by reference to a particular subsector of democratization, civil society will generally be employed as the example, for this is the area where the author has been working most recently.

2. Again in the disclosure spirit, the author should confess to having received tenure before launching into his first extended stint at USAID in the early 1980s.

3. One manifestation of this trend has been the virtual disappearance of earlier career

development training opportunities at USAID, through which midcareer officers in the past were supported in attending university programs in development.

4. Quite a few would argue that there is little interest as well. Attacking something as "too academic" or "merely academic" often (though certainly not always) serves as a telling charge at USAID, enough to stand by itself and obviating any need to show other shortcomings. Thomas Carothers in *Aiding Democracy Abroad: The Learning Curve* (Washington, DC: Carnegie Endowment for International Peace, 1999), 95–96, would also add ideological tensions lingering from the Vietnam War, when so many academics became estranged from what they saw as subservience of ideals to Cold War agendas. This may still constitute a factor for many older academics but appears to be much less in evidence among younger ones. See also the observations of Kevin F. F. Quigley on the academic–practitioner divide more generally, in his "Political Scientists and Assisting Democracy: Too Tenuous Links," *PS: Political Science and Politics* 30, no. 3 (September 1997): 564–567.

5. The faster rate of increase for civil society than for the DG sector as a whole reflects its increasing importance as a DG enterprise—growing from about 18 percent of all DG activity in FY 1991 to around 36 percent in FY 2000. In Figures 12.1 and 12.2, no data are reported for FY 1996. This was one of the consequences of USAID's move to a new budgetary management system in the mid-1990s.

6. "Civil society" represented a reasonably comprehensive and at the same time discrete as well as relatively recent term (in its current usage), thus permitting a relatively straightforward DG subsector search on the databases, although it included analyses of the advanced countries as well as developing ones. For example, see Robert Putnam, *Bowling Alone: The Collapse and Revival of American Community* (New York: Simon and Schuster, 2000). Other subsectors would have been much less manageable. "Elections" and "political parties" have constituted a major research area in political science for decades, and additions to this literature from the current democratization wave would be hard to distill from that mass. "Rule of law," in contrast, would be hard to comprehend in a search, since relatively few analyses of the topic include this exact term in their titles or abstracts. The net would have to be extended to combinations like "judicial administration" with "reform," which would be difficult to plumb satisfactorily. In contrast, "civil society" proved both easy and instructive.

7. The rapid increase in civil society articles has been fueled, in part, by the emergence of two specialized journals during the decade—*The Journal of Democracy*, edited in the United States, and *Democratization*, edited in England. But the vast majority of the articles cited in the databases appeared in journals already established in the social sciences.

8. David Osborne and Ted Gaebler, *Reinventing Government: How the Entrepreneurial Spirit Is Transforming the Public Sector* (Reading, MA: Addison-Wesley, 1992).

9. Office of the Vice President, Agency for International Development: Accompanying Report of the National Performance Review, *From Red Tape to Results: Creating a Government That Works Better and Costs Less* (Washington, DC: U.S. Government Printing Office, September 1993), 37–44.

10. For the democracy sector, the DG Center created and widely distributed an ambitious collection of illustrative SOs, IRs, and indicators—some 256 pages in all, comprising twenty-two IRs, seventy-six sub-IRs, and hundreds of "candidate" indicators. See USAID, *Handbook of Democracy and Governance Program Indicators* (Washington, DC: USAID, Bureau for Global Programs, Field Support and Research, Center for De-

mocracy and Governance, August 1998). The agency itself volunteered to become a GPRA model within the federal government, going considerably beyond the actual requirements of GPRA itself, in what appears to have been part of an effort to convince outside constituencies—especially Congress—that it could meet the most exacting scrutiny in its work.

11. For example, see USAID, *FY 2000 Accountability Report* (Washington, DC: USAID, 2001).

12. These remarks must be hedged by reference to USAID's system of report collecting, which depends on field missions and contractors sending in their work. There have always been lapses in this system, as some took on this task more conscientiously than others and as calls from Washington to send in reports turned stronger or weaker over the years. Moreover, the data presented in Figure 12.5 include evaluations of all types, not just project/program evaluations (the data for the figure were gathered simply by searching for the word "evaluation" in the agency's archival database). Still, the pattern does appear quite clear over the course of the 1990s. It can also be observed that USAID overall has collected successively less material in recent years. The total number of documents coming into the agency's Development Experience Clearinghouse dropped every year from just over 5,000 in 1993 to slightly over 2,000 in 2000.

13. "Effective citizen participation" was defined to mean "some process that allows ordinary citizens to express their views early enough in the planning process to make a difference, and [in which] the government expresses its judgment about whether it will take these views into account. This participation cannot be just a comment on something that already has so much momentum that citizen views cannot be taken into account." See Associates in Rural Development (ARD), *Governance and Local Democracy (GOLD) Sites Indicator Results: Final Report 1995, 1996, 1997, 1998, 1999, 2000* (Manila: ARD, December 2000), 12–13.

14. For a more extended analysis of GPRA as a measurement tool, see Harry Blair, "USAID and Democratic Decentralization: Taking the Measure of an Assistance Program," in *Democracy Assistance: International Co-operation for Democratization*, ed. Peter Burnell (London: Frank Cass, 2000), 226–240; for a heavier critique, see Carothers, *Aiding Democracy Abroad*, 281–302. McMahon's analysis is also useful here; see Edward R. McMahon, "Assessing USAID's Assistance for Democratic Development: Is It Quantity versus Quality?" *Evaluation* 7, no. 4 (2001): 43–367. USAID has not been the only donor agency concerned with democracy assistance evaluation. For a lengthy analysis of the Swedish International Development Authority's grappling with these matters, see Derek Poate et al., "The Evaluability of Democracy and Human Rights Projects: A Logframe-Related Assessment," *Sida Studies in Evaluation 2000*, vol. 3 (Stockholm: Swedish International Development Cooperation Agency, 2000).

15. The Philippines mission, for example, ceased including the indicator on citizen participation in environmental planning shown in Figure 12.7 for years after 1997. The GOLD contractor (Associates in Rural Development), however, continued to collect and report the data shown in Figure 12.7 in its own publications, even though the USAID mission in Manila didn't send the information on to Washington. See Associates in Rural Development (ARD), *Governance and Local Democracy (GOLD) Sites Indicator Results*, 14–15.

16. For more on using this approach, see Blair, "USAID and Democratic Decentralization" and "Intermediate Result Reporting as a Management Tool: Promise and Lim-

itations in the DG Sector," unpublished report (Washington, DC: United States Agency for International Development, DG Center, 30 August 1999).

17. USAID, *FY 2000 Accountability Report.*

18. Freedom House issued three rankings for some 192 countries in its 2000–2001 round—one overall rating using a three-point scale and then two more specific measures for civil liberties and political rights, each on a seven-point scale. For the Europe and Eurasia region beginning with 1998, Freedom House has compiled a more detailed set of rankings with six major categories, which come considerably closer to USAID's DG subsectors, but it is not clear that they could be used as agency program outcome measures. See, for example, Freedom House, *Freedom in the World* (New York: Freedom House, 2001). In addition, USAID's Bureau for Europe and Eurasia has over the past several years developed an "NGO sustainability index" that incorporates a number of more finely tuned measures, such as NGO advocacy capacity (e.g., USAID, *The 2000 NGO Sustainability Index for Central and Eastern Europe and Eurasia*, 4th ed. [Washington, DC: Bureau for Europe and Eurasia, Office of Democracy and Governance, January 2001]). But neither the Freedom House nor the sustainability index has been taken up by other USAID regional bureaus.

19. See USAID, *1997 Agency Performance Report* (Washington, DC: USAID, Center for Development Information and Evaluation, January 1998); USAID, *1998 Agency Performance Report* (Washington, DC: USAID, Center for Development Information and Evaluation, 31 March 1999); USAID, *1999 Agency Performance Report* (Washington, DC: USAID, Center for Development Information and Evaluation, 28 February 2000).

20. USAID, *1999 Agency Performance Report*, 49.

21. For example, see Eduardo C. Gamarra, Michele Schimpp, and George Gray Molina, "The Transition to Sustainable Democracy in Bolivia and the Strategic Role of USAID," *Case Studies in Program Impact* (Washington, DC: Management Systems International, June 2001); also Lynn Carter, *On the Crest of the Third Wave: Linking USAID Democracy Program Impact to Political Change; A Synthesis of Findings from Three Case Studies: Bolivia, Bulgaria and South Africa* (Washington, DC: Management Systems International, for USAID, Office of Democracy and Governance, October 2001).

22. These were among the results reported in ibid., 30f.

23. Ibid., 43–44.

24. Juan J. Linz and Alfred Stepan, *Problems of Democratic Transition and Consolidation: Southern Europe, South America, and Post-Communist Europe* (Baltimore: Johns Hopkins University Press, 1996).

25. This analysis of Bolivia draws on Harry W. Blair, *Civil Society Strategy Assessment for Bolivia and El Salvador* (Washington, DC: USAID, Democracy and Governance Center 16 February 2001); and "Institutional Pluralism in Public Administration and Politics: Applications in Bolivia and Beyond," *Public Administration and Development* 21, no. 2 (May 2001): 119–129, as well as the DG team's country-level analysis in Gamarra, Schimpp, and Molina, "The Transition to Sustainable Democracy."

26. USAID, *FY 2000 Accountability Report.*

Chapter 13

The Research–Policy Nexus and U.S. Democracy Assistance

Shaheen Mozaffar

This chapter examines the impact of scholarly research on U.S. democracy assistance programs. It focuses specifically on the ways in which scholarship has informed and shaped the democracy assistance programs administered by the U.S. Agency for International Development (USAID), the principal U.S. government (USG) instrument responsible for delivering American democracy assistance worldwide. In examining this impact of the research–policy nexus on U.S. democracy assistance, the chapter draws on empirical materials related to the formulation and delivery of USAID democracy assistance in Africa.

It should be stressed that the chapter does not provide either a comprehensive account of U.S. democracy assistance policy[1] or an in-depth examination of USAID democracy assistance programs in Africa. The principal objective of the chapter is a conceptual one, namely, to clarify the structure of the research–policy nexus and its impact on the conceptualization, formulation, and implementation of U.S. democracy assistance. To illustrate this relationship, the chapter draws selectively on USAID democracy programs in Africa.

The central argument of the chapter is that scholarly research has had an important, but indirect and irregular, impact on the shape and content of USAID democracy assistance programs. Scholarly research has impacted democracy assistance programs principally as a diagnostic tool, contributing substantively to the development of conceptual frameworks for designing democracy aid programs and strategies and identifying targets of opportunity to implement them effectively. It has had limited impact on prescribing the substantive content of democracy aid programs and even lesser impact on designing the projects and the technical assistance for implementing them.

This uneven impact obscures the important contribution of scholarship to democracy assistance. It also highlights an important weakness in the conceptualization of the research–policy nexus that seriously hampers theoretically systematic analysis and empirically relevant understanding of that contribution. This weakness involves the erroneous view of a reflexive and uniform link between research and policy that motivates the often simplistic criticisms of many, if not all, scholars about policymakers' failure to use research as a basis for policy. However, both studies and experience show that several factors mediate the impact of research on policy,[2] two of which are especially crucial for the present discussion.

The first concerns the type of knowledge produced by scholarship and the extent to which this knowledge has policy relevance. The second concerns the intrinsic incoherence of the research–policy nexus that derives from (1) the wider political-institutional context that structures the formulation and execution of American foreign policy and (2) the different organizational cultures in which academics and practitioners work and the different institutional incentives that motivate their professional interests. The first factor is obviously the more important because it concerns the production of knowledge that makes up the substantive content of policy. The second factor shapes how this knowledge enters the policy arena and is used in policy formulation.

Together, these two factors constitute a useful analytical framework for theoretically systematic analysis and empirically accurate understanding of the complex and varied ways in which research impacts the formulation of democracy assistance programs. In particular, they offer a realistic conceptualization of the research–policy nexus that emphasizes its intrinsic incoherence rooted in the diversity of purpose and the incrementalism of decision making that typify both academic research and policy making, the much-vaunted claims of cumulative theory-building and disciplined production of knowledge in academe notwithstanding.[3] Such a realistic conceptualization is important because it encourages an appropriate recognition of the opportunities that exist for research to impact policy as well as the constraints on them. Such a recognition, in turn, is absolutely crucial for an appreciation of the fact that scholars and practitioners occupy fundamentally different organizational cultures and are motivated by correspondingly different professional interests and institutional incentives and that these differences cannot and should not be eliminated. *But they can and should be bridged to the mutual benefit of both communities.*[4]

The raw materials for constructing this bridge are to be found in the substantive knowledge that academic research routinely produces because scholars are by training best equipped to do so. However, scholars studying democracy and democratization have not exploited this comparative advantage in part because they are often unaware of the policy relevance of their work, but principally because they lack an adequate understanding of policy-relevant knowledge. What, then, is policy-relevant knowledge? How has it informed USAID democracy assistance programs?

Before answering these questions, the chapter focuses on the second factor, namely, the incoherence of the research–policy nexus and how it mediates the impact of research on policy. A prior understanding of this factor is important because it defines the wider context that structures (facilitates and constrains) the production of policy-relevant knowledge and the way that this knowledge enters the policy process and is incorporated in the substantive content of democracy assistance programs. The chapter then explains the three key features that constitute policy-relevant knowledge and illustrates how research has impacted the development and application of the strategic assessments framework, a key diagnostic tool utilized by USAID to design its democracy assistance programs. The conclusion summarizes the central arguments and situates them in the theoretical literature on the complex and ambiguous relationship of social science research to policy making and the inchoate utilization of information in decision making. Figure 13.1 portrays how the key factors discussed in the chapter interact to constitute the complex process by which research impacts democracy assistance policy.

CONCEPTUALIZING THE RESEARCH–POLICY NEXUS

The production of policy-relevant knowledge is no guarantee that it will enter the policy process, much less impact decision making and substantive policy outcomes. How policy-relevant knowledge enters the policy process and impacts democracy assistance depends a great deal on the intrinsic features of the research–policy nexus. These features reflect the combined effects of (1) the characteristic fragmentation of the wider political-institutional context that shapes the U.S. foreign policy process and (2) the different organizational cultures and institutional incentives that shape the work, professional interests, and expectations of scholars and practitioners. Together, these two factors produce a fractured nexus between research and policy that, in turn, vitiates the uniform impact of research on policy.

The Political-Institutional Context

The advancement of democracy across the world has been a leitmotif of American foreign policy for the past century, reaching its greatest triumph in the post–World War II democratic reconstruction of Germany and Japan.[5] In Africa, however, the American record of support for democracy reflects a "sorry history."[6] Rhetorical support of democracy in Africa was rarely translated into practice, as the United States made pragmatic accommodations with the continent's authoritarian rulers as part of its global struggle with the Soviet Union.[7] Around 1989–1990, the end of the Cold War and the global spread of democracy's Third Wave[8] reverberated through Africa, precipitating widespread popular protest that quickly replaced authoritarian regimes with hurriedly constituted democratic government in some African countries and preemptive political liberalization by authoritarian rulers in others.[9] These historical transformations led to a dramatic change in U.S. foreign policy toward a greater concern with de-

Figure 13.1
How Research Impacts Democracy Assistance Policy

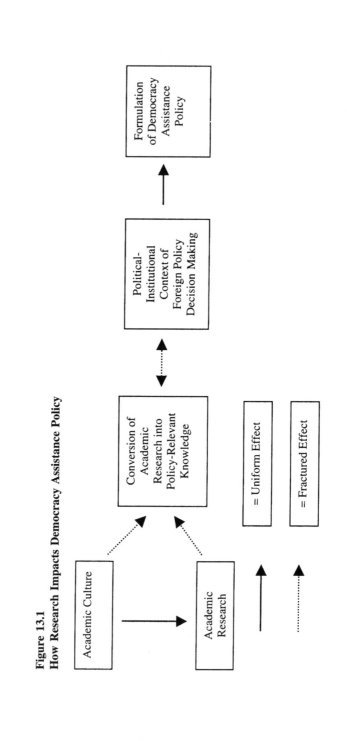

mocracy, accountability, and human rights and launched systematic and, for a while, well-funded U.S. democracy assistance programs.[10]

However, while the U.S. foreign policy goals in Africa have shifted in emphasis, the basic process by which they are established and the strategies devised to achieve them have not—neither has Africa's traditional marginal position in U.S. foreign policy priorities. As a result, in the absence of any major crisis on the continent that might seriously affect U.S. strategic interests, the basic process of U.S. foreign policy toward Africa continues to reflect the influence of bureaucratic routines and the competing organizational interests and missions of respective bureaucracies, ranging from the principal diplomatic and national security agencies, such as the Department of State (DOS), the Department of Defense (DOD), and the Central Intelligence Agency (CIA), to the social and economic development agencies such as USAID.[11] The result is the well-known fragmentation that typifies the U.S. foreign policy process.[12]

This has paradoxical consequences for the impact of research on democracy assistance. On the one hand, it gives scholars access to midlevel career policymakers in USAID who, free from the partisan influences that constrain decisions by the president or the secretary of state, tend to be more receptive than political appointees to the ideas and insights produced by academic research. Moreover, because these policymakers are also responsible for formulating the democracy programs and designing the technical assistance for implementing them, scholars are potentially able to have a substantial and meaningful impact on democracy assistance at this level. Indeed, some of the most productive effects of research on democracy assistance programs have occurred at this level. For example, when democracy assistance became a foreign policy priority for the United States at the end of the Cold War, USAID as the principal U.S. government (USG) agency responsible for promoting international development was charged with formulating and implementing the democracy assistance programs. But the agency, which had traditionally focused on social and economic development and had carefully, even if somewhat disingenuously, defined its programs as "apolitical," did not possess the requisite in-house expertise in democracy. As a result, it relied heavily on outside academic experts to develop a sound intellectual foundation for conceptualizing and designing its democracy assistance programs. The agency's Africa Bureau, in fact, took the lead in recruiting academics either through direct personal service contracts or indirectly through large-scale, multiyear contracts to consulting firms, such as the Associates in Rural Development (ARD), to conduct research and provide technical assistance. These activities contributed substantially to the development of conceptual frameworks and analytical tools for assessing the needs of individual African countries for democratic assistance on the basis of which country-specific democracy aid programs could be designed and implemented.

On the other hand, USAID is not a policy-making agency and therefore does not set policy priorities. That responsibility rests with the State Department. As an arm of the State Department, USAID's principal task is the implementation of development policies through the provision of technical assistance. While it exercises considerable autonomy in how it performs this task, it has to operate within the policy (and hence the political) as well as the bureaucratic constraints associated with its location in the overall organizational framework of the U.S. foreign policy establishment. USAID democracy assistance programs thus have to compete with USAID development programs as well as with strategically more important U.S. foreign policy priorities for attention and especially scarce resources. Additionally, USAID's position in policy debates derived from its comparative advantage in technical assistance and could be overridden by larger strategic considerations. For instance, USAID opposed direct financial assistance and commodity support (faxes, computers, etc.) for political parties in the 1994 transitional elections in Mozambique and the 1996 elections in Bosnia-Herzegovina. This opposition was based, among other things, on technical grounds; for example, the political parties did not possess the requisite accounting mechanisms required by U.S. law. But the Department of State, citing larger U.S. strategic interests in both countries, as well as congressional pressure in the case of Bosnia-Herzegovina, overrode USAID opposition.[13]

A particularly crucial aspect of bureaucratic politics that mitigates the direct impact of research on policy concerns the relationship between USAID Missions and U.S. Embassies overseas. This relationship derives from the considerable autonomy delegated to them by Washington and varies according to the personnel involved.[14] In 1992–1994, for example, the vigorous and vocal pro-democracy stance of U.S. Ambassador Smith Hempstone in Kenya gave the first USAID Regional Economic Development Services Organization (REDSO) adviser, a prominent academic African specialist, considerable leeway in his work over the objection of his superior, the USAID mission director.[15] Hempstone's successor, however, adopted a less vigorous pro-democracy position and severely curtailed the work of the second REDSO officer. In Ethiopia, the embassy's less than enthusiastic support for democracy limited the impact of an otherwise activist USAID democracy portfolio there.

Finally, in Ghana in 1992, Ambassador Kenneth Brown's quiet but firm support for democratic transition in that country over the objection of the USAID mission there is especially instructive in how bureaucratic politics conditions the impact of academic research on the substantive content of democracy assistance programs. After the problematic transitional elections in Ghana in 1991, the USAID Africa Bureau in Washington, armed with a new mandate to provide democracy assistance, sent a team of five academics to conduct a standard strategic assessment exercise aimed at developing a general assessment of the prospects for democratic consolidation in the country and identifying targets of opportunity for disbursing financial assistance in support of that process. The team was charged with recommending a range of options for allocating the funds. However, at its first meeting with embassy and USAID personnel, the team was informed that the decision had already been made to spend $10 million to improve Ghana's election administration system, which was held responsible for the problems that marred the otherwise successful transitional election the year before. In response to this unanticipated situation and unwilling to insert itself in bureaucratic politics, the team reorganized its work plan and proceeded to complete its original task of conducting the assessment but tailored its final recommendation to accommodate the fait accompli presented to it by the embassy. In the end, the program turned out to be a spectacular success, a rare and unheralded outcome for USAID democracy assistance, but that was due in no small measure to the embassy's strong support for it against the objection of the USAID country mission.

The fragmentation of the internal organizational structure of USAID for formulating and delivering democracy assistance programs also mitigates the direct impact of research on policy. While this fragmentation reflects the typical division of labor in any bureaucracy, it contributes to the incoherence in the formulation and execution of democracy assistance programs. Two aspects of this fragmentation are especially important for the present discussion. The first concerns the division between the Center for Democracy and Governance (henceforth, DG Center) and the regional bureaus. Established in 1994 as the organizational manifestation of the elevation of democracy assistance as a major U.S. foreign policy priority, the DG Center's principal purpose is to provide technical and intellectual leadership in the field of democracy development, but it also helps short-staffed field missions design and implement democracy strategies and directly manages some democracy assistance programs from Washington.[16] The regional bureaus are responsible for the provision of technical assistance and the delivery of the full range of development portfolios (of which democracy assistance is one) tailored to the needs of the specific regions for which they are responsible.[17] While coordination between the DG Center and the regional bureaus over democracy assistance does occur, albeit not routinely, the inevitable duplication of efforts and their respective organizational interests, reinforced by issues of turf protection and budget imperatives, tend to diminish the coherence of democracy assistance programs.[18]

The second aspect of the fragmented internal organizational structure concerns the division of the DG Center's democracy assistance programs into four areas that it considers to be the building blocks of democracy: rule of law, elections and political process, civil society, and governance. The DG Center recognizes that the four areas are not mutually exclusive and supports programs that crosscut them, but its basic staff and money allocations reflect their mutual separation. Moreover, an implicit and unwarranted assumption of synergy and homeostatic equilibrium in the relationship among these four areas informs the center's work. Recognition of and serious attention to the inherent tension between them, analyzed in extensive research and validated by historical evidence, are not reflected in either the analytical or the technical work of the center.

Finally, even as they define an incoherent process that mitigates the uniform impact of research on policy, the characteristic fragmentation of the U.S. foreign policy structure and the associated organizational politics and competing foreign policy priorities do create multiple opportunities for researchers to influence democracy assistance programs. However, this very multiplicity of opportunities is both a source and a symptom of the frayed nexus between research and policy. On the one hand, the varied opportunities expand the number of entry points for researchers to access practitioners involved in democracy assistance programs. On the other, they overwhelm academics unfamiliar with the intricacies of bureaucratic structures and procedures with a mind-boggling array of seemingly disjointed access points defined by mystifying acronyms. The result is that only a limited number of scholars who have developed skills combining substantive professional and area expertise, intellectual entrepreneurialism, and mastery of the bureaucratic maze are able to impact USAID democracy assistance programs.[19] This, in turn, produces a highly personalized and idiosyncratic pattern of linkages between individual academics and practitioners that is cultivated and sustained over time. There is, in other words, no institutionalized mechanism for research to impact policy.

The Different Worlds of Research and Policy

Scholars and practitioners occupy different organizational cultures that influence their work, provide different institutional incentives, and shape their different mind-sets.[20] These differences, which are generally viewed as inherently irreconcilable, are best exemplified by the stereotypical perceptions that scholars and practitioners have of each other.[21]

For practitioners, scholars (1) impute far too much rationality to the policy process; (2) produce arcane knowledge replete with esoteric jargon understood only by them and their colleagues; (3) are misguided in their attempt to examine the otherwise inchoate policy process on a scientific basis; (4) produce quantitative studies about trivial issues, but when such studies do produce important policy-relevant results, these are lost in abstract theorizing and not presented in ways that are useful for policymakers; and (5) are not as objective and free from ideological biases as they claim. For scholars, practitioners: (1) are caught up in the incrementalism of bureaucratic routines and are unable and unwilling to take a look at the larger picture; (2) are atheroetical and ahistorical and tend to treat each issue as unique, with no theoretical reference point for analyzing and interpreting it; (3) incorrectly claim that intuitive judgment and experience are sounder bases for policy decisions because they do have their unacknowledged theoretical perspectives that they use implicitly; and (4) are swayed far too much by shifting political considerations.

What is striking about these mutual criticisms is that they are mirror images and totally misdirected. That is, practitioners criticize scholars for doing precisely what scholars are professionally trained to do and therefore ought to be doing. Similarly, scholars criticize practitioners for doing precisely what practitioners are professionally trained to do and therefore ought to be doing. The result is that scholars and practitioners fail to recognize the *specific ways* in which their otherwise distinctive skills and substantive work are compatible and can foster mutually beneficial exchanges.

THE MEANING OF POLICY-RELEVANT KNOWLEDGE

Clarifying the meaning of policy-relevant knowledge requires a prior understanding of the general relationship between knowledge and action.[22] Knowledge is not a substitute for action but is the raw material that both shapes the actions of policymakers and informs the substantive content of those actions. The dominant criterion of appropriate actions (good policy), in other words, is not the much-vaunted objective *analytical rationality* espoused by academic researchers but the *political rationality* of practitioners that necessarily encompasses a broader range of political interests and idiosyncratic concerns that animate the decision-making process and eventually become embedded in the substantive content of policy. Policy informed by knowledge but motivated by interests necessarily involves judgments by policymakers about trade-offs between (1) a search for high-quality decisions, (2) the need for acceptability, consensus and support, and (3) the prudent management of time and other policy-making resources.[23]

Research, in other words, produces knowledge that has an important but indirect impact on policy. For research to have this impact on policy, however, it must produce policy-relevant knowledge that has three key components: (1) a conceptual model of the range of strategies likely to solve a policy problem; (2) context-specific knowledge about the conditions that are likely to contribute to the success or failure of the strategies; and (3) actor-specific models as opposed to the generalized rational-choice models.

Conceptual Model

Policy-relevant knowledge provides a general conceptual model that serves policy first as a diagnostic tool by clarifying for policymakers the "nature of the problem they face, the trend they may be observing, and the incipient warning signs they may be sensing."[24] Second, the conceptual model serves as a prescriptive tool by contributing to the conceptualization of strategies for dealing effectively with the problem at hand and specifying the theoretical rationale for using the strategy, that is, how and why the strategy is likely to be successful. It is important to recognize that the model itself is not a strategy but the conceptual and theoretical foundation for policymakers to design their preferred strategy.

Two literatures in extant political science scholarship are especially suitable in providing such a conceptual model for democracy assistance programs. The first is the literature on the crucial distinction and the inherent structured tension between populism and liberalism that underpin and animate all modern democracies. A useful contribution that research can make in this respect would be to clarify the practical implications of the two views of democracy for the design of new democratic institutions and the potential strategies that could be devised to accommodate their conflicting imperatives in emerging democracies.[25] Acknowledgment, much less an understanding, of the two definitions of democracy and the inherent tension between them does not exist in USAID. Indeed, over the past few years, USAID democracy programming has shifted substantially toward strengthening civil society in emerging democracies.[26] This shift is heavily informed by an implicit populism that is not even recognized within the agency and is curiously at odds with the agency's efforts in other areas of democracy programming, for example, the support designed in the governance component to strengthen policy-making capacities of new and fragile democratic governments.

A telling example of this paradox occurred during the Second USAID Legislative Strengthening Conference that the DG Center organized in June 2000. The central theme of the conference was that *representation was the most important function of democratic legislatures*, and the conference presentations were mostly aimed at analyzing and devising ways to strengthen the representation function of legislatures in emerging democracies. That modern democratic legislatures located as they are at the interface of state and society perform governance functions as well, such as lawmaking, investigative, and oversight functions, that inherent tensions exist among these functions and between them and representation, that the effectiveness and legitimacy of democratic legislatures derive from their ability to negotiate the inherent tensions between these essential functions, that all modern democracies have designed and sustained institutional mechanisms to negotiate these tensions with varying degrees of success, and that these tensions relate to the larger contradictory imperatives of representation and governance—all these issues were largely ignored in the conference presentation. More egregiously, the misguided emphasis on representation as the most important function of democratic legislatures is now institutionalized in USAID's *Handbook on Legislative Strengthening*, prepared by the DG Center. This handbook includes detailed recommendations on strategies for improving the representation of legislatures in emerging democracies with no consideration of how this might impact the other functions that democratic legislatures perform as well as the USAID programs aimed at improving them.

The second literature is the burgeoning scholarship inspired by the new institutionalism. This literature remains highly varied in quantity and quality, but many of its central insights about institutional design variations that distinguish democracies and their relative capacities for governance and peaceful conflict management are now beginning to coalesce around a limited number of core themes. For example, an impressive theoretical and empirical literature has emerged on the consequences of presidential and parliamentary regimes and different electoral systems designs for accommodating the inherent tensions between broad-based representation and creating stable governing majorities.[27] Yet these themes have not been synthesized and converted into policy-relevant knowledge. Doing so would provide some semblance of theoretical grounding to the otherwise ad hoc development of USAID democracy aid programs in such areas as elections and political process and legislative strengthening. For instance, USAID's democracy assistance programs in elections and political process almost invariably aim to improve individualized, candidate-based (as opposed to party-based) campaigning and postelection representation. This goal, however, is best realized in countries that have adopted plurality electoral systems with single-member districts, an institutional design that encourages such political strategies. Yet, some USAID past and current programs have been implemented in countries that have adopted party-list, multimember proportional representation electoral systems, an institutional design that is profoundly at odds with the candidate-based strategy of election campaign and political representation.[28]

Context-Specific Knowledge

Policy-relevant knowledge provides generic knowledge of strategy based on past experience to develop improved understanding of the conditions on which the effectiveness of that strategy depends. The emphasis here is on context-specific knowledge and conditional generalization. Context-specific knowledge requires a "thick description" approach in which area specialists excel.[29] Conditional generalization requires specifying the contextual conditions under which a strategy is likely to be successful or not, an approach that most area specialists reject. Yet combining the approaches is absolutely essential for producing policy-relevant knowledge. Bureaucrats working especially at the level of project design and implementation usually do not have detailed local knowledge and will find the expertise of area specialists particularly helpful. However, they are also interested in knowledge about the conditions under which a particular strategy is likely to work. This combination of generic knowledge and conditional generalization is productively generated through "lessons learned" exercises that USAID occasionally undertakes but has not integrated as an essential component of its decision-making process because of time and personnel limitations. In the few instances that such exercises have been completed and reports produced, it is not clear that the lessons have been seriously considered and incorporated in subsequent programming.

The last few years have witnessed an increasing number of comparative studies dealing broadly with the process of democratic transitions as well as more narrowly with how specific democratic institutions are selected and perform across regions and countries in Africa. These works typically aim to discover context-rich explanations that specify the empirical limits of extant theoretical propositions[30] as well as the empirical conditions that shape the choice, performance, and outcomes of new democratic institutions, such as electoral systems, in expected and unexpected ways. For instance, while it is widely recognized that proportional representation is ideally suited for securing equitable political representation in multiethnic societies,[31] more contextually sensitive analysis shows that plurality systems with single-member districts can also secure equitable representation in multiethnic societies if ethnopolitical groups are regionally concentrated and vote as a cohesive bloc.[32] The policy implication of this body of research suggests that USAID democracy assistance aimed at improving candidate-based election campaigns and postelection representation is more likely to succeed in the latter group of countries than the former.

Actor-Specific Knowledge

Policy-relevant knowledge provides actor-specific behavioral models. Standard, rational-choice models portray political leaders as disembodied actors free from strategic and contextual constraints. Actor-specific behavioral models provide detailed knowledge of how individuals or groups in specific cultural contexts are likely to respond to uncertain and rapidly changing political situations that typify democratic transitions. Particularly useful here is the emphasis of the political economy approach on the role of power and interest groups and the centrality of individual leaders in shaping political outcomes in the absence of strong institutions in transitional democracies. This approach is useful in identifying potential constraints and opportunities for targeting democracy assistance. This approach, in fact, has been successfully integrated with the earlier institutional approach in USAID to create a more effective strategic assessment framework, an important diagnostic tool for developing an overall assessment of the prospects for democratic consolidation in individual countries and identifying targets of opportunity for channeling scarce democracy assistance funds.[33]

In sum, within the constraints of the frayed research–policy nexus that mitigates the consistent impact of research on policy, as discussed in the previous section, research can have an important impact on policy. To have this impact, however, researchers must develop a broader understanding of the relationship between knowledge and action and a more rigorous conceptualization of what constitutes policy-relevant knowledge. The latter requirements are especially critical because the conversion of information produced by research into usable knowledge by policymakers is an absolutely essential condition for improving the impact of research and policy. In other words, the production of policy-relevant knowledge is a way to smooth the frayed nexus between research and policy and bridge the gap between the academic and policy communities.

RESEARCH AND STRATEGIC ASSESSMENTS

As mentioned above, one of the more critical functions of policy-relevant knowledge in democracy assistance is to serve as a diagnostic tool that can provide policymakers with an overall assessment of the situation in a particular country that can also identify targets of opportunity for devising democracy assistance programs tailored to the specific needs and situation of that country. For USAID, strategic assessments are an important diagnostic tool for prioritizing its democracy assistance portfolio. From the inception of democracy assistance programs in the late 1980s, USAID has relied on academic experts to assist in developing an analytical framework for strategic assessments that is sufficiently broad-based to encompass the key political, structural, and historical factors that are likely to affect the process of democratic transitions and the prospects for democratic consolidation. Application of this framework in specific countries could then be used to design country-appropriate assistance programs.

This effort to incorporate the insights of academic research into the development of a strategic assessment framework involved reconciling two competing theoretical approaches to explaining political behavior generally and democratic transitions in particular. One approach was the institutional analysis and development (IAD) approach, and the other was the political economy (PE) approach. The IAD approach emphasized the importance of institutions as sets of rules and institutional incentives in structuring political behavior and shaping political outcomes.[34] The principal policy lesson of the approach was to "get the institutions right." The PE approach stressed the importance of power, group interests, and the role of individual leaders, especially in the context of weak institutions typically found in developing countries, in shaping political processes and determining political outcomes.[35] The principal policy lesson of the PE approach was to stress the importance of groups and interests that supported political liberalization. In USAID, the Africa Bureau favored the IAD approach, while the Near East Bureau and, to a lesser extent, the Latin American Bureau favored the PE approach.[36]

The Africa Bureau took the lead in developing a strategic assessment framework grounded in the IAD approach. The approach informed the development of the framework in two ways: (1) through the establishment of a small group of political scientists who were specialists in the IAD approach to develop a strategic assessment framework and (2) field-testing the framework in five countries (Ghana, Mali, Niger, Tanzania, and Madagascar). The substantive components of the IAD framework were anchored by the concept of "democratic disciplines" that emphasized a multidimensional set of institutional rules to constrain (discipline) the arbitrary exercise of public power by the state. These rules included (1) a written constitution; (2) rule of law; (3) elections; (4) legislative deliberation; (5) civil society; and (6) decentralization.[37]

This framework was envisaged as the common basis for conducting the country assessments in the five countries, with team members for each assessment responsible for at least one and occasionally two democratic disciplines. But the framework was never uniformly utilized because some of the academic country specialists (mostly political scientists) recruited to conduct the country assessments were either unfamiliar with the framework or strong adherents of the PE approach and thus did not agree with its central assumptions and logic. This was not a major obstacle, however, because the academics were selected for their country expertise, not their expertise in the IAD framework. However, the team leader responsible for writing the final report was an IAD specialist and synthesized the various components of the team's report within the framework. In the end, all five reports included a uniform structure and provided the basis for a synthetic analysis at the end of the project.[38]

The impact of the IAD framework and the country assessments that it spawned on the content and design of democracy assistance programs, however, was rather limited in USAID generally and even within the Africa Bureau. One reason was that the complexity of the framework and the expense involved in designing programs consistent with its findings often proved to be prohibitive. This was especially true at the level of the country missions, which were responsible for incorporating new democracy assistance programs in their portfolios. The IAD approach never acquired wide acceptance within USAID; the Near East Bureau, in particular, remained implacably opposed to it, perhaps reflecting the continued strong influence of the PE approach in Middle Eastern scholarship. The project under which the IAD framework was developed and tested came to an end in 1994, coinciding with the transfer and subsequent retirement of the senior officer in the Africa Bureau, who was committed to the approach and had supported and spearheaded the development and field-testing of the framework based on it. The end of the project also coincided with the internal reorganization of USAID that led to the creation of the DG Center in the new Global Bureau as the main repository of intellectual and technical leadership in democracy assistance and the attendant decline in the ability of regional bureaus to devise their own approaches to democracy assistance. The new personnel in the DG Center had little commitment to the IAD approach; as a result, it failed to acquire its erstwhile prominence in shaping USAID thinking about democracy assistance.

Even so, the IAD framework introduced important insights about the centrality of institutions and institutional incentives into the organizational process governing the conceptualization of democracy assistance programs and into the next iteration of the strategic assessment framework. Since it was established in 1994 to provide intellectual and technical leadership to USAID democracy assistance program, the DG Center began an incremental process of developing conceptual frameworks for technical assistance for specific programs (e.g., media support and political party support) in each of its four broad programmatic areas, rule of law, elections and political process, civil society, and governance. As part of this overall attempt to institutionalize its intellectual and technical leadership, the center used both field experience and analytical studies conducted by academics to develop over a period of five years a new strategic assessment framework.[39] This framework consists of four sequential but related steps by which each country is analyzed, its democratic transition and prospects for democratic consolidation assessed, and targets of opportunity for democratic assistance identified.

Substantively, the framework combines elements of both the IAD and PE approaches. These elements define the analytically sequential topics for conducting the assessment: the political system, the key actors and their interests, the institutions, and distilling the framework and the institutions. The first step in the assessment process involves identifying the prevailing strengths and weaknesses of the country along five key elements of a democratic political system: (1) consensus over the basic rules of the game, (2) the extent of rule of law as a functional process beyond the formal trappings of courts and judges, (3) the degree of political competition permitted, (4) the extent of inclusion of diverse groups, and (5) good governance, defined as the capacity of both public and private social institutions to govern effectively. These five elements define the basic structural foundation of a democratic system.

The second step is to assess their operational effectiveness by examining the key actors and their interests who constitute the players in the political game. The emphasis here is on identifying the central players, their interests, the resources (both domestic and international) that are available to them for deployment in the political game, the alliances that they are likely to form, and the strategies that they are likely to adopt to pursue their goals. The key to this step is the identification of the quantity and quality of political support or opposition for democratization in the country.

The third step is to identify the institutions, the sets of rules that structure the political game and the strategic interactions of the players. Here, the emphasis is first on the basic legal environment comprising the constitutional sphere, the substantive law sphere of statues and regulations, and the judicial sphere for the peaceful adjudication of disputes. A second emphasis is on the competitive arena, both electoral and nonelectoral. The third emphasis is on the arena of governance, including the legislature, the executive, and the administrative, and the local government spheres. The fourth area of emphasis is on civil society, broadly defined as the institutional arena, encompassing all associational life beyond the state.

These three steps constitute the analytical components of the assessment strategy. In an important and useful departure from the previous strategic assessment framework, this framework adds a fourth pragmatic step for distilling the framework to make it usable for designing programs. The key to this step is close attention to the political, bureaucratic, and financial constraints on USAID's and other donors' support for democracy assistance as well as practical constraints on the ability of recipient countries to utilize that assistance effectively.

In sum, the purpose of the strategic assessment is "to lay out the problems and possible solutions, to explain and order them, to recommend a strategy and subordinate tactics, and to suggest results and impacts."[40] Because this framework has been utilized in only two countries, Morocco and Peru, its utility in helping to design specific assistance programs remains to be tested. What is clear, however, is that the substantive components of the framework reflect the combined insights of the IAD and the PE approaches.[41] This combination, in turn, parallels the growing integration of the two approaches in extant comparative political science scholarship on democracy and democratization.

CONCLUSION AND IMPLICATIONS

This chapter has argued that academic research has had an important, but inconsistent, impact on U.S. democracy assistance programs administered by USAID. Academic research has had a visible impact as a diagnostic tool, informing the development of strategic assessment frameworks that are used by USAID to develop an overall assessment of the status of democratic transition and the prospect for democratic consolidation in a country. This assessment is ideally conducted to assist the agency in identifying targets of opportunity and designing country-appropriate democracy assistance programs. The two main theoretical approaches—the IAD and the PE approaches—in extant political science scholarship informed the substantive content of the framework. However, the standard operating procedures, competing organizational interests, and incrementalism that typically animate bureaucratic processes mediated their impact. The conflicting commitment of the Africa Bureau to the IAD approach and of the Near East Bureau to the PE approach, for instance, vitiated the full acceptance of the initial framework based on the former approach. Personnel turnover and internal reorganization contributed to the diminished impact of the IAD approach but also led to the integration of some of its insights with the PE approach to shape the development and inform the content of the current strategic assessment framework in USAID.

The uneven impact of academic research on democracy assistance policy can be attributed to the disjointed character of the research–policy nexus associated with the complexity and incoherence of the overall structure and process of U.S. foreign policy and with the different organizational cultures in which academics and practitioners work. Within the constraint of the disjointed research–policy nexus, however, research can have a significant impact on policy to the extent that both researchers and academics recognize that the differences in their respective professional worlds cannot be eliminated but can be bridged to their mutual benefit. The key to building and sustaining this bridge is the ability of researchers to convert their research products into policy-relevant knowledge that offers practitioners (1) a general conceptual model of strategies that can assist policymakers to devise appropriate policies, (2) context-sensitive analysis and conditional explanations of the prospects for success and failure of alternative policies, and (3) actor-specific models that identify the key players in the political game who are the likely supporters and opponents of democratization.

The analysis presented in this chapter contains an important, perhaps even a painful lesson for academics who insist that the dominant criterion for determining the relevance of research for policy should be its pristine analytical rationality instead of the more messy political rationality that animates policy decisions. In the real world of policy, however, such an insistence sounds unrealistic at best and naive at worst. Moreover, to paraphrase Alexander George's writing on the impact of research on foreign policy, scientific theory and knowledge are not essential for sensible implementation of democracy assistance programs.[42] Two implications follow. The first, according to George, is that just as ordinary people cope with life's routine chores without the benefit of sophisticated scientific knowledge, policymakers can, do, and must rely on the best available knowledge and experience to make reasonably intelligent judgments about complex issues that they routinely confront. Even the most scientifically sound research cannot substitute for such judgment. The second implication is that no inevitable isomorphic relationship exists between scientific knowledge and policy-relevant knowledge. Sound science may be necessary for the production of policy-relevant knowledge, but it is certainly not sufficient. The transformation of scientifically sound knowledge into policy-relevant knowledge is the key to the productive impact of research on policy, but that transformation itself is independent of the scientific enterprise and requires a close understanding of policy-relevant knowledge.

The need for a close understanding of policy-relevant knowledge revealed by the analysis presented in the chapter also points up an important theoretical implication of that analysis. The indirect and uneven impact of democratization research on democracy assistance policy reflects the more general pattern of complex and ambiguous relationship of social science research to policy making[43] as well as the more general pattern of inchoate information utilization in decision making.[44] Policymakers routinely have to balance conflicting imperatives under conditions of incomplete information, time constraints, and resource scarcity to arrive at feasible (as opposed to desirable or optimum) policy options with uncertain outcomes. Decision makers, moreover, are bombarded with a bewildering variety of information from a corresponding variety of sources, including information from academic research. They employ a series of implicit filters defined by bureaucratic structures and procedures to process the information. They discard the information that fails to pass the filters, and they retain the information that passes through the filters as residues that augment their stock of knowledge on which they draw when action becomes necessary.[45]

The analysis presented in this chapter suggests that these processes that animate all policy making and the realistic conception of the link between knowledge production and knowledge utilization that they engender help to clarify U.S. democracy assistance policy making as well. To the extent that scholars are inclined to use their comparative advantage in knowledge production and influence U.S. democracy assistance policy, a realistic appreciation of the inherent complexity and incoherence of U.S. foreign policy is essential if they are to speak truth to power. Speaking truth to power requires both an understanding that policies are essentially experiments with uncertain outcomes and a self-conscious attempt to incorporate this understanding into systematic policy analysis.[46] But it also requires a close understanding of those factors that mediate the relationship between knowledge production and knowledge utilization and constrain the direct and uniform impact of research on policy.

Finally, policy relevance need not be a criterion, either exclusively or in combination with other criteria, for evaluating knowledge produced by scholars. A combination of professional training, intellectual interest, and institutional incentives motivates most scholars to produce works that have no intrinsic policy relevance and that they would prefer to be judged exclusively on analytical and professional merits.[47] At the same time, however, Stokes[48] has brilliantly pointed out (1) that the distinction between basic and applied research that has underpinned scientific enterprise for the past fifty years in the United States has had deleterious effects on both and (2) that some of the major scientific discoveries of the past century originated in attempts to devise policy solutions to social problems. Thus, while this chapter has focused on the impact of research on policy, it is also important to recognize that policies and the problems that they are designed to resolve can and do become sources for the production and accumulation of scientific knowledge. In comparative democratization scholarship, this impact of policy on research is evident in the recent attempt to develop an analytical framework for the systematic analysis and understanding of the role of electoral governance in the process of democratization. This attempt draws on the experience of practitioners over the past two decades in international election observation and international assistance provided principally, but not exclusively, by USAID to establish effective and credible systems of electoral governance in emerging democracies.[49]

NOTES

Some materials for this chapter are drawn from a larger project funded by the National Science Foundation. The author thanks the Boston University African Studies Center for continued research support. The final responsibility for the chapter rests with the author.

    1. For such an account, see Thomas Carothers, *Aiding Democracy Abroad: The Learning Curve* (Washington, DC: Carnegie Endowment for International Peace, 1999).

    2. See Nathan Caplan, Andrea Morrison, and Russell J. Stambaugh, *The Use of Social Science Knowledge in Policy Decisions at the National Level* (Ann Arbor: University of Michigan Press, 1975); Carol F. Weiss and Michael J. Bucuvalas, *Social Science Research and Decision-Making* (New York: Columbia University Press, 1980).

    3. On incrementalism, see Herbert A. Simon, *Administrative Behavior: A Study of Decision-Making Processes in Administrative Organization* (New York: Free Press, 1976). On the problems of cumulative theory-building, see Thomas S. Kuhn, *The Structure of Scientific Revolutions*, 3rd ed. (Chicago: University of Chicago Press, 1996).

    4. Alexander G. George, *Bridging the Gap: Theory and Practice in Foreign Policy* (Washington, DC: U.S. Institute of Peace, 1993).

    5. Tony Smith, *America's Mission: The United States and the Worldwide Struggle for Democracy in the Twentieth Century* (Princeton, NJ: Princeton University Press, 1994).

    6. Larry Diamond, "Promoting Democracy in Africa: U.S. and International Policies

in Transition," in *Africa in World Politics: Post–Cold War Challenges*, 2nd ed., ed. John W. Harbeson and Donald Rothchild (Boulder, CO: Westview Press, 1995), 250–252.

7. Peter J. Schraeder, *United States Foreign Policy toward Africa: Incrementalism, Crisis, and Change* (New York: Cambridge University Press, 1994).

8. Samuel P. Huntington, *The Third Wave: Democratization in the Late Twentieth Century* (Norman: University of Oklahoma Press, 1991).

9. Michael Bratton and Nicolas van de Walle, *Democratic Experiments in Africa: Regime Transitions in Comparative Perspective* (New York: Cambridge University Press, 1997).

10. Carothers, *Aiding Democracy Abroad*.

11. Presidential involvement in African policy has been largely limited to crisis situations that might affect strategic U.S. interests (e.g., Angola and Mozambique in the 1970s) or that might lead to severe regional instability and potential American commitment and involvement (e.g., the current crisis in the Great Lakes region). Extended political crises, such as the antiapartheid struggle in South Africa, have also contributed to increased involvement of Congress and the public. Schraeder, *United States Foreign Policy*, 11–50, offers an excellent account of these variations in patterns and processes of U.S. foreign policy toward Africa.

12. Graham T. Allison, *Essence of Decision: Explaining the Cuban Missile Crisis* (Boston: Little, Brown, 1971); Morton H. Halperin, *Bureaucratic Politics and Foreign Policy* (Washington, DC: Brookings Institution, 1974); Charles W. Kegley Jr. and Eugene R. Wittkopf, *American Foreign Policy: Pattern and Process* (New York: St. Martin's Press, 1996).

13. In a telling indication of the inverse correlation between U.S. strategic priorities and USAID influence, USAID was successful in opposing embassy request for direct support to political parties in the 2000 elections in Haiti.

14. According to protocol, the ambassador, as the president's representative, is the overall chief of country posts with authority over all U.S. foreign policy personnel.

15. The REDSO adviser provides technical assistance in response to requests by USAID country missions. Most country missions did not initially have resident democracy specialists to handle the addition of democracy assistance programs to their portfolios. REDSO officers were appointed in part to fill the gap. In 1992, two REDSO officers were appointed, one based in Nairobi for servicing missions in East and Southern Africa and the second based in Abidjan for servicing missions in West Africa. The first two REDSO officers in Nairobi and the first REDSO officer in Abidjan were prominent American political scientists and African specialists.

16. Center for Democracy and Governance home page: http://www.usaid.gov/democracy/center/index.html.

17. The four regional bureaus include Africa, Asia and the Near East, Europe and Eurasia (covering the former communist countries), and Latin America and the Caribbean.

18. Compounding the fragmentation, the Office of Transition Initiatives, established in 1994 as a rapid response unit to assist in the reconstruction of countries coming out of violent internal wars, also provides democracy assistance programs.

19. This situation with respect to democracy assistance reflects a larger and longer pattern of relationship between academics and USAID. See Michael Bratton, "Academic Analyses and U.S. Economic Assistance Policy on Africa," *Issue: A Journal of Opinion* 19, no. 1 (Winter 1990): 21–37.

20. See Caplan, Morrison, and Stambaugh, *The Use of Social Science Knowledge in Policy Decisions at the National Level*; George, *Bridging the Gap*, 3–18; Weiss and Bucuvalas, *Social Science Research and Decision-Making*.

21. These stylized and somewhat simplified perceptions are drawn liberally from George, *Bridging the Gap*, 3–18.

22. This section draws heavily on George's excellent, pragmatic yet analytically rigorous explication of policy-relevant knowledge.

23. George, *Bridging the Gap*, 19–29.

24. Bruce W. Jentleson, "In Pursuit of Praxis: Applying International Relations Theory to Foreign Policy-Making," in *Being Useful: Policy Relevance and International Relations Theory*, ed. Miroslav Nincic and Joseph Lepgold (Ann Arbor: University of Michigan Press, 2000), 131.

25. Quigley makes a similar point. Kevin F. F. Quigley, "Political Scientists and Assisting Democracy: Too Tenuous Links," *PS: Political Science and Politics* 30, no. 3 (September 1997): 564–567.

26. Blair provides data and analysis of the dramatic increase in funding and programming for support of civil society in emerging democracies. Harry W. Blair, "Research and Practice and Democratization: Cross-Fertilization or Cross Purposes?" paper presented at the "Conference on Democratic Performance," Center on Democratic Performance, State University of New York at Binghamton, 7–9 June 2001.

27. See, among others, Joel Barkan, "Rethinking the Applicability of Proportional Representation for Africa," in *Elections and Conflict Management in Africa*, ed. Timothy D. Sisk and Andrew Reynolds (Washington, DC: U.S. Institute of Peace, 1998), 57–70; Arend Lijphart, *Electoral Systems and Party Systems: A Study of Twenty-Seven Democracies, 1945–1990* (New York: Oxford University Press, 1994); Shaheen Mozaffar, "Electoral Systems and Their Political Effects in Africa: A Preliminary Analysis," *Representation* 34, nos. 3–4 (Autumn/Winter 1997): 148–156; Shaheen Mozaffar, "Electoral Systems and Conflict Management in Africa: A Twenty-Eight State Comparison," in *Elections and Conflict Management in Africa*, ed. Timothy D. Sisk and Andrew Reynolds (Washington, DC: U.S. Institute of Peace, 1998), 81–98; Andrew Reynolds, "Elections in Southern Africa: The Case for Proportionality, a Rebuttal," in *Elections and Conflict Management in Africa*, ed. Timothy D. Sisk and Andrew Reynolds (Washington, DC: U.S. Institute of Peace, 1998), 71–80; Matthew S. Shugart and John M. Carey, *Presidents and Assemblies: Constitutional Design and Electoral Systems* (New York: Cambridge University Press, 1992); Matthew S. Shugart and Scott Mainwaring, eds., *Presidentialism and Democracy in Latin America* (New York: Cambridge University Press, 1997).

28. In fairness to USAID, such programs are designed and implemented by two USAID partners, the National Democratic Institute (NDI), associated with the Democratic Party and the International Republican Institute (IRI), associated with the Republican Party. The programs clearly reflect the bias of the two main American political parties. Yet, while NDI and IRI enjoy considerable autonomy in designing their projects, USAID retains the final authority over them and can require better theoretical grounding for the projects.

29. Thick description refers to the detailed explication of the cultural and social context of human behavior. For elaboration of the concept, see Clifford Geertz, *The Interpretation of Cultures: Selected Essays* (New York: Basic Books, 1973).

30. Bratton and van de Walle, *Democratic Experiments in Africa*.

31. Reynolds, "Elections in Southern Africa."

32. Mozaffar, "Electoral Systems and Their Political Effects in Africa"; Mozaffar, "Electoral Systems and Conflict Management in Africa."

33. See USAID, *Conducting DG Assessment: A Framework for Strategy Development* (Washington, DC: USAID, Center for Democracy and Governance, 2000).

34. Elinor Ostrom, *Governing the Commons: The Evolution of Institutions for Collective Actions* (New York: Cambridge University Press, 1990).

35. Stephan Haggard and Robert R. Kaufman, *The Political Economy of Democratic Transition* (Princeton, NJ: Princeton University Press, 1995).

36. The precise reasons for this correspondence between bureaucratic and theoretical compartmentalization are not entirely clear but probably had to do with the respective academic training of the individuals who headed the democracy assistance programs in the Africa and the Near East Bureaus. In the Africa Bureau, that individual's previous portfolio had been the decentralization and financial management portfolio, in which the IAD framework heavily informed the analytical and technical work.

37. Ronald Oakerson, "Democracy as a Discipline," typescript, 1994.

38. Shaheen Mozaffar, *Institutional Analysis and the Assessment of Democratic Governance in Africa* (Burlington, VT: Associates in Rural Development, 1994). The individual country assessments are reported in the following publications: Associates in Rural Development (ARD), *Governance in Mali: An Assessment of Transition and Consolidation and Guidelines for Near-Term Action* (Burlington, VT: ARD, 1994); Robert Charlick, *Improving Democratic Governance for Sustainable Development: An Assessment of Change and Continuity in Niger* (Burlington, VT: Associates in Rural Development, 1994); Leslie Fox et al., *An Assessment of Politics and Governance in Madagascar* (Burlington, VT: Associates in Rural Development, 1994); Tina West, *The Consolidation of Democratic Governance in Ghana: How Can USAID Respond?* (Burlington, VT: Associates in Rural Development, 1992); Tina West, *The Transition to Democratic Governance in Tanzania: An Assessment and Guidelines for Near-Term Action* (Burlington, VT: Associates in Rural Development, 1994).

39. USAID, *Conducting DG Assessment*.

40. Ibid., 55.

41. A team of political scientists with country expertise and comparative analytical skills participated in the development of the framework.

42. George's full statement reads: "It should be recognized that scientific theory and knowledge are not essential for sensible conduct of foreign policy." George, *Bridging the Gap*, 139.

43. Caplan, Morrison, and Stambaugh, *The Use of Social Science Knowledge*; Weiss and Bucuvalas, *Social Science Research and Decision-Making*; Aaron Wildavsky, *Speaking Truth to Power: The Art and Craft of Policy Analysis* (Boston: Little, Brown, 1979).

44. Michael D. Cohen, James G. March, and Johan P. Olsen, "A Garbage Can Model of Organizational Choice," *Administrative Science Quarterly* 17 (1972): 1–25; James G. March and Johan P. Olsen, *Ambiguity and Choice and Organizations* (Bergen: Universitetsforlaget, 1976); Simon, *Administrative Behavior*.

45. Weiss and Bucuvalas, *Social Science Research and Decision-Making*, 249.

46. Wildavsky, *Speaking Truth to Power*.

47. Anecdotal evidence also suggests that many political science departments do not treat "applied" research reported, for example, in consulting reports as legitimate "scholarly" works in tenure and promotion decisions. A number of professional colleagues

inform the author that they do not even list works resulting from applied research in their résumés, especially when compiling their tenure and promotion files.

48. Donald E. Stokes, *Pasteur's Quadrant: Basic Science and Technological Innovation* (Washington, DC: Brookings Institution, 1997).

49. Shaheen Mozaffar and Andreas Schedler, "Introduction: The Comparative Study of Electoral Governance," *International Political Science Review*, Special Issue on "Electoral Governance and Democratization," vol. 23, no. 1 (January 2002).

Part IV

Conclusion

Chapter 14

The Art of Democratic Crafting and Its Limits

Edward Friedman

INTRODUCTION

The literature on democratization, which, like democracy itself, flourished in the last decade of the twentieth century, reached new levels of practical sophistication both quantitatively and qualitatively. No one person can fully command this burgeoning subfield of the political science discipline. Yet there have already been important, almost heroic efforts to synthesize some of the new knowledge and to draw it together so as to derive lessons from the experiences of the various governments and nongovernmental organizations that have been actively promoting democratization.[1]

Given the achievements to date and the importance of the issue of democratization to decent human lives, professional analysts should be hoping for and working for further advances and syntheses, a project that requires yet greater cooperation, including taking each other's ideas seriously. The conference leading to this volume and the book itself are further efforts to keep moving ahead, to help crafters make the best possible institutional choices.

Because the academic study of democratic crafting has flourished as never before starting around 1990, in part a response to the demands of democratic peoples all around the world trying to build a constitutional order that would guarantee the blessings of political liberty, there is now a record of practice and the evaluation of performance to examine in order to learn how well or poorly analysts have done in helping fledgling democracies better institutionalize fragile democratic breakthroughs.[2]

While the actual record and the analytical literature are too voluminous for a thorough investigation in a short article or even this book, it is possible to sketch some of the important things that have and have not been learned about building a democracy. The greatest error, in a political science quest for systemic knowledge, would be to forget how much of politics is an art dependent on timing and contingent particulars, matters that, if overlooked in the quest for general theory, would undermine all the great good that can indeed be won by improving our systemic knowledge. Political crafting is an art with limits.

PARADIGMATIC SHIFTS

Before 1990, the mainstream approach to democratization highlighted evolutionary preconditions, both economic and sociocultural. That approach did not leave much space for democratic crafters. Instead, the view was that over a long period of time, behind people's backs, conditions evolved that eventually facilitated a ready democratic transition. With larger structural dynamics taken as decisive, the impact of mere human agency and institution-building was treated as virtually a residual factor, something not worthy of much sustained work, the error of voluntarism.

In the economic approach to structural preconditions, a democratic breakthrough followed upon the prior slow growth of private property, a market-oriented economy, a literate population, a middle-class society, independent professionals, relative autonomy in the legal system, and the rise of robust civil societies. With all such structural preconditions met, democratization happened. Put in its most simplified and yet most elegant form, Barrington Moore Jr., in his 1966 class study of the *Social Origins of Dictatorship and Democracy*, famously noted, "[N]o bourgeoisie, no democracy."[3]

Political agents that tried to build the institutions of democracy in barren soil, in societies lacking temperate water and proper nutrients and a moderate climate, all required for a fruitful harvest, of course, failed, from this point of view. Consequently, the modern world was replete with diverse political forms but few democracies. Postcolonial democracies, lacking the needed preconditions, had, of course, to implode in most of the world. Indeed, rapid economic growth, a priority for the poor, seemed to demand authoritarian political mobilization. Virtually all analysts agreed that supposed Chinese developmental success in the Mao era and Indian economic failure in the Nehru era testified to how the democratic project was irrelevant to or even an obstacle to poor people in developing nations gaining the material blessings of modernity.[4]

Of course, not all democracies met the paradigm's claimed preconditions. Consequently, time and again, political scientist Samuel Huntington, a leader in the study of the relation of political system to political development, dismissed democratic India, with its population mainly poor, rural, illiterate, and landless, as doomed. It was assumed that democracy in India could not last. Since Indian democracy thrives, any theory of democracy that cannot encompass the experience of India's 1 billion people should be seen as inadequate. In democracy, numbers count. That 1 billion Indians have long lived in freedom should be central to any theory of democracy.[5]

Anomalies aside, the paradigm of preconditions was assumed to be unassailable, reason incarnate. Given such assumptions about imperative conditions, a central question about Indian democracy was how and when it would fail. The momentary mid-1970s declaration of Emergency Rule by Indian Prime Minister Indira Gandhi was swiftly touted as the essential and eventual truth about an India that lacked the needed economic preconditions.

What India did have was a single dominant party, the Congress with a mass popular base, largely because of Mahatma Gandhi, a party founded in 1885 that was committed to making democracy work, and a Congress Party in power with a policy commitment of positive discriminations that gave the poorest of the poor a stake in democracy's success, such that, surveys show, in India, the poor, far more than the rich, are satisfied with and committed to democracy. Systemic theory did not heed such decisive political particulars and, therefore, was misleading. Institutions, policies, and political commitments were matters of great moment.

Another preconditions approach to democratization slighted economic factors and stressed sociocultural preconditions. This structuralist paradigm assumed that the basis for a democratic breakthrough required proper values that flowed from cultural experiences such as the Protestant religion with its emphasis on tolerance for individual consciences and/or a deep historical relation to a liberal constitutional order such as in Britain. In addition, this shaped political attitudes among the colonized and thereby transferred democracy-friendly ways of life. Seymour Martin Lipset was the most prominent proponent of this Anglo-Protestant political culture approach. If constitutional government in Burma failed by 1962 while neighboring India's democracy grew ever more entrenched, the causal reason for democracy's demise was that Burma had too short a colonial experience with the British.[6] One presumed that colonies that suffered rule by Catholic authoritarianism spreading cultural values exported from Portugal, Spain, and France would not be able to democratize. Costa Rica was just another anomaly.

In this perspective, a British experience could compensate for Indians being mainly Hindu rather than Protestant. Few bothered to inquire why the Dutch in Indonesia, despite their Protestantism, had not bequeathed Indonesians a robust democracy. Or why the Dutch in South Africa were the source of a racist apartheid tyranny. Or why Anglo-Saxon Protestants in America could promote the racist terrorism of the Ku Klux Klan. As is well known, hegemonic ideologies render invisible contradictory data.

The American occupation experience for Japan was, for political culturalists, too short to be more than superficial. In fact, British Japan specialists told American General Douglas MacArthur during the American postwar occupation of Japan that, given Japan's authoritarian Shinto culture, Japan could not be democratized.[7] The famous Canadian Marxist historian of Japan, E. H. Norman, vacillated on whether the Japanese emperor could, if that institution were democratized, serve the cause of democratization. At first, Norman found "that the monarchy would be an unsafe foundation upon which to build a new Japan," since it "played the same role as Fuhrerism in Nazi Germany." But Norman believed that "the Japanese are not yet ready" for "overthrowing the Emperor." This "made the policy of using the Emperor politically practical and hence sensible." Yet Norman insisted that "the Japanese should be encouraged to abolish the Emperor Institution or to reform it along more democratic lines."[8]

As with Spain, constitutional monarchies can facilitate conservative adherence to democracy. Japanese soon thought of the 1931–1945 war as a fifteen-year exception to continuous constitutional progress since the Meiji Era. Culture and history can always be reimagined to serve democratic purposes. The partial democratization of the imperial institution in Japan probably helped institutionalize democracy.

Not seeing culture as ambiguous and contested but treating political culture, rather, as deeply structured and embedded, Samuel Huntington confidently predicted in the mid-1950s that "*samurai*" "*Bushido*" Japan's democracy would fail and that Japan would again soon become a military despotism.[9] No one noticed that social surveys from Japan and Germany showed far more Japanese embracing democracy as the best form of government. The "West" apparently was less democratic than the "East."

Or institutional choice matters. Like Imperial Japan, so, too, Imperial Germany was democratizable. If Imperial "Germany had . . . embarked on a gradual liberalization in 1914 . . . there could have been a transition to democracy unburdened by the humiliation of a lost war and the stab-in-the-back legend and by a ruined economy."[10] As with the similarities of Germany and Japan, in general, knowledge about democratic crafting is constrained by approaches that are merely regional or limited to area studies.

Before the 1990s, alternative institutional choice approaches were hidden by the paradigm of cultural structuralism that did not notice the many anomalies challenging its theory. That democratic France or Belgium was Catholic did not merit serious attention. Given their analytical presuppositions, political scientists, left and right, developed theories of authoritarian modernizers for developing nations, whereas, since the careful work of Adam Przeworski and his colleagues, it is obvious that democracy does not impact economic performance. The allegedly suitable and successful modernizing military regime in Muslim Pakistan was paradigmatic for realists such as Samuel Huntington in 1968 as the democracy in multicultural India (Hindu, Muslims, Sikhs, Jains, Christians) was not. That is, it was claimed by analysts such as Huntington that the supposedly narrow Westernized ruling elite in India had imposed alien political forms that would soon have to be rejected by the Indian body politic.

Perhaps a critical political sociology of our profession is required. Conservative analysts tended to identify with—and accept the antidemocratic categories of—old antidemocratic elites, as with the specialists advising MacArthur in Japan, while Marxist-influenced analysts treated political democracy as almost epiphenomenal, explaining how socioeconomic transformations that ended the exploitation of capitalist imperialism were what mattered. The profession very much mirrored the Cold War. It therefore may not be surprising that the end of the Cold War brought, at long last, a respect for and a profound interest in democratization as such, suddenly treated as the normal way to pursue a less inhuman politics.

In prior approaches to democratization stressing structural preconditions, economic or sociocultural, there was little space for a democratic crafting approach focused on matters such as institutional choice. Deep structure was almost everything. No one asked theoretically interesting questions for democratic theory about Catholic Costa Rica's democracy or Hindu India's democracy, why the post–World War II American occupation was successful in democratizing Nazi Germany, fascist Austria, and Shinto/Buddhist/Confucian militarist Japan, why democracy entrenched itself only in certain former British colonies and not in others. Within the old paradigm of structural preconditions, there were no lessons for democratic crafters other than, perhaps, change your religion, become dependent on America or Britain, develop your economy for some generations, and, meanwhile, be silent or patient.

In retrospect, one might argue that the dominant trend in political science rationalized a Cold War era American preference for anticommunist military dictatorships, with a Marxist minority taking the other side in the Cold War. Policy preference was rationalized as structural inevitability. The alternatives seemed to be South Korea's dictator Park Chung Hee or North Korea's dictator Kim Il Sung, the Republic of China on Taiwan's dictator Chiang Kai-shek versus communist China's dictator Mao Zedong. Realists such as Huntington argued that right authoritarians were needed to take on left authoritarians since democrats were culturally alien to the non-West.

There was little challenge from a perspective of democratic crafting. In Asia, India's democracy was expected to fail, and Japan's democracy was treated as Asian authoritarianism. No one asked why the first and third most populous democracies in the post–World War II era were Hindi and Shinto and not the evolutionary result of a rising urban middle class influenced by Anglo Protestantism.

China can be taken as a case study testing the validity of the structural approach to democratization. Since market-oriented reforms exploded in 1978, China has become the world's most rapidly growing emerging market economy. Its middle class is larger than India's. Some among ruling elites in China argued that the path to stable democratization was through an era of political repression combined with market expansion. "The marketization of the economy would lead to the growth of a middle class, which in turn would foster the growth of democratic governance."[11]

Yet, instead, repression in China intensified in the 1990s, and democracy did not evolve. From Latin America to Asia, business classes have often backed authoritarians.[12] This is because democracy, actually, is not an epiphenomenon of deeper structures, economic or otherwise, but because democracy is a matter of the semiautonomous political realm and therefore can be created only by political struggles and creations in that political arena. The theory of economic structural dynamics as the cause of a democratic breakthrough is not confirmed by the Chinese experience. All that can be affirmed for economic preconditions theory is that in China, household farmers and independent businesses might provide a helpful support base for democratizers should political conflict lead a pro-democracy elite faction to appeal for popular support. In sum, because democracy is the consequence of events in a political realm, there is much to learn from crafters who focus on political institution building.

ELECTION SYSTEMS

The political science literature that first challenged the proponents of structural preconditions and opened the way to a robust study of democratic crafting came from analysts who investigated electoral systems, party systems, and political institutions. In retrospect, this position was, at first, also dominated by critics of American Cold War practices. It is not easy to escape the hegemonic preoccupations of one's era. Infused with a lot of knee-jerk anti-Americanism, the assumption of analysts of electoral and party systems was that democratization in the developing world was possible, but only once one understood that the American system was not a positive model for anything or anyone. It was claimed that to copy America was to guarantee failure for one's nation. If one wanted to understand why the attempts to craft democracy since the early nineteenth century in the independent countries of Latin America had failed, it was not because of Catholicism or from suffering from Iberian colonialism rather than benefiting from a transfer of British attitudes, values, and cultural practices but because of the error of copying the American model of democracy, especially presidentialism. Certain institutional choices were better for democratic success. It just happened that the United States had it all wrong. Whatever the naïveté in a promotion of parliamentarism regardless of prior institutional historical experience, the focus on crafting should be understood as a tremendous achievement, albeit one that should be purged of its parochial prejudices.

These anti-American analysts also argued that first-past-the-post voting, as in America, was destabilizing, while proportional representation brought stability. Similar contrasting results followed from mistakenly implanting a supposedly destabilizing two-party system, as in poor, misled America, rather than an inclusionist multiparty system.[13] For successful democratization, in this anti-American liturgy, one needed a multiparty system, a voting system of proportional representation, and a political system of parliamentarism. Indeed, given the real cancer of racism gnawing at America, a political system as far from America's as possible, that is, consociationalism, was touted as the solution to communalist tensions. Such professional prejudices remain rife among analysts. Much of that work, however, is quite unconvincing when closely and objectively examined.[14]

The first synthesis of the quantitative, large N studies of democratic experience that attempted to transcend the parochial anti-American bias was that of Giovanni Sartori's *Comparative Constitutional Engineering*.[15] He challenged Duverger (as well as New Zealand, Australia, Canada, and Britain itself[16]; India practiced first-past-the-post voting in single-member districts but did not produce a two-party system) and Lijphart ("untenable"; India would have fragmented had it practiced proportional representation [PR]).[17] He pointed to crucial topics that had received insufficient attention, such as the size of voting districts and the drawing of district lines, and to dilemmas of crafting such as party primaries, which, on the one hand, could challenge old oligarchies, yet, on the other hand, strengthened the extremist wings of parties.

Given Sartori's sensitivities to the ambiguities of constitutional engineering, a trait lacking in some of his more fully quantitatively oriented colleagues who went on to do yet more global and systemic work,[18] Sartori called attention to both the importance and difficulty of democratic deepening. Concessions to elites to permit an institutionalization of the original breakthrough to democracy swiftly become sacred traditions blocking a deepening of what is, almost from its compromised origins, a very shallow democracy. "[R]eform is always difficult. Once an electoral arrangement is in place, its beneficiaries protect their vested interests and struggle to go on playing the game by the rules that they know."[19] This limiting institutional reality permits Marxists and other realists to find political democracy to be merely bourgeois dictatorship or only electoral formal democracy. A topic that is relatively unstudied is why popular forces are, nonetheless, often able, as with Solidarity in Poland in 1989 or Marcos' "quickie election" in the Philippines, to turn the actual uncertainty in a political game where numbers are counted in the direction of a deepening of democracy. Single-dimension determinism obscures the dynamics of democratization.

Given greater awareness now of the compromises and shallowness inherent in fledgling democracies, it is surprising that more work is not done on the processes of deepening—ending limitations on the suffrage by wealth, birth, property, gender, literacy, religion, language, and national origin. Deepening is not necessarily easy or peaceful, as the American Civil War and the prolonged struggle to make the ballot universal in Britain both reveal. Making the United States and United Kingdom more a part of the general approach to the problem of deepening is possible once one abandons an approach in which the two countries were contrasting ideal democratic models, one of a presidential and the other of a parliamentary political system.

Taking early democracies as full and consolidated democracies obscures the issue of deepening. There is no comparative work on the late inclusion of first peoples, the indigenes who tend to be peripheralized or exterminated by modernizers. Given the rising at Chiapas and the media attention that it won, this is startling. The pioneers in including indigenous peoples in special ways in the democratic political system were India and Japan, followed by Taiwan and New Zealand. There are compelling struggles and innovations on this issue from

Canada to Finland to Guatemala. For progress in democratic crafting, analysts have to break with the expectation that getting democratization right results from comparing the backward rest to the advanced West, especially to Britain and America.

The profession, for a long time, was locked into outmoded debates, worrying too much over whether presidentialism or parliamentarism works best in so-called Third Wave democracies, not asking how the experiments in all parts of the planet to adapt Germany's electoral system (partial PR) and France's semipresidentalism have worked out. No new nation has recently tried to emulate U.S. presidentialism or U.K. parliamentarism. Comparisons that break outmoded paradigms, such as Yu-shan Wu's comparison of democratization in Taiwan and East Europe,[20] do not receive the attention that they merit. Latin America and Europe are still too often treated as paradigmatic in ways that exclude most of the people who live in democracies, more of whom reside in Asia rather than in any other continent.

COMMUNALISMS

The crafting problem that most rose to consciousness in the 1990s, the issue that most worried Sartori, was communalist divisions and passionately divided societies. Could one have successfully crafted a democracy for Afghanistan in 1989, with all its angry and mistrustful divisions, when the Soviet invaders left? Insufficient attention has been paid to the magisterial work on democratic crafting in divided societies by the pioneering Donald Horowitz, who was virtually alone entering the 1990s in arguing that South Africa could craft the institutions of a fully functioning democracy.

Horowitz has led the way in granting the communalist issue the attention that it merits. Grappling with communalism highlights how difficult it is to define democracy. Specialists contest its meaning because, among other reasons, democracy actually signifies two things. It is both a set of procedures and a project. It is, on the one hand, experientially fair rules that hold rulers publicly accountable and allow for their periodic removal from power and, on the other hand, a project, the political commitment "to the proposition," as President Abraham Lincoln put it, to constitute an ever more perfect republic to make real democracy's promise "that all men are created equal." And yet democratic crafters often cannot succeed unless they treat the differential needs of communities in asymmetric ways, as the experience of India suggests.

The proceduralist meaning of democracy is embodied in Robert Dahl's idea of democracy as a peace pact, a set of institutionalized compromises; in Giuseppi DiPalma's notion of "coexistence in diversity," procedural rules that allow different communities to live in peace; in the popular adage of "majority rule, minority rights," a political system of institutions and rules that feel fair to losers as well as winners; and in street philosopher Rodney King's plaint, "Can't we all get along?"

Research agendas follow from an appreciation of the proceduralist dimension of democracy. Are the rules fair if military and security forces can intimidate voters and elected officials? If not, how are the forces of coercion to be kept under civilian democratic control? A disdain among academics for police state torturers has made this crucial item of the security forces a lower priority of research than it should be. Addressing that issue is the best part of realist Samuel Huntington's *The Third Wave*.[21]

Most analysts by now are supremely conscious of the centrality of communalist division to a proper crafting of stable democratic institutions. But there, too, often remains a preconception that these difficulties are not serious problems in "the West," only "the rest." A moment's contemplation of the multicentury violent struggle of the British against the Irish and of the horrors of America's Civil War and its inhuman racist prologue and century-long repressive aftermath should discredit that euphoric and misleading binary. More work is needed to integrate the experience of places like Switzerland, where, in the nineteenth century, there were religious massacres and bloody violence over issues of regional representation. Anxiety, mistrust, and cries for vengeance or justice among such groups may make democratic crafting a far more iffy project everywhere than those seeking magic silver bullet formulas might prefer. Howard Brown's chapter in this book on terror and vengeance is illuminating in this regard.

Communalist splits are invitations to demagogic antidemocratic mobilization. Even the most brilliant minds working to craft Fiji's democratic constitution could not easily succeed. Why?[22]

Perhaps specialists in constitutional engineering must respectfully revisit the literature on preconditions of democracy. What is striking is not that there are socioeconomic or cultural preconditions to democracy but that the divisions among groups fostered by prior events become obstacles to democracy when old elites or groups tied to them prefer violence in defense of authoritarianism to accepting fair procedural rules in a democracy. It may be that nothing short of prolonged hellish experiences can inoculate such people against the deadly virus of preferring power through repression over democratic proceduralism.

Democracy becomes possible, Robert Dahl argued, when the costs of further repression seem higher to those in power than do the costs of conciliation. That is, there is a strict limit to what crafters can achieve until a significant set of the dominant political actors can find a reason to see democratic accommodation as a superior path. Communalist divisions, reflected in dehumanizing ideologies and attached to organs of coercion, cannot readily be wished—or crafted—out of existence.

This principle holds from Fiji at the end of the twentieth century to the United States at the middle of the nineteenth century. The Republic of China on Taiwan, usually treated as a Spain-like successful peaceful consolidation of democratization, is worth contemplating. After all, many believe that without the king's intervention to hold the loyalty of conservatives, a military coup in Spain was quite possible.

Taiwan lacks a monarch to hold anxious conservatives to democratic outcomes. On Taiwan, the army and security forces were, since 1945, the coercive arms of an ethnic minority, Nationalist Party mainlanders, in a fascistlike regime. While the democratic breakthrough of 1988 has supposedly broken the Nationalist Party's bond with the army and led soldiers to be loyal, instead, to the government won in 1999 by a party of nonmainlander challengers to the previous ruling party, the Nationalists, analysts in the People's Republic of China (PRC) believed that a mainlander coup was quite possible to prevent permanent subordination of mainland exiles (13 percent of the population) to a detested and previously subordinated majority of islanders. Many Taiwanese, likewise, fear that the senior officer corps descended from mainland families might not vigorously defend Taiwan against mainland Chinese (PRC) attack.

Taiwan has done virtually nothing, compared to South Africa, to accommodate the anxieties of the old communalist elite. Hopefully nothing ill will occur in the short run, and, over a long term, Taiwanese mainlanders will lose their anxieties and accommodate the new reality. That may, however, depend on international factors beyond the control of crafters. Crafting has limits.

This unsettled case highlights the importance of time and timing, conjunctural and contingent matters, and crucial forces that cannot be subsumed in general and systemic theory. But the crucial contribution of analysts is to clarify the impact of systemic matters of constitutional engineering. Studies of elections show that when the president and parliament are elected at the same time, then, more than 90 percent of the time, the same party wins both. This enhances governmental effectiveness. This has implications for Taiwan.

Taiwan elects its president and members of the legislature in different years. This has facilitated divided governments in a political system of semipresidentialism similar to that of France. Critics would say that this produces inefficiency. A stalemate between the two branches of government, president and parliament, made it difficult for the government to respond to a deep economic crisis in 2001. In general, the globalized new economy with 24/7 instantaneous finance greatly increases the price of procrastination (e.g., Argentina in 2001–2002), thereby putting a premium on efficiency. Consequently, Taiwan should change its election timing.

Or should it? Isn't success in the art of communalist conciliation more important than political effectiveness? Given the ethnic divide involving a long and deeply held demeaning racist attitude of mainlanders toward Taiwanese and given the historic mainlander control of the organs of culture and coercion, is efficiency—whose weight is enhanced by the globalized new economy—more important than reducing ethnic mistrust and precluding the mainlander-dominated military from turning against the fledgling democracy? It may well be that the imperative of conciliation almost always trumps the logic of efficiency or justice. If that is the case, then the globalized new economy works against successful democratization.

This is a political judgment call: something to be decided only by politicians with their fingers on the irregular pulse beat of the people, something far beyond the competence of outside analysts no matter how well trained or how profoundly knowledgeable. In short, analysts of democratic crafting should approach their topic with great humility and self-restraint, cognizant of the limited value of general theory.

TOWARD NEW AGENDAS

Only after the fact could Japan specialist E. H. Norman see that in Japan as, indeed, one should find in all cultures, people could discover and draw on "the warm and generous traditions in their history."[23] So, too, can Afghans or Iranians or any people. Democratization is premised in a faith in democracy, the power of a liberated people to reimagine their nation and to make institutions work in new ways, as Brazil began to do in the 1990s, so as to avoid the deadly plague of ancient tyrannical evils.

The big question is: Why do losers, either prior elites or challengers who never win, accept defeat, especially when the division between ins and outs has an emotive content from things such as region and religion and culture and speech? It is important, as Kristi Andersen does in this volume, to address this question first to supposedly stable democracies; otherwise, new democracies will be perceived myopically as exotics. Why did the ethnically, lingually, and religiously distinct people of Scotland accept English rulers for so long, especially since there was no important federalist decentralization in Great Britain? Did it matter that, first, Scot Presbyterians were guaranteed their religion as an established religion? Did it matter that merit mattered in education, civil service exams, and business and that government did not intervene in culturally sensitive realms? That is, does it turn out, when one looks at the United Kingdom from the perspective that one has learned from studying new democracies outside of Western Europe, that the relative success of the British system has precious little to do with conventional notions about Parliament or Anglo-Saxon culture or Protestant consciences? Crafting on religion for the people of Scotland and for Muslims in India may have similarities hidden by conventional historicist and area studies preconceptions.

One thing for sure has been learned: democratization is not a matter of a zeitgeist or a Third Wave but is a very difficult matter of institution building.[24] The purpose of learning the art of crafting is to make it no more difficult than it has to be. That would be a great achievement.

This means that analysts must be self-critical of the biases of their systemic work. Comparison is iffy. The moment of democratization matters. Democracies crafted before World War I tended to exclude the working poor from the suffrage, facilitating the rise of a Labor or Socialist Party, the instrument of democratic empowerment for working people. But democracies set up after World War II began with universal suffrage, making it difficult for a labor party to rise, facilitating a very different logic of interparty conflict. Given the centrality of party and party system to a democratic politics, this conjunctural factor complicates a comparative politics of democratization.

Likewise, in the post–Bretton Woods era of a new kind of globalization where people can best move up economically by moving to a richer country, immigration, aliens, guest workers, and openness to citizenship are more important issues in the national political debate touching on matters of national identity and citizen loyalty.[25] Consequently, there is a strict limit to what can be generalized from one era and party system to another. Systemic theorizing carried too far is counterproductive. Or, as Sartori had it, "There is no getting away from context."[26]

This has been obvious to practitioners who do not pay much heed to the work of systemic political science. Practitioners know how much democratic crafting is an art, not a mechanical matter of plugging in the formulas of constitutional engineering. Systemic political science should not treat the little that it contributes as everything. Much is a matter of path dependency (e.g., given how much authoritarians manipulated the decision for chief executive in the Republic of Korea when it was a military dictatorship, South Koreans generally felt that democratization required the election of a president in a single ballot with no complicating interference, resulting in French-type semipresidentialism), of timing conjunctures, of international contingencies, and of judgment calls on trade-offs. How much does one concede to reconciling elite forces to the new democracy? How much does one sacrifice justice in the higher interest of reconciliation?

Had the Indian Congress Party at the outset promoted land reform in the interest of equity, would it have alienated rural elites, split the Congress Party, and thereby destabilized India's democracy as right-wing forces were strengthened? If the Congress Party had not held on to power for decades as a dominant single party winning Muslim support because of constitutional concessions on Muslim private law, could India have promoted the positive discriminations to peripheralized castes that have deepened India's democracy and held the allegiance of the poor? If Indian crafters had listened to those who insisted that constitutions should be difficult to amend so that minorities, as in South Africa subsequently, can be assured that their rights will be protected, would India have split from the pressure of linguistic regional groups for their own state, a pressure that turned out to be easy to accommodate given the simplicity of amending India's constitution?

No crafting theory suggested that India should guarantee the Muslims their own religious courts in private matters. Yet a study of Scotland in Great Britain might have yielded such an insight. To understand Indian success as paradigmatic, one must accept that general theory cannot be allowed to override the art of politics, which gets what is possible now and does not attempt to craft the true and just democracy. Fledgling democracies are almost inescapably shallow. That makes the issue of the deepening of democracy far more crucial than the present scholarly literature warrants. Is a systemic theory of deepening possible?

Systemic theory, generalizing from the set of cases available throughout history, is what academic analysts have to offer. This contribution is crucial. It can save crafters from error, open them to new and better possibilities, and leave more margin for error in other realms. This matters. But systemic theory can and must be enriched.

This requires that analysts tackle taboo topics such as religion[27] and learn from experiences such as India's. Religion is always and everywhere a potential threat to democracy because whatever religion asserts about all humans as God's creatures, in fact, a religion invariably contends that its people are specially blessed and that some ultimate ends of life are sacred givens and not matters for debate and voting. Indigenous people were exterminated in the Americas, among other reasons, because Christians insisted on the godly way as the only life worth living. That is, religion has tendencies that can implode the notion that all are substantively equal and also procedurally free to choose their own dignity. It is a threat to both aspects of democracy.

It is worth returning to the experience of Holland and England to learn how long and slowly it took religious toleration and universal human rights to evolve in those Protestant nations. In short, the most dangerous hubris of political scientists studying the democratic experiences of the diverse nations of the world is not too much faith in political science but too little knowledge of the "West's" actual history, an ignorance that produces misleading assessments of the valuable experiences of the variety of democracies throughout the world, the almost 2 billion people, say, of India, Japan, Brazil, South Africa, Indonesia, and Nigeria. This reality should be mined for its positive lessons.

Is there new knowledge on how to contain military and other security forces? How important is it that constitutions be legitimated by national referenda? With supermajoritarianism? Preceded by national conferences? What, besides the wisdom of holding national elections before local elections, do we know about organizing first elections? Specialists have so much to learn from a conversation with each other.

After one acknowledges the wisdom in so much of South Africa's crafting, with South Africa representative of places where communalist divisions and wealth inequalities supposedly made democracy impossible, how much credit goes to systemic factors such as the crafting of a federalist polity that institutionalized language and educational diversity with local communalist self-determination, and how much credit goes, rather, to the extraordinary leadership of Nelson Mandela or to the path-dependent causes of compromise following from a long, monstrous, and unwinnable civil war or to the conjuncture of crafting occurring after the Soviet system had imploded and lost its attraction?

And yet democracy in South Africa could erode. Despite policies to woo foreign direct investment, little has come. There has instead been much capital flight. Racist fears and fantasies of the rich, despite an independent judiciary, balanced budget, and low inflation, strengthen the voice of those crying out for a seizure and redistribution of ill-gotten gains. There is much that national crafting cannot control, including the explosion of wealth among the richest, concomitant to the post–Bretton Woods era of globalization, money that can be spent significantly and disproportionately to impact electoral knowledge and voter choice not in the interest of the poor majority.

If the premodern political philosophy that concluded that republics succeed in small polities has some validity, as suggested by how many small islands in the Pacific and Caribbean are democratic, then the issue of federalism may deserve far more weight than it has hitherto received. A lack of federalism and a commitment to concentrated central power may then be seen as a source of Irish-English communalist tensions over the centuries and of the difficulties in institutionalizing democracy in France. A prerequisite of paradigmatic breakthroughs in knowledge may yet follow from the implosion of the conventional wisdom about a supposedly known and exemplary "West."

It should be obvious by now that the crucial decisions for crafters are not between presidentialism and parliamentarism, not between a two-party system and a multiparty system, and not between first-past-the-post voting and proportional representation. The field of democratic crafting, like this volume, is now mining a much richer vein of political ore. Even if knowledge about democratic crafting is a bit more like gambling than a controlled natural science laboratory experiment, it is vital that the crafters' odds be increased by making available all the best knowledge on democratic crafting. At the Machiavellian moment when people are crafting a democratic polity, ending authoritarianism and civil war, they should be able to know how to enhance trust among contending parties (release political prisoners? allow political organizing? reform the security forces? dismantle the national police? get the military out of domestic intelligence? make police forces locally based?). But what if these institutions and their constituent interests resist? There is a limit to what crafting can achieve.

Given the knowledge explosion and its commercially driven distortions (publishers do not readily welcome work on India or Africa), the importance of gatekeepers heightens. Journal editors, program coordinators at annual meetings, foundation funders, and directors of relevant centers should help synthesize knowledge and focus important debates. How does the profession foster a conversation among those working on communalisms, on religion, on gender, and on indigenous peoples? How does one factor in the inordinate impact of the ever-changing global moment in international politics and international political economy?

While today's new globalization enhances the weight of the international factor, it has long been obvious that international forces impact domestic democratic possibilities. Plato's dialogues on Socrates' death long ago highlighted how much international tensions can foster local chauvinism that subverts the toleration required by democracy.

South Africa's democratic transition was eased by the failure of Leninist socialism, the implosion of the Soviet Union, China's market-opening, and so on. The antimarket left, which once denounced political democracy as the class dictatorship of the bourgeoisie, no longer had credible policies to grow the economy. Had Fidel Castro come to power in 1989 rather than 1959, Cuban governance would most likely have taken a very different course, one friendlier to openness and democracy. Timing conjunctures are weighty.

Yet, globalization has also unleashed profoundly undemocratic forces. Intolerant religious revivalisms and purifying nativisms pervade the planet in an age when people feel increasingly threatened by seemingly incomprehensible, all-powerful alien forces. While this suggests that international peace, growth, and international financial stability offer an architectural foundation for successful democratization, there is no escape from the priority of domestic issues. What makes all key groups in a nation believe that the democratic rules of the game are fair and can work for them?

Despite profound consciousness of the dangers inherent in sensitive societal divisions, there is precious little analysis of the key crafting issues in grappling with poisonously divided societies. Donald Horowitz, the leading student of this topic, has grown pessimistic about how much crafters can achieve.[28] Clues perhaps can be found in the magnificent collection of papers edited by Jorgen Elklit and published by the Ministry of Foreign Affairs in Copenhagen. The following are some quotes from that international work sponsored by the government of Denmark.

Care needs to be taken not to introduce too many changes into electoral systems during the early years . . . which . . . increases the importance of the initial decisions.[29]

One key initial decision is the rule to change the rules. There is a wide gap between the United States, where amending the Constitution is almost impossible, and India, where it is so easy that many hundreds of amendments have passed, including a changing of provincial boundaries to accommodate language communalisms. Is there a rule to decide which rule to choose? How decisive are particulars that do not necessarily logically follow from a general finding? Sartori touts the double ballot as democratizing, but that technique is the tool of white racists in primaries in the American South. Politics is an art. The weight of the local is heavy. Systemic comparative politics is limited by the power of ever-changing particulars. Still, even particulars can be stated in a general form.

. . . those in power may fear that proportional representation might make it more difficult to create stable government.

. . . A parliament which has minimal representation of large minorities in society ridicules and marginalizes those groups.

. . . electoral geography is crucial with regard to the extent to which a first-past-the-post system distorts representation. It is extremely important how the constituencies are actually delineated; it is here, however, that the ability to manage the transitional process of those in power is located.

. . . The introduction of a federal system . . . can ease tension and resolve the political impasse.[30]

In other words, it matters very much how power is centralized or decentralized, where boundaries are drawn, how much representation is given to each unit, and how all of this relates to the variously politically marked communalist identities that seek a share of power and that fear vulnerability from a lack of any power as they see who controls the security forces. The consensus of students of constitutional engineering is that we know how to craft, to achieve sufficient stability and representativeness, and to accommodate all communities with democratic rules. The recent failure of the constitutional arrangement in Fiji, crafted by the world's most brilliant students of the topic, however, suggests a sobering limitation to what mechanical engineers can achieve. Democracy is an art. Science has its limits.

The supposedly old-fashioned structuralists based their analyses on an indubitable truth that analysts of institution-crafting forget at their peril. If elites with control of wealth, prestige, and force do not like the outcomes of democracy, they may have the capacity to end democratic rule. How to deepen democracy and not threaten democracy, given the intractable realities of power, remains as challenging as ever. This dilemma can be put in the words of George Bush the elder's famously ineloquent vice president, Dan Quayle. He noted on May 22, 1989, "We are on an irreversible trend toward more . . . democracy—but that could change."

NOTES

1. The editors of the *Journal of Democracy* and *Democratization*, Marc Plattner and Larry Diamond, have played major roles in this synthetic effort. Peter Burnell, ed., *Democracy Assistance* (London: Frank Cass, 2000) brings together work about diverse governments in promoting democracy.

2. When a major work, such as Juan Linz and Alfred Stepan, *Problems of Democratic: Southern Europe, South America; and Post-Communist Europe Transition and Consolidation* (Baltimore: Johns Hopkins University Press, 1996), is published, other specialists should be invited for symposia to discuss the contribution and its problems. The members of the subdiscipline should engage the work of their colleagues far more than is now the case. I thought the best part of the book was its insights on sequencing.

3. For an analysis of what Moore actually meant by this phrase, which was not that a rising bourgeoisie guaranteed successful democratization, see Edward Friedman, "Development, Revolution, Democracy and Dictatorship," in *Democracy, Revolution and History*, ed. Theda Skocpol (Ithaca, NY: Cornell University Press, 1998), 102–123.

4. Literatures spread on topics from military modernizers and developmental dictators to the Soviet model and Asian authoritarianism. The military tyranny of Pakistan was Samuel Huntington's model in his classic *Political Order in Changing Societies* (New Haven, CT: Yale University Press, 1968).

5. The literature on Indian democracy is voluminous. One recent effort that engages the general theoretical literature is Maya Chadda, *Building Democracy in South Asia* (Boulder, CO: Lynne Rienner, 2000).

6. Daniel Chirot, *Modern Tyrannies* (Princeton, NJ: Princeton University Press, 1994), 322.

7. John Dower, *Embracing Defeat* (New York: Norton, 1999), 217–224.

8. John Price, "E. H. Norman, Canada and Japan's Postwar Constitution," *Pacific Affairs* 74, no. 3 (2001): 387, 388, 391, 394, 398.

9. Samuel P. Huntington, "Japan: The Continuity of Political Militarism," in *The Soldier and the State* (Cambridge, MA: Harvard University Press, 1957), 124–139. This error alone should discredit the political culture approach to democracy.

10. Sheri Berman, "Modernization in Historical Perspective," *World Politics* J3 (April 2001): 462. An alternative hypothesis on a successful early German democratization is Niall Ferguson, *The Pity of War* (New York: Basic Books, 1999).

11. Joseph Fewsmith, *China since Tiananmen* (New York: Cambridge University Press, 2001), 86.

12. David Martin Jones, "Democratization, Civil Society and Illiberal Middle Class Culture in Pacific Asia," *Comparative Politics* 30, no. 2 (1998): 147–170.

13. Donald Horowitz's critique of the purported data supporting the antipresidential bias is persuasive. Cf. Horowitz, "Comparing Democratic Systems," in *The Global Resurgence of Democracy*, ed. Larry Diamond and Marc Plattner (Baltimore: Johns Hopkins University Press, 1996), 143–149.

14. For thorough and persuasive critiques of Lijphart's promotion of consociationalism, see Liam Anderson, "The Implications of Institutional Design for Macroeconomic Performance: Reassessing the Claims of Consensus Democracy," *Comparative Political Studies* 34, no. 4 (May 2001): 429–452; Ian Lustick, "Lijphart, Lakatos and Consociationalism," *World Politics* 50 (October 1997): 88–117.

15. Giovanni Sartori, *Comparative Constitutional Engineering*, 2nd ed. (New York: New York University Press, 1997).

16. Ibid., 38.

17. Ibid., 56.

18. Gary Cox, *Making Votes Count* (New York: Cambridge University Press, 1997).

19. Sartori, *Comparative Constitutional Engineering*, 28.

20. Wu Yu-Shan, "Comparing Third-Wave Democracies," *Issues and Studies* 37, no. 4 (Taipei, Taiwan) (July/August 2001): 1–37.

21. Samuel P. Huntington, *The Third Wave* (Norman: University of Oklahoma Press, 1991), chapter 5 sections, "The Torturer Problem" and "The Praetorian Problem."

22. Brij V. Lal, *Fiji before the Storm* (Canberra: Asia Pacific Press, 2000); John Kelly and Martha Kaplan, *Represented Communities: Fiji and World Decolonization* (Chicago: University of Chicago Press, 2000).

23. Cited in Price, "E. H. Norman," 405.

24. Because surveys offer quantitative data, and numbers make research results seem objective or scientific, the significance of attitudes to successful democratization is probably overestimated. Opinion can be volatile, especially in times of war and economic

crises. Hence, high evaluations of democracy at moment 1 are no guarantor of similar opinion at moment 2. What is worthy of study is democratic continuity despite hard times and despite popular attitudes that devalue the worth of democracy.

25. Bonnie Honig, *Democracy and the Foreigner* (Princeton, NJ: Princeton University Press, 2001).

26. Sartori, *Comparative Constitutional Engineering*, 135.

27. Nancy Rosenblum, ed., *Obligations of Citizenship and Demands of Faith* (Princeton, NJ: Princeton University Press, 2000); Jeff Spinner-Haley, *Surviving Diversity* (Baltimore: Johns Hopkins University Press, 2000).

28. In Ian Shapiro and Stephen Macedo, eds., *Nomos XLII: Designing Democratic Institutions* (New York: New York University Press, 2000).

29. Jørgen Elklit, *Electoral Systems for Emerging Democracies: Experiences and Suggestions* (Copenhagen: Danida, 1997), 10.

30. Ibid., 11, 138.

Bibliography

Adams, Roy J. "Regulating Unions and Collective Bargaining: A Global, Historical Analysis of Determinants and Consequences." *Comparative Labor Law Journal* 14 (1993): 272–301.

Ake, Claude. "Globalization, Multilateralism and the Shrinking Democratic Space." Unpublished manuscript, James Madison College, Michigan State University, 1996.

Allison, Graham T. *Essence of Decision: Explaining the Cuban Missile Crisis.* Boston: Little, Brown, 1971.

Allswang, John M. *A House for All Peoples: Ethnic Politics in Chicago, 1890–1936.* Lexington: University Press of Kentucky, 1971.

Anderson, Liam. "The Implications of Institutional Design for Macroeconomic Performance: Reassessing the Claims of Consensus Democracy." *Comparative Political Studies* 34, no. 4 (May 2001): 429–452.

Anderson, Sarah and John Cavanagh with Thea Lee. *Field Guide to the Global Economy.* New York: New Press, 2000.

Anstee, Margaret Joan. *Orphan of the Cold War: The Inside Story of the Collapse of the Angolan Peace Process, 1992–1993.* New York: St. Martin's Press, 1996.

Aron, Janine. "The Institutional Foundations of Growth." In *Africa Now: People, Policies and Institutions,* ed. Stephen Ellis. London: James Currey, 1995.

Associates in Rural Development (ARD). *Governance and Local Democracy (GOLD) Sites Indicator Results: Final Report 1995, 1996, 1997, 1998, 1999, 2000.* Manila: ARD, 2000.

———. *Governance in Mali: An Assessment of Transition and Consolidation and Guidelines for Near-Term Action.* Burlington, VT: ARD, 1994.

Austin, Dennis. *Democracy and Violence in India and Sri Lanka.* New York: Council on Foreign Relations Press, 1995.

Awonusi, V. O. "Regional Accents and Internal Variability in Nigerian English: A Historical Analysis." *English Studies* 67 (December 1986): 555–560.

Baczko, Bronislaw. *Comment sortir de la Terreur. Thermidor et la Révolution*. Paris: Gallimard, 1989.

Bamgbose, Ayo. "Post-Imperial English in Nigeria, 1940–1990." In *Post-Imperial English: Status Change in Former British and American Colonies, 1940–1990*, ed. Joshua A. Fishman, Andrew Conrad, and Alma Rubal-Lopez. Berlin and New York: Mouton de Gruyter, 1996.

Barber, Benjamin R. *Jihad v. McWorld: How Globalism and Tribalism Are Reshaping the World*. New York: Ballantine Books, 1996.

Bardhan, Pranab. "Method in the Madness? A Political-Economy Analysis of Ethnic Conflicts in Less Developed Countries." *World Development* 25, no. 9 (September 1997): 1381–1398.

Barkan, Joel. "Rethinking the Applicability of Proportional Representation for Africa." In *Elections and Conflict Management in Africa*, ed. Timothy D. Sisk and Andrew Reynolds. Washington, DC: U.S. Institute of Peace, 1998.

Barretto, Amilcar A. *Language, Elites, and the State: Nationalism in Puerto Rico and Quebec*. Westport, CT: Praeger, 1998.

Bayart, Jean-Francois. "Civil Society in Africa." In *Political Domination in Africa: Reflections on the Limits of Power*, ed. Patrick Chabal. Cambridge: Cambridge University Press, 1986.

Berger, Suzanne and Ronald Dore, eds. *National Diversity and Global Capitalism*. Ithaca, NY: Cornell University Press, 1996.

Berman, Sheri. "Modernization in Historical Perspective." *World Politics* J3 (April 2001): 462.

Berry, Jeffrey M. and Deborah Schildkraut. "Citizen Groups, Political Parties, and Electoral Coalitions." In *Social Movements and American Political Institutions*, ed. Anne N. Costain and Andrew S. McFarland. Lanham, MD: Rowman and Littlefield, 1998.

Blair, Harry W. "Research and Practice in Democratization: Cross-Fertilization or Cross Purposes?" Paper presented at the "Conference on Democratic Performance," Center on Democratic Performance, State University of New York at Binghamton, 7–9 June 2001.

———. "Institutional Pluralism in Public Administration and Politics: Applications in Bolivia and Beyond." *Public Administration and Development* 21, no. 2 (May 2001): 119–129.

———. *Civil Society Strategy Assessment for Bolivia and El Salvador*. Washington, DC: USAID, Democracy and Governance Center, 16 February 2001.

———. "USAID and Democratic Decentralization: Taking the Measure of an Assistance Program." In *Democracy Assistance: International Co-operation for Democratization*, ed. Peter Burnell. London: Frank Cass, 2000.

———. "Intermediate Result Reporting as a Management Tool: Promise and Limitations in the DG Sector." Unpublished report. Washington, DC: U.S. Agency for International Development, DG Center, 30 August 1999.

Bojičić, Vesna and Mary Kaldor. "The 'Abnormal' Economy of Bosnia-Herzegovina." In *Scramble for the Balkans: Nationalism, Globalism, and the Political Economy of Reconstruction*, ed. Carl-Ulrik Schierup. New York: St. Martin's Press in association with the Centre for Research in Ethnic Relations, University of Warwick, 1999.

Borneman, John. *Settling Accounts: Violence, Justice, and Accountability in Postsocialist States.* Princeton, NJ: Princeton University Press, 1997.

Bostwick, Kate M. "Women's Political Clubs." *Monthly Illustrator* 13 (1913): 304–308.

Bourdin, Philippe. "Les 'Jacobins' du Bois de Cros (Clermont-Ferrand, an V): Chronique d'un massacre annoncé." *Annales historiques de la Révolution française* (1997): 249–304.

Boyce, James K. and Manuel Pastor Jr. "Aid for Peace: Can International Financial Institutions Help Prevent Conflict?" *World Policy Journal* 15 (1998): 42–50.

Bradbury, Jonathan and James Mitchell. "Devolution: New Politics for Old?" *Parliamentary Affairs* (April 2001): 257–275.

Brady, Henry E., Kay Lehman Schlozman, and Sidney Verba. "Prospecting for Participants: Rational Expectations and the Recruitment of Political Activists." *American Political Science Review* 93, no. 1 (1999): 153–168.

Bratton, Michael. "Academic Analysis and U.S. Economic Assistance Policy on Africa." *Issue: A Journal of Opinion* 19, no. 1 (Winter 1990): 21–37.

Bratton, Michael and Robert Mattes. "Support for Democracy in Africa: Intrinsic or Instrumental?" *British Journal of Political Science* 31 (July 2001): 447–474.

Bratton, Michael and Nicolas van de Walle. *Democratic Experiments in Africa: Regime Transitions in Comparative Perspective.* New York: Cambridge University Press, 1997.

Bräutigam, Deborah. "Institutions, Economic Reform, and Democratic Consolidation in Mauritius." *Comparative Politics* 30, no. 1 (October 1997): 45–62.

Brown, Howard G. "Domestic State Violence: Repression from the Croquants to the Commune." *The Historical Journal* 42 (1999): 597–622.

———. "From Organic Society to Security State: The War on Brigandage in France, 1797–1802." *Journal of Modern History* 69 (1997): 661–695.

Brysk, Alison. "Globalization and Human Rights: Transnational Threats and Opportunities." Paper presented at the conference "Transnationalism," UCLA, 5–8 May 1999.

Buchez, Philippe-Joseph-Benjamin and Prosper-Charles Roux. *Histoire parlementaire de la Révolution française.* Paris: Paulin, 1838.

Burgerman, S. D. "Mobilizing Principles: The Role of Transnational Activists in Promoting Human Rights Principles." *Human Rights Quarterly* 20, no. 4 (November 1998): 905–923.

Burkhart, Richard. "The Capitalist Political Economy and Human Rights: Cross-National Evidence." Paper presented at the "Hinman Symposium on Democratization and Human Rights," Binghamton University, State University of New York, 1998.

Burnell, Peter, ed. *Democracy Assistance.* London: Frank Cass, 2000.

Burnell, Peter and Peter Calvert, eds. *The Resilience of Democracy.* Portland, OR: Frank Cass, 1999.

Burstein, Paul. "Interest Organizations, Political Parties, and the Study of Democratic Politics." In *Social Movements and American Political Institutions*, ed. Anne N. Costain and Andrew S. McFarland. Lanham, MD: Rowman and Littlefield, 1998.

Byington, Kaa. *Bantay ng Bayan: Stories from the NAMFREL Crusade, 1984–1986.* Manila: Bookmark, 1988.

Cable, Vincent. "The Diminished Nation-State: A Study in the Loss of Economic Power." *Deadalus* 124, no. 2 (Spring 1995): 55–74.

Caplan, Nathan, Andrea Morrison, and Russell J. Stambaugh. *The Use of Social Science*

Knowledge in Policy Decisions at the National Level. Ann Arbor: University of Michigan Press, 1975.

Carleton, David. "The New International Division of Labor, Export-Oriented Growth and State Repression in Latin America." In *Dependence, Development, and State Repression*, ed. George Lopez and Michael Stohl. Westport, CT: Greenwood, 1989.

Carleton, David and Michael Stohl. "The Role of Human Rights in U.S. Foreign Assistance Policy." *American Journal of Political Science* 31, no. 2 (1987): 1002–1018.

Carothers, Thomas. *Aiding Democracy Abroad: The Learning Curve.* Washington, DC: Carnegie Endowment for International Peace, 1999.

———. *The Clinton Record on Democracy Promotion, Working Paper No. 16.* Washington, DC: Carnegie Endowment for International Peace, September 2000.

Carter, Lynn. *On the Crest of the Third Wave: Linking USAID Democracy Program Impact to Political Change; A Synthesis of Findings from Three Case Studies: Bolivia, Bulgaria and South Africa.* Washington, DC: Management Systems International, for U.S. Agency for International Development, Office of Democracy and Governance, October 2001.

Castan, Yves. *Honnêteté et relations sociales en Languedoc, 1715–1780.* Paris: Plon, 1974.

Chadda, Maya. *Building Democracy in South Asia.* Boulder, CO: Lynne Rienner, 2000.

Charlick, Robert. *Improving Democratic Governance for Sustainable Development: An Assessment of Change and Continuity in Niger.* Burlington, VT: Associates in Rural Development, 1994.

Chhibber, Ajay. "The State in a Changing World." *Finance & Development* 34, no. 3 (1997): 17–20.

Chirot, Daniel. *Modern Tyrannies.* Princeton, NJ: Princeton University Press, 1994.

Church, Clive. "Switzerland: A Paradigm in Evolution." *Parliamentary Affairs* 53, no. 1 (January 2000): 96–113.

Cingranelli, David L. and Thomas Pasquerello. "Human Rights Practices and the U.S. Distribution of Foreign Aid to Latin American Countries." *American Journal of Political Science* 29 (1985): 539–563.

Cingranelli, David L. and David L. Richards. "Measuring the Level, Pattern, and Sequence of Government Respect for Physical Integrity Rights." *International Studies Quarterly* 43 (1999): 407–417.

———. "Respect for Human Rights after the End of the Cold War." *Journal of Peace Research* 36, no. 5 (1999): 511–534.

Clapham, Christopher. "Rwanda: The Perils of Peacemaking." *Journal of Peace Research* 35, no. 2 (1998): 195.

Clark, Elizabeth Spiro. "Why Elections Matter." *The Washington Quarterly* (Summer 2000): 27–40.

Clemens, Elisabeth S. "Organizational Repertoires and Institutional Change: Women's Groups and the Transformation of American Politics, 1890–1920." In *Civic Engagement in American Democracy*, ed. Theda Skocpol and Morris P. Fiorina. Washington, DC: Brookings Institution, 1999.

Cobb, Richard. *Les armées révolutionnaires.* Paris: Mouton et Co., 1962.

———. "Note sur la répression contre le personnel sans-culotte de 1795 à 1801." In *Terreur et subsistances (1793–1795).* Paris: Librairie Clavreuil, 1964.

————. *The Police and the People: French Popular Protest, 1789–1820*. Oxford: Oxford University Press, 1970.

————. *Reactions to the French Revolution*. London and New York: Oxford University Press, 1972.

Coffey, Thomas M. *The Long Thirst: Prohibition in America 1920–1933*. New York: W. W. Norton, 1975.

Cohen, Benjamin. "Phoenix Risen: The Resurrection of Global Finance." *World Politics* 48, no. 2 (January 1996): 268–296.

Cohen, Lizabeth. *Making a New Deal: Industrial Workers in Chicago, 1919–1939*. Cambridge: Cambridge University Press, 1990.

Cohen, Michael D., James G. March, and Johan P. Olsen. "A Garbage Can Model of Organizational Choice." *Administrative Science Quarterly* 17 (1972): 1–25.

Colletta, Nat J., Markus Kostner, and Ingo Wiederhofer. "Disarmament, Demobilization, and the Social and Economic Reintegration of Ex-Combatants: Lessons and Liabilities in State Transition." Paper presented at the "Conference on Reinvigorating and Resuscitating Weak, Vulnerable, and Collapsing States," World Peace Foundation, Cambridge, MA, June 2001.

Collier, David and Steven Levitsky. "Democracy with Adjectives: Conceptual Innovation in Comparative Research." *World Politics* 49 (April): 430–451.

Comaroff, John L. and Jean Comaroff, eds. *Civil Society and the Political Imagination in Africa*. Chicago: University of Chicago Press, 1999.

Cornell, Svante E. "Democratization Falters in Azerbaijan." *Journal of Democracy* 12, no. 2 (April 2001): 118–131.

Cotter, Cornelius P. et al. *Party Organizations and American Politics*. New York: Praeger, 1984.

Cox, Gary. *Making Votes Count*. New York: Cambridge University Press, 1997.

Crowder, Michael. "Lugard and Colonial Nigeria: Towards an Identity." *History Today* 36 (February 1986): 23–29.

Dadmehr, Nasrin. "Tajikistan: A Vulnerable State in a Post-War Society." Paper presented at the "Conference on Reinvigorating and Resuscitating Weak, Vulnerable, and Collapsing States," World Peace Foundation, Cambridge, MA, June 2001.

Dahl, Robert A. *On Democracy*. New Haven, CT: Yale Nota Bene Books, 2000.

————. *Polyarchy: Participation and Opposition*. New Haven, CT: Yale University Press, 1971.

Dalton, Russell J. "Political Support in Advanced Industrial Democracies." In *Critical Citizens: Global Support for Democratic Governance*, ed. Pippa Norris. Oxford: Oxford University Press, 1999.

Davenport, Christian and Kathy Barbieri. "Pacific Inducement or Terroristic Impulse: Investigating the Relationship between Trade-Dependency and the Violation of Human Rights." Paper presented at the "1997 annual meeting of the American Political Science Association," Washington, DC.

Debidour, A., ed. *Recueil des actes du Directoire exécutif*. Paris: Imprimerie nationale, 1910–1917.

Dent, Martin. "Nigeria: Federalism and Ethnic Rivalry." *Parliamentary Affairs* 53, no. 1 (January 2000): 157–168.

Diamond, Larry. *Developing Democracy: Toward Consolidation*. Baltimore: Johns Hopkins University Press, 1999.

————. "Promoting Democracy in Africa: U.S. and International Policies in Transition."

In *Africa in World Politics: Post–Cold War Challenges*, 2nd ed., ed. John W. Harbeson and Donald Rothchild. Boulder, CO: Westview Press, 1995.

Diamond, Larry and Seymour Martin Lipset, eds. *Politics in Developing Countries: Comparing Experiences in Developing Countries.* Boulder, CO: Lynne Rienner, 1990.

Diamond, Larry and Marc Plattner. *The Global Resurgence of Democracy.* Baltimore: Johns Hopkins University Press, 1996.

Dicken, Peter. *Global Shift: Transforming the World Economy*, 3rd ed. New York: Guilford Press, 1998.

Djamba, Yanyi K. "African Immigrants in the United States of America: Socio-Demographic Profile in Comparison to Native Blacks." *Journal of Asian and African Studies* 34, no. 2 (June 1999): 210–215.

Doornbos, Martin. "African Multipartyism and the Quest for Democratic Alternatives: Ugandan Elections, Past and Present." In *Chasing a Mirage? Observing Elections and Democratization in Africa*, ed. Jan Abbink and Gerti Hesseling. New York: St. Martin's Press, 1999.

Douarche, Aristide. *Les tribunaux civils de Paris pendant la Révolution (1791–1800)*, vol. 2. Paris: L. Cerf, 1905–1907.

Dower, John. *Embracing Defeat.* New York: Norton, 1999.

Doyle, Charles. "Internal Counter-Revolution: The Judicial Reaction in Southern France, 1794–1800." *Renaissance and Modern Studies* 33 (1989): 114.

Dubofsky, Melvyn. *The State and Labor in Modern America.* Chapel Hill: University of North Carolina Press, 1994.

Duval-Jouve, Joseph. *Montpellier pendant la Révolution, 1789-an VIII*, 4 vols. Montpellier: C. Coulet, 1879–1881.

Duvergier, J.-B. *Collection complète des lois*, 2e éd. Paris: Chez A. Guyot et Scribe, 1834.

Easton, David. "A Reassessment of the Concept of Political Support." *Journal of Political Science* 5 (1975): 435–437.

———. *A Systems Analysis of Political Life.* Chicago: University of Chicago Press, 1965.

The Economist. "The World Economy: The Hitchhiker's Guide to Cybernomics." *The Economist*, 28 September 1996.

———. "The World Economy: Who's in the Driving Seat?" *The Economist*, 7 October 1995.

Edwards, Rebecca. *Angels in the Machinery: Gender in American Party Politics from the Civil War to the Progressive Era.* New York: Oxford University Press, 1997.

Eisenstadt, Todd and Daniel Garcia. "Colombia: Negotiations in a Shifting Pattern of Insurgency." In *Elusive Peace: Negotiating an End to Civil Wars*, ed. I. William Zartman. Washington, DC: Brookings Institution, 1995.

Ejobowah, John B. "Who Owns the Oil: The Politics of Ethnicity in the Niger Delta of Nigeria." *Africa Today* 47 (Winter 2000): 37.

Eldersveld, Samuel J. "The Party Activist in Detroit and Los Angeles: A Longitudinal View, 1956–1980." In *Political Parties in Local Areas*, ed. William Crotty. Knoxville: University of Tennessee Press, 1986.

———. *Political Parties: A Behavioral Analysis.* Chicago: Rand McNally, 1964.

Ellis, Stephen. *The Mask of Anarchy: The Destruction of Liberia and the Religious Dimensions of an African Civil War.* New York: New York University Press, 1999.

Elklit, Jørgen. *Electoral Systems for Emerging Democracies: Experiences and Suggestions.* Copenhagen: Danida, 1997.

Falola, Toyin. *Violence in Nigeria: The Crisis of Religious Politics and Secular Ideologies.* Rochester, NY: University of Rochester Press, 1998.

Fenno, Richard F., Jr. *Home Style: House Members in Their Districts.* Boston: Little, Brown, 1978.

Ferguson, Niall. *The Pity of War.* New York: Basic Books, 1999.

Fewsmith, Joseph. *China since Tiananmen.* New York: Cambridge University Press, 2001.

Fieldhouse, D. K. *Economic and Empire, 1830–1914.* London: Weidenfield and Nicholson, 1973.

Florini, Ann M. *The Third Force: The Rise of Transnational Civil Society.* Washington, DC: Carnegie Endowment for International Peace, 2000.

Fournier, Georges. "Réalité et limites de la réaction thermidorienne dans l'Hérault, L'Aude, et la Haute-Garonne." In *Tournant de l'an III*, ed. Michel Vovelle. Paris: Editions du CTHS, 1997, 490.

Fox, Leslie et al. *An Assessment of Politics and Governance in Madagascar.* Burlington, VT: Associates in Rural Development, 1994.

Francis, John G. and Robert C. Benedict. "Issue Group Activists at the Conventions." In *The Life of the Parties: Activists in Presidential Politics*, ed. Ronald B. Rapoport, Alan A. Abramowitz, and John McGlennon. Lexington: University Press of Kentucky, 1986.

Franck, Thomas M. *Fairness in International Law and Institutions.* New York: Oxford University Press, 1995.

Freedman, Estelle. "Separatism as Strategy: Female Institution Building and American Feminism, 1870–1930." *Feminist Studies* 5 (Fall 1979): 512–529.

Freeman, Jo. *A Room at a Time: How Women Entered Party Politics.* Lanham, MD: Rowman and Littlefield, 1999.

Freedom House. *Freedom in the World.* New York: Freedom House, 2001.

Fried, Amy and David Schultz. "Alexis DeTocqueville and Empirical Political Science: How the Pluralists and the Social Capital Scholars Read *Democracy in America*." Paper delivered at the meeting of the Midwest Political Science Association, April 2000.

Frieden, Jeffrey. "Invested Interests: The Politics of National Economic Policies in a World of Global Finance." *International Organizations* 45 (1991): 425–451.

Friedman, Edward. "Development, Revolution, Democracy and Dictatorship." In *Democracy, Revolution and History*, ed. Theda Skocpol. Ithaca, NY: Cornell University Press, 1998.

Frieson, Kate. "The Politics of Getting the Vote in Cambodia." In *Propaganda, Politics, and Violence in Cambodia: Democratic Transition under United Nations Peacekeeping*, ed. Steve Heder and Judy Ledgerwood. Armonk, NY: M. E. Sharpe, 1996.

Frundt, Henry J. *Refreshing Pauses.* New York: Praeger, 1987.

Gamarra, Eduardo C., Michele Schimpp, and George Gray Molina. "The Transition to Sustainable Democracy in Bolivia and the Strategic Role of USAID." In *Case Studies in Program Impact.* Washington, DC: Management Systems International, June 2001.

Gamm, Gerald and Robert D. Putnam. "Association-Building in America, 1840–1940." *Journal of Interdisciplinary History* 29, no. 3 (1999): 511–557.

Garapon, Antoine. "La justice reconstructive." In *Et ce sera justice: punir en démocratie*, ed. Antoine Garapon, Frédéric Gros, and Thierry Pech. Paris: Éditions Odile Jacob, 2001.

Garrett, Geoffrey. *Partisan Politics in the Global Economy*. New York: Cambridge University Press, 1998.

Geertz, Clifford. *The Interpretation of Cultures: Selected Essays*. New York: Basic Books, 1973.

George, Alexander G. *Bridging the Gap: Theory and Practice in Foreign Policy*. Washington, DC: U.S. Institute of Peace, 1993.

Gérard, Pierre. "L'armée révolutionnaire de la Haute-Garonne." *Annales historiques de la Révolution française* (1959): 155.

Gibney, Mark and Matthew Dalton. "The Political Terror Scale." In *Human Rights and Developing Countries*, ed. David L. Cingranelli. Greenwich, CT: JAI Press, 1996.

Giliomee, Hermann and Charles Simkins, eds. *The Awkward Embrace: One-Party Dominance and Democracy*. Cape Town: Tafelberg, 1999.

Ginsberg, Benjamin. "How Polling Transforms Public Opinion." In *Manipulating Public Opinion: Essays on Public Opinion as a Dependent Variable*, ed. Michael Margolis and Gary A. Mauser. Pacific Grove, CA: Brooks/Cole, 1989.

Gleavy, R. and E. Kermeli, eds. *Islamic Law: Theory and Practice*. London and New York: I. B. Tauris, 1997.

Gosnell, Harold F. *Machine Politics: Chicago Model*. Chicago: University of Chicago Press, 1937.

Gough, Hugh. *The Newspaper Press in the French Revolution*. Chicago: Lyceum Books, 1988.

Green, John C. "The Christian Right and the 1994 Elections: A View from the States." *PS: Political Science and Politics* 28 (1995): 5–8.

Green, John C., James L. Guth, and Clyde Wilcox. "Less Than Conquerors: The Christian Right in State Republican Parties." In *Social Movements and American Political Institutions*, ed. Anne N. Costain and Andrew S. McFarland. Lanham, MD: Rowman and Littlefield, 1998.

Greer, Donald. *The Incidence of the Terror during the French Revolution*. Cambridge, MA: Harvard University Press, 1935.

Guilhaumou, Jacques. "Fragments of a Discourse on Denunciation (1789–1794)." In *The Terror*, vol. 4 of *The French Revolution and the Creation of Modern Political Culture*, ed. Keith Michael Baker. Oxford: Pergamon Press, 1994.

Haggard, Stephan. *Developing Nations and the Politics of Global Integration*. Washington, DC: Brookings Institution, 1995.

———. "The Political Economy of the East Asian Financial Crisis." Manuscript, 1 March 2000.

Haggard, Stephan and Robert R. Kaufman. *The Political Economy of Democratic Transition*. Princeton, NJ: Princeton University Press, 1995.

Haggard, Stephan and Sylvia Maxfield. "The Political Economy of Financial Internationalization in the Developing World." *International Organization* 50, no. 1 (1996): 35–68.

Hall, Peter A. *Governing the Economy: The Politics of State Intervention in Britain and France*. New York: Oxford University Press, 1986.

Hall, Peter Dobkin. "Vital Signs: Organizational Population Trends and Civic Engagement in New Haven, Connecticut, 1850–1998." In *Civic Engagement in American Democracy*, ed. Theda Skocpol and Morris P. Fiorina. Washington, DC: Brookings Institution, 1999.

Halperin, Morton H. *Bureaucratic Politics and Foreign Policy*. Washington, DC: Brookings Institution, 1974.

Hansen, Gary and Harry Blair. *Civil Society and Democratic Reform: Strategic Approaches for International Donors*. Washington, DC: U.S. Agency for International Development, 1995.

Harbeson, John W. "Externally Assisted Democratization: Theoretical Issues and African Realities." In *Africa in World Politics: The African State in Flux*, 3rd ed., ed. John W. Harbeson and Donald Rothchild. Boulder, CO: Westview Press, 2000.

Harbeson, John W., Donald Rothchild, and Naomi Chazan, eds. *Civil Society and the State in Africa*. Boulder, CO: Lynne Rienner, 1994.

Hays, Samuel P. "Political Parties and the Community-Society Continuum." In *The American Party Systems: Stages of Political Development*, ed. William Nisbet Chambers and Walter Dean Burnham. New York: Oxford University Press, 1967.

Held, David et al. *Global Transformations: Politics, Economics and Culture*. Stanford, CA: Stanford University Press, 1999.

Henderson, Conway. "Conditions Affecting the Use of Political Repression." *Journal of Conflict Resolution* 35 (1991): 120–142.

———. "Dependency and Political Repression: A Caveat on Research Expectations." In *Human Rights in Developing Countries*, ed. David Louis Cingranelli. Greenwich, CT: JAI Press, 1996.

———. "Population Pressures and Political Repression." *Social Science Quarterly* 74 (1993): 322–333.

Herman, Edward S. and Frank Brodhead. *Demonstration Elections: U.S.-Staged Elections in the Dominican Republic, Vietnam, and El Salvador*. Boston: South End Press, 1984.

Hirschfield, Robert S., Bert E. Swanson, and Blanche D. Blank. "A Profile of Political Activists, Manhattan." *Western Political Quarterly* 15 (September 1962): 489–506.

Honig, Bonnie. *Democracy and the Foreigner*. Princeton, NJ: Princeton University Press, 2001.

Horowitz, Donald. "Comparing Democratic Systems." In *The Global Resurgence of Democracy*, ed. Larry Diamond and Marc Plattner. Baltimore: Johns Hopkins University Press, 1996.

Huang, Chang-Ling. "Learning the New Game: Labor Politics in the Newly Democratized South Korea and Taiwan." Paper presented at the 2000 annual meeting of the American Political Science Association, Washington, DC.

Human Rights Watch. *Divide and Rule: State-Sponsored Ethnic Violence in Kenya*. New York: Human Rights Watch, 1993.

Huntington, Samuel P. *Political Order in Changing Societies*. New Haven, CT: Yale University Press, 1968.

———. *The Soldier and the State*. Cambridge, MA: Harvard University Press, 1957.

———. *The Third Wave: Democratization in the Late Twentieth Century*. Norman: University of Oklahoma Press, 1991.

Ibelema, Minabere. "Nigeria: The Politics of Marginalization." *Current History* 99, no. 637 (May 2000): 213.

Ilesanmi, Simeon O. *Religious Pluralism and the Nigerian State*. Athens: Ohio University Center for International Studies, 1997.

International Crisis Group. *Central Asia: Crisis Conditions in Three States, ICG Asia Report 7*. New York: International Crisis Group, 7 August 2000.

———. "Consensual Democracy in Post-Genocide Rwanda: Evaluating the March 2001 District Elections." *International Crisis Group, Africa Report* 34 (9 October 2001).

———. *Elections in Bosnia and Herzegovina, ICG Report 16*. New York: International Crisis Group, 22 September 1996.

International Labor Organization (ILO). *International Labor Standards*. Geneva: ILO, 1998.

International Monetary Fund (IMF). *International Capital Markets: Developments, Prospects and Key Policy Issues*. World Economic and Financial Surveys. Washington, DC: IMF, 1996.

Jacobs, Antoine. "Collective Self-Regulation." In *Making of Labor Law in Europe: A Comparative Study of Nine Countries up to 1945*, ed. Bob Hepple. New York: Continuum International, 1986.

Jaume, Lucien. *Le discours jacobin et la démocratie*. Paris: Fayard, 1989.

Jenkins, Rob. *Democratic Politics and Economic Reform in India*. New York: Cambridge University Press, 1999.

Jentleson, Bruce W. "In Pursuit of Praxis: Applying International Relations Theory to Foreign Policy-Making." In *Being Useful: Policy Relevance and International Relations Theory*, ed. Miroslav Nincic and Joseph Lepgold. Ann Arbor: University of Michigan Press, 2000.

Jewell, Malcolm E. and David M. Olson. *American State Political Parties and Elections*. Homewood, IL: Dorsey Press, 1978.

Jones, David Martin. "Democratization, Civil Society and Illiberal Middle Class Culture in Pacific Asia." *Comparative Politics* 30, no. 2 (1998): 147–170.

Karatnycky, Adrian, Alexander Motyl, and Aili Piano. *Nations in Transit 1999–2000: Civil Society, Democracy, and Markets in East Central Europe and the Newly Independent States*. New Brunswick, NJ: Transaction and Freedom House, 2001.

Karl, Terry. "Imposing Consent? Electoralism vs. Democratization in El Salvador." In *Elections and Democratization in Latin America, 1980–85*, ed. Paul Drake and Eduardo Silva. San Diego: CLAS/Center for US-Mexican Studies, 1986.

Kasfir, Nelson, ed. *Civil Society and Democracy in Africa: Critical Perspectives*. London: Frank Cass, 1998.

Katzenstein, Peter. *Small States in World Markets: Industrial Policy in Western Europe*. Ithaca, NY: Cornell University Press, 1985.

Keane, John. *Civil Society: Old Images, New Visions*. Stanford, CA: Stanford University Press, 1998.

———. *Democracy and Civil Society*. London: Verso, 1988.

Kegley, Charles W. Jr. and Eugene R. Wittkopf. *American Foreign Policy: Pattern and Process*. New York: St. Martin's Press, 1996.

Kelly, John and Martha Kaplan. *Represented Communities: Fiji and World Decolonization*. Chicago: University of Chicago Press, 2000.

Kenen, Peter. *The International Economy.* Cambridge: Cambridge University Press, 1994.

Kerr, K. Austin. *Organizing for Prohibition: A New History of the Anti-Saloon League.* New Haven, CT, and London: Yale University Press, 1985.

Khan, M. N. "Ijma: Third Source of Islamic Law." *Hamdard Islamicus* 22 (January 1999): 84–86.

Khan, Sarah Ahmed. *Nigeria: The Political Economy of Oil.* Oxford: Oxford University Press for the Oxford Institute of Energy Studies, 1994.

Kleppner, Paul. *Chicago Divided: The Making of a Black Mayor.* DeKalb: Northern Illinois University Press, 1985.

Klingemann, Hans-Dieter. "Mapping Political Support in 1990s: A Global Analysis." In *Critical Citizens: Global Support for Democratic Governance,* ed. Pippa Norris. Oxford: Oxford University Press, 1999.

Koonings, Kees and Dirk Kruijt, eds. *Societies of Fear: The Legacy of Civil War, Violence and Terror in Latin America.* London and New York: Zed Books, 1999.

Kritz, Neil J., ed. *Transitional Justice: How Emerging Democracies Reckon with Former Regimes,* 3 vols. Washington, DC: U.S. Institute of Peace, 1995.

Kuhn, Thomas S. *The Structure of Scientific Revolutions,* 3rd ed. Chicago: University of Chicago Press, 1996.

Kukah, M. H. and Toyin Falola. *Religious Militancy and Self-Assertion: Islam and Politics in Nigeria.* Aldershot, U.K., and Brookfield, VT: Avebury Press, 1996.

Kumar, Krishna and Marina Ottaway. "General Conclusions and Priorities for Policy Research." In *Postconflict Elections, Democratization, and International Assistance,* ed. Krishna Kumar. Boulder, CO: Lynne Rienner, 1998.

Kweit, Robert W. and Mary Grisez Kweit. In *The Life of the Parties: Activists in Presidential Politics,* ed. Ronald B. Rapoport, Alan A. Abramowitz, and John McGlennon. Lexington: University Press of Kentucky, 1986.

Ladd, Everett C. "The Data Just Don't Show Erosion of America's 'Social Capital.' " *Public Perspective* 7, no. 4 (1996): 5–22.

Lagos, Marta. "Between Stability and Crisis in Latin America." *Journal of Democracy* 12, no. 1 (January 2001): 138.

Lake, David A. and Donald Rothchild. "Containing Fear: The Origins and Management of Ethnic Conflict." *International Security* 21, no. 2 (Fall 1996): 41–75.

Lal, Brij V. *Fiji before the Storm.* Canberra: Asia Pacific Press, 2000.

Latzer, Barry, ed. *Death Penalty Cases: Leading U.S. Supreme Court Cases on Capital Punishment.* Boston and Oxford: Butterworth-Heinemann, 1998.

Leary, Virginia A. "The Paradox of Workers' Rights as Human Rights." In *Human Rights, Labor Rights, and International Trade,* ed. Lance A. Compa and Stephen F. Diamond. Philadelphia: University of Pennsylvania Press, 1996.

Ledgerwood, Judy. "Patterns of CPP Political Repression and Violence during the UNTAC Period." In *Propaganda, Politics, and Violence in Cambodia: Democratic Transition under United Nations Peace-keeping,* ed. Steve Heder and Judy Ledgerwood. Armonk, NY: M. E. Sharpe, 1996.

Lewis, Gwynne. *The Second Vendée: The Continuity of Counter-revolution in the Department of the Gard, 1789–1815.* Oxford: Oxford University Press, 1978.

Lewis, John P. "Some Consequences of Giantism: The Case of India." *World Politics* 43, no. 3 (April 1991): 367–399.

Lezhnev, Sasha. "Can Democracy Successfully Manage Ethnic Conflict? A Proposed

Three Step Process Using Nigeria as a Case Study." Unpublished paper, April 2001.

Licklider, Roy, ed. *Stopping the Killing: How Civil Wars End.* New York: New York University Press, 1993.

Lijphart, Arend. *Electoral Systems and Party Systems: A Study of Twenty-Seven Democracies, 1945–1990.* New York: Oxford University Press, 1994.

Linz, Juan J. and Alfred Stepan. *Problems of Democratic Transition and Consolidation: Southern Europe, South America, and Post-Communist Europe.* Baltimore: Johns Hopkins University Press, 1996.

Lipset, Seymour Martin. "Introduction." In *Encyclopedia of Democracy,* ed. Seymour Martin Lipset. Washington, DC: Congressional Quarterly Press, 1995.

Lizée, Pierre P. *Peace, Power, and Resistance in Cambodia: Global Governance and the Failure of International Conflict Resolution.* New York: St. Martin's Press, 2000.

Loimeier, Roman. *Islamic Reform and Political Change in Northern Nigeria.* Evanston, IL: Northwestern University Press, 1997.

Longman, Timothy. "State, Civil Society and Genocide in Rwanda." In *State, Conflict and Democracy in Africa,* ed. Richard Joseph. Boulder, CO: Lynne Rienner, 1998.

Lucas, Colin. "The First Directory and the Rule of Law." *French Historical Studies* 10 (1977): 231–260.

———. "Themes in Southern Violence after 9 Thermider." In *Beyond the Terror: Essays in French Regional and Social History, 1794–1815,* ed. Colin Lucas and Gwynne Lewis. Cambridge: Cambridge University Press, 1983.

———. "The Theory and Practice of Denunciation in the French Revolution." *Journal of Modern History* 68 (1996): 768–785.

Lustick, Ian. "Lijphart, Lakatos and Consociationalism." *World Politics* 50 (October 1997): 88–117.

Luzatto, Sergio. "Comment entrer dans le Directoire? Le problème de l'amnistie." In *La République directoriale: Actes du colloque de Clermont-Ferrand, 22–24 mai 1997,* ed. Philippe Bourdin and Bernard Gainot. Clermont-Ferrand: Société des études robespierristes, 1998.

Lyons, Martyn. *Revolution in Toulouse. An Essay on Provincial Terrorism.* Berne: Peter Lang, 1978.

Lyons, Terrence. "Closing the Transition: The May 1995 Elections in Ethiopia." *Journal of Modern African Studies* 34 (1996): 121–142.

———. "The Role of Postsettlement Elections." In *Ending Civil Wars,* ed. Stephen John Stedman, Donald Rothchild, and Elizabeth Cousens. Boulder, CO: Lynne Rienner, 2002.

———. *Voting for Peace: Postconflict Elections in Liberia.* Washington, DC: Brookings Institution, 1999.

Maddison, Angus. *The World Economy in the 20th Century.* Paris: OECD Development Center, 1989.

Manning, Carrie. "Constructing Opposition in Mozambique: Renamo as Political Party." *Journal of Southern African Studies* 24, no. 1 (March 1998): 161–190.

Mansfield, Edward and Jack Snyder. "Democratization and War." *International Security* 20, no. 1 (Summer 1995): 5–38.

March, James G. and Johan P. Olsen. *Ambiguity and Choice in Organizations.* Bergen: Universitetsforlaget, 1976.

Marshall, Ann. "Organizing across the Divide: Everyday Life, Feminists Activism, and the Election of Women to Public Office." Ph.D. thesis, Syracuse University, 2000.

Marshall, Don D. "Understanding Late-Twentieth Century Capitalism: Reassessing the Globalization Theme." *Government and Opposition* 31, no. 2 (1996): 193–215.

Mathiez, Albert. *La réaction thermidorienne*. Paris: A. Colin, 1929.

Mazrui, Ali A. and Pio Zirimu. "The Secularization of an Afro-Islamic Language: Church, State and Marketplace in the Spread of Kiswahili." In *The Power of Babel: Language and Governance in the African Experience*, ed. Ali A. Mazrui and Alamin A. Mazrui. Oxford, Nairobi, Kampala, Cape Town, and Chicago: James Currey, E.A.E.P, Fountain, David Philip, and the University of Chicago Press, 1998.

McAdams, A. James, ed. *Transitional Justice and the Rule of Law in New Democracies*. Notre Dame, IN: University of Notre Dame Press, 1997.

McCormick, James M. *American Foreign Policy and Process*. Itasca, IL: Peacock, 1992.

McCreadie, Robert. "Scottish Identity and the Constitution." In *National Identities: The Constitution of the United Kingdom*, ed. Bernard Crick. Cambridge, MA, and Oxford: Blackwell, 1991.

McGrew, Anthony G. and Paul Lewis, eds. *Global Politics: Globalization and the Nation-State*. Oxford: Polity Press, 1992.

McLaren, L. M. "The Effect of IMF Austerity Programs on Human Rights Violations: An Exploratory Analysis of Peru, Argentina, and Brazil." Paper presented at the 1998 annual meeting of the Midwest Political Science Association, Chicago.

McMahon, Edward R. "Assessing USAID's Assistance for Democratic Development: Is It Quantity versus Quality?" *Evaluation* 7, no. 4 (2001): 43–367.

Meyer, William H. *Human Rights and International Political Economy in Third World Nations*. Westport, CT: Praeger, 1998.

———. "Human Rights and MNCs: Theory versus Quantitative Analysis." *Human Rights Quarterly* 18, no. 2 (1996): 368–397.

Mitchell, Neil J. and James M. McCormick. "Economic and Political Explanations of Human Rights Violations." *World Politics* 40 (1988): 476–498.

Mkandawire, Thandike. "Economic Policy-Making and the Consolidation of Democratic Institutions in Africa." In *Domination or Dialogue? Experiences and Prospects for African Development Cooperation*, ed. Kjell Havnevik and Brian Van Arkadie. Uppsala, Sweden: Nordic Institute for African Studies, 1966.

Montgomery, Tommie Sue. *Revolution in El Salvador: From Civil Strife to Civil Peace*. Boulder, CO: Westview Press, 1995.

Mortimer-Ternaux, Louis. *Histoire de la Terreur, 1792–1794*, vol. 8. Paris: Lévy, 1862–1881.

Moses, Jonathon W. "Love It or Leave It: Exit, Voice and Loyalty with Global Labor Mobility." Paper presented at the 2000 annual meeting of the American Political Science Association, Washington, DC.

Moulinas, René. "Le département de Vaucluse en 1795: la contre-révolution en marche?" In *Le Tournant de l'an III: Réaction et Terreur blanche dans la France révolutionnaire*, ed. Michel Vovelle. Paris: Éditions du CTHS, 1997.

Mozaffar, Shaheen. "Electoral Systems and Conflict Management in Africa: A Twenty-Eight State Comparison." In *Elections and Conflict Management in Africa*, ed. Timothy D. Sisk and Andrew Reynolds. Washington, DC: U.S. Institute of Peace, 1998.

———. "Electoral Systems and Their Political Effects in Africa: A Preliminary Analysis." *Representation* 34, nos. 3–4 (Autumn/Winter 1997): 148–156.

———. *Institutional Analysis and the Assessment of Democratic Governance in Africa.* Burlington, VT: Associates in Rural Development, 1994.

Mozaffar, Shaheen and Andreas Schedler. "Introduction: The Comparative Study of Electoral Governance." *International Political Science Review* 23, no. 1, Special Issue on "Electoral Governance and Democratization" (January 2002).

Munro, J. Forbes. *Africa and the International Economy.* London: J. M. Dent and Sons, 1976.

National Democratic Institute (NDI). *Making Every Vote Count: Domestic Election Monitoring in Asia.* Washington, DC: NDI, 1996.

———. *Reforming the Philippine Electoral Process, 1986–1988.* Washington, DC: NDI, 1991.

Nelson, Joan. "The Political Economy of Stabilization: Commitment, Capacity, and Public Response." *World Development* 12, no. 10 (1984): 983–1006.

Newbury, Catherine. "Rwanda: Recent Debates over Governance and Rural Development." In *Governance and Politics in Africa*, ed. Goran Hyden and Michael Bratton. Boulder, CO: Lynne Rienner, 1992.

Niwanko, A. A. *Nigeria: The Stolen Billions.* Enugu, Nigeria: Fourth Dimension, 1999.

Norris, Pippa, ed. *Critical Citizens: Global Support for Democratic Governance.* Oxford: Oxford University Press, 1999.

Nozick, Robert. *Philosophical Explanations.* Oxford: Clarendon Press, 1981.

Nyerere, Julius K. *Ujamaa: Essays on Socialism.* Oxford: Oxford University Press, 1977.

Oakerson, Ronald. "Democracy as a Discipline." Typescript, 1994.

O'Donnell, Guillermo. "Illusions about Consolidation." *Journal of Democracy* 7, no. 2 (1996): 34–51.

O'Donnell, Guillermo and Philippe C. Schmitter. *Transitions from Authoritarian Rule: Tentative Conclusions about Uncertain Democracies.* Baltimore: Johns Hopkins University Press, 1986.

Office of the Vice President. Agency for International Development: Accompanying Report of the National Performance Review. *From Red Tape to Results: Creating a Government That Works Better and Costs Less.* Washington, DC: Government Publication Office, September 1993.

Ohmae, Kenichi. *The End of the Nation State.* New York: Free Press, 1995.

Oman, Charles. *Globalisation and Regionalism: The Challenge for Developing Countries.* Paris: OECD, 1994.

Osabu-Kle, Daniel. *Compatible Cultural Democracy: The Key to Development in Africa.* Peterborough, Ontario: Broadview Press, 2000.

Osborne, David and Ted Gaebler. *Reinventing Government: How the Entrepreneurial Spirit Is Transforming the Public Sector.* Reading, MA: Addison-Wesley, 1992.

Organization for Security and Cooperation in Europe (OSCE). *The Republic of Tajikistan Elections to the Parliament, 27 February 2000: Final Report.* Warsaw: OSCE, Office for Democratic Institutions and Human Rights, 17 May 2000.

Ostrom, Elinor. *Governing the Commons: The Evolution of Institutions for Collective Actions.* New York: Cambridge University Press, 1990.

Ottaway, Marina. "Angola's Failed Elections." In *Postconflict Elections, Democratization, and International Assistance*, ed. Krishna Kumar. Boulder, CO: Lynne Rienner, 1998.

————. "Should Elections Be the Criterion of Democratization in Africa?" *CSIS Africa Notes* no. 145. Washington, DC: Center for Strategic and International Studies, 1993.

Parenti, Michael. *The Sword and the Dollar*. New York: St. Martin's Press, 1989.

Paris, Roland. "Peacebuilding and the Limits of Liberal Internationalism." *International Security* 22, no. 2 (Fall 1997): 56.

Payne, Tony. "Multi-Party Politics in Jamaica." In *Political Parties in the Third World*, ed. Vicky Randal. London: Sage, 1988.

Petit, Jean-Claude. *Ces peines obscures: la prison pénale en France, 1780–1875*. Paris: Fayard, 1990.

Peyrard, Christine. *Les Jacobins de l'Ouest*. Paris: Publications de la Sorbonne, 1996.

Piano, Aili. *Freedom in the World, 2000–2001*. New York: Freedom House, 2001.

Plattner, Marc F. "The Democratic Moment." In *The Global Resurgence of Democracy* (2nd ed.), ed. Larry Diamond and Marc F. Plattner. Baltimore: The Johns Hopkins University Press, 1996.

Poate, Derek et al. "The Evaluability of Democracy and Human Rights Projects: A Logframe-related Assessment." *Sida Studies in Evaluation 2000, vol. 3*. Stockholm: Swedish International Development Cooperation Agency, 2000.

Poe, Steven C. "Human Rights and the Allocation of U.S. Military Assistance." *Journal of Peace Research* 28 (1991): 205–216.

————. "Human Rights and Economic Aid under Ronald Reagan and Jimmy Carter." *American Journal of Political Science* 36 (1992): 147–167.

Poe, Steven C. and C. Neal Tate. "Repression of Rights to Personal Integrity in the 1980s: A Global Analysis." *American Political Science Review* 88 (1994): 853–872.

Poe, Steven C., C. Neal Tate, and Linda Camp Keith. "Repression of the Human Right to Personal Integrity Revisited: A Global Cross-National Study Covering the Years 1976–1993." *International Studies Quarterly* 43, no. 2 (1999): 291–313.

Poe, Steven C., Tanya Vazquez, and Sabine Carey. "How Are These Pictures Different? A Quantitative Comparison of the U.S. State Department and Amnesty International Human Rights Reports, 1976–1995." *Human Rights Quarterly* 23, no. 3 (2001): 650–677.

Polsby, Nelson W. *Consequences of Party Reform*. New York: Oxford University Press, 1983.

Pomper, Gerald. "New Jersey Party Chairmen." *Western Political Quarterly* 18 (1965): 186–197.

Popkin, Jeremy D. *The Right-Wing Press in France, 1792–1800*. Chapel Hill: University of North Carolina Press, 1980.

Posen, Barry R. "The Security Dilemma and Ethnic Conflict." In *Ethnic Conflict and International Security*, ed. Michael E. Brown. Princeton, NJ: Princeton University Press, 1993.

Price, John. "E. H. Norman, Canada and Japan's Postwar Constitution." *Pacific Affairs* 74, no. 3 (2001): 387–405.

Protess, David L. and Alan R. Gitelson. "Political Stability, Reform Clubs, and the Amateur Democrat." In *The Party Symbol: Readings on Political Parties*, ed. William Crotty. San Francisco: W. H. Freeman, 1990.

Przeworski, Adam et al. *Democracy and Development*. New York: Cambridge University Press, 1998.

Przeworski, Adam, Adam Alvarez, José Antonio Cheibub, and Fernando Limongi. "What Makes Democracies Endure." *Journal of Democracy* 7 (1996): 39–55.

Putnam, Robert D. *Bowling Alone: The Collapse and Revival of American Community.* New York: Simon and Schuster, 2000.

———. *Making Democracy Work: Civic Traditions in Modern Italy.* Princeton, NJ: Princeton University Press, 1993.

Quigley, Kevin F. F. "Political Scientists and Assisting Democracy: Too Tenuous Links." *PS: Political Science and Politics* 30, no. 3 (September 1997): 564–567.

Rahman, H.H.A. "The Origin and Development of Ijtihad to Solve Complex Modern Legal Problems." *Bulletin of the Henry Martyn Institute of Islamic Studies* 17 (January–June 1998): 7–21.

Rahn, Wendy M., John Brehm, and Neil Carlson. "National Elections as Institutions for Generating Social Capital." In *Civic Engagement in American Democracy*, ed. Theda Skocpol and Morris P. Fiorina. Washington, DC: Brookings Institution, 1999.

Rapoport, David C. and Leonard Weinberg, eds. *The Democratic Experience and Political Violence.* London: Frank Cass, 2001.

Rapoport, Ronald B., Alan A. Abramowitz, and John McGlennon. *The Life of the Parties: Activists in Presidential Politics.* Lexington: University Press of Kentucky, 1986.

Regan, Patrick M. "U.S. Economic Aid and Political Repression: An Empirical Evaluation of U.S. Foreign Policy." *Political Research Quarterly* 48, no. 3 (1995): 613–628.

Reinhard, Marcel. *Le Département de la Sarthe sous le régime directoriale.* Saint Brieuc: Les Presses Bretonnes, 1935.

Reynolds, Andrew. "Elections in Southern Africa: The Case for Proportionality, a Rebuttal." In *Elections and Conflict Management in Africa*, ed. Timothy D. Sisk and Andrew Reynolds. Washington, DC: U.S. Institute of Peace, 1998.

———. *Electoral Systems and Democratization in Southern Africa.* New York: Oxford University Press, 1999.

Richards, David L. "Perilous Proxy: Human Rights and the Presence of National Elections." *Social Science Quarterly* 80, no. 4 (Winter 1999): 648–665.

Richards, David L. and Ronald D. Gelleny. "Is It a Small World After All? Economic Globalization and Human Rights in Developing Countries." In *Coping with Globalization*, ed. Steven Chan and James Scarritt. Essex: Frank Cass, 2002.

Richards, David L., Ronald D. Gelleny, and David H. Sacko. "Money with a Mean Streak? Foreign Economic Penetration and Government Respect for Human Rights in Developing Countries." *International Studies Quarterly* 45, no. 2 (2001): 219–239.

Roberts, David W. *Political Transition in Cambodia, 1991–99: Power, Elitism, and Democracy.* New York: St. Martin's Press, 2001.

Roblot, René. *La justice criminelle en France sous la Terreur.* Paris: Librairie de droit et de jurisprudence, 1938.

Rodrik, Dani. *The New Global Economy and Developing Countries: Making Openness Work.* Washington, DC: Overseas Development Council, 1999.

———. "Understanding Economic Policy Reform." *Journal of Economic Literature* 34 (March 1996): 9–41.

Rosenblum, Nancy L. "Political Parties as Membership Groups." *Columbia Law Review* 100, no. 3 (2000): 813–844.

————. "*Primus Inter Pares*: Political Parties and Civil Society." *Chicago Kent Law Review* 75, no. 2 (2000): 493–529.

————, ed. *Obligations of Citizenship and Demands of Faith*. Princeton, NJ: Princeton University Press, 2000.

Rosenstone, Steven J. and John Mark Hansen. *Mobilization, Participation, and Democracy in America*. New York: Macmillan, 1993.

Rotberg, Robert I. "Africa's Mess, Mugabe's Mayhem." *Foreign Affairs* vol. 79, no. 5 (September–October 2000): 47–61.

Ryan, Mary P. "Civil Society as Democratic Practice: North American Cities during the Nineteenth Century." *Journal of Interdisciplinary History* 29 (1999): 559–584.

Salmore, Stephen A. and Barbara G. Salmore. *Candidates, Parties, and Campaigns: Electoral Politics in America*. Washington, DC: CQ Press, 1985.

Sartori, Giovanni. *Comparative Constitutional Engineering*. New York: New York University Press, 1994.

Saulawa, Abdullah Mu'aza. "Islam and Its Anti-Colonial and Educational Contribution in West Africa and Northern Nigeria, 1800–1960." *Hamdard Islamicus* 19, no. 1 (1996): 69–79.

Schaffer, Frederic. *Democracy in Translation: Understanding Politics in an Unfamiliar Culture*. Ithaca, NY: Cornell University Press, 1998.

Schmidt, Vivien A. "The New World Order, Incorporated: The Rise of Business and the Decline of the Nation-State." *Daedalus* 124, no. 2 (Spring 1995): 75–106.

Schmitter, Philippe C. and Terry Lynn Karl. "What Democracy Is . . . and Is Not." In *The Global Resurgence of Democracy*, 2nd ed., ed. Larry Diamond and Marc F. Plattner. Baltimore: Johns Hopkins University Press, 1996.

Schoultz, Lars. "U.S. Foreign Policy and Human Rights." *Comparative Politics* 13 (1981): 149–170.

Schraeder, Peter J. *United States Foreign Policy toward Africa: Incrementalism, Crisis, and Change*. New York: Cambridge University Press, 1994.

Shapiro, Ian and Stephen Macedo, eds. *Nomos XLII: Designing Democratic Institutions*. New York: New York University Press, 2000.

Shugart, Matthew S. and John M. Carey. *Presidents and Assemblies: Constitutional Design and Electoral Systems*. New York: Cambridge University Press, 1992.

Shugart, Matthew S. and Scott Mainwaring, eds. *Presidentialism and Democracy in Latin America*. New York: Cambridge University Press, 1997.

Sikkink, Katherine and Margaret E. Keck. *Activists beyond Borders: Advocacy Network in International Politics*. Ithaca, NY: Cornell University Press, 1998.

Silbey, Joel. "Party Organization in Nineteenth Century America." In *Parties and Politics in American History: A Reader*, ed. L. Sandy Maisel and William G. Shade. New York: Garland, 1994.

Simon, Herbert A. *Administrative Behavior: A Study of Decision-Making Processes in Administrative Organization*. New York: Free Press, 1976.

Sisk, Timothy D. "Elections and Conflict Management in Africa: Conclusions and Recommendations." In *Elections and Conflict Management in Africa*, ed. Timothy D. Sisk and Andrew Reynolds. Washington, DC: U.S. Institute of Peace Press, 1998.

Skocpol, Theda. "Advocates without Members: The Recent Transformation of American Civic Life." In *Civic Engagement in American Democracy*, ed. Theda Skocpol and Morris P. Fiorina. Washington, DC: Brookings Institution, 1999.

————. "How Americans Became Civic." In *Civic Engagement in American Democracy*, ed. Theda Skocpol and Morris P. Fiorina. Washington, DC: Brookings Institution, 1999.

Skocpol, Theda and Morris P. Fiorina, eds. *Civic Engagement in American Democracy*. Washington, DC: Brookings Institution, 1999.

Smith, Tony. *America's Mission: The United States and the Worldwide Struggle for Democracy in the Twentieth Century*. Princeton, NJ: Princeton University Press, 1994.

Snyder, Jack. *From Voting to Violence: Democratization and Nationalist Conflict*. New York: W. W. Norton, 2000.

Snyder, Jack and Robert Jervis. "Civil War and the Security Dilemma." In *Civil Wars, Insecurity, and Intervention*, ed. Barbara F. Walter and Jack Snyder. New York: Columbia University Press, 1999.

Sorauf, Frank J. "Political Parties and Political Analysis." In *The American Party Systems: Stages of Political Development*, ed. William Nisbet Chambers and Walter Dean Burnham. New York: Oxford University Press, 1967.

Sorsa, Piritta. "Sub-Saharan African Own Commitments in the Uruguay Round—Myth or Reality?" *The World Economy* 19, no. 3 (May 1996): 287–306.

Southall, Roger and Roddy Fox. "Lesotho's General Election of 1998: Rigged or de Riguer?" *Journal of Modern African Studies* 37, no. 4 (1999): 669–696.

Spar, Debora L. "The Spotlight and the Bottom Line: How Multinationals Export Human Rights." *Foreign Affairs* 77, no. 2 (1998): 7–12.

Spencer, Thomas T. "Auxiliary and Non-Party Politics: The 1936 Democratic Presidential Campaign in Ohio." *Ohio History* 90 (1981): 114–128.

Spinner-Haley, Jeff. *Surviving Diversity*. Baltimore: Johns Hopkins University Press, 2000.

Stallings, Barbara, ed. *Global Change, Regional Response: The New International Context of Development*. New York: Cambridge University Press, 1995.

Stedman, Stephen John. "Spoiler Problems in Peace Processes." *International Security* 22, no. 5 (Fall 1997): 5–53.

Stedman, Stephen John, Donald Rothchild, and Elizabeth Cousens, eds. *Ending Civil Wars: The Implementation of Peace Agreements*. Boulder, CO: Lynne Rienner, 2002.

Stohl, Michael, David Carleton, and Steven E. Johnson. "Human Rights and U.S. Foreign Assistance: From Nixon to Carter." *Journal of Peace Research* 21 (1984): 215–226.

Stokes, Donald E. *Pasteur's Quadrant: Basic Science and Technological Innovation*. Washington, DC: Brookings Institution, 1997.

Strange, Susan. "The Defective State." *Daedalus* 124, no. 2 (Spring 1995): 55–74.

Tanner, Victor. "Liberia: Railroading Peace." *Review of African Political Economy* 25 (1998): 140.

Tanzi, Vito and Ludger Schuknecht. *The Growth of Government and the Reform of the State in Industrial Countries, IMF Working Paper*. Washington, DC: International Monetary Fund, December 1995.

Tarrow, Sidney. "Making Social Science Work across Space and Time: A Critical Reflection on Robert Putnam's Making Democracy Work." *American Political Science Review* 90, no. 2 (1996): 389–397.

Teitel, Ruti G. *Transitional Justice*. New York: Oxford University Press, 2000.

Ten, Chin Liew. *Crime, Guilt, and Punishment*. Oxford: Clarendon Press, 1987.

Thompson, Kenneth W. *The U.S. Constitution and Constitutionalism in Africa.* Lanham, MD: University Press of America, 1990.

Timberman, David. *A Changeless Land: Continuity and Change in Philippine Politics.* Manila and Singapore: Bookmark and Institute of Southeast Asian Studies, 1991.

Tocqueville, Alexis de. *Democracy in America.* Trans. Henry Reeve. New York: Knopf, 1945.

UNCTAD. *Trade and Development Report, 1997.* Geneva: United Nations Conference on Trade and Development, 1997.

———. *World Investment Report, 1995.* Geneva: United Nations Conference on Trade and Development, 1995.

U.S. Agency for International Development (USAID). *Civil Society and Democratic Reform: Strategic Approaches for International Donors.* Washington, DC: USAID, 1995.

———. *Conducting DG Assessment: A Framework for Strategy Development.* Washington, DC: USAID, Center for Democracy and Governance, 2000.

———. *FY 2000 Performance Review.* Washington, DC: USAID, 2001.

———. *Handbook of Democracy and Governance Program Indicators.* Washington, DC: USAID, Bureau for Global Programs, Field Support and Research, Center for Democracy and Governance, August 1998.

———. *Handbook on Legislative Strengthening.* Washington, DC: USAID, Center for Democracy and Governance, 2000.

———. *1998 Agency Performance Report.* Washington, DC: USAID, Center for Development Information and Evaluation, 31 March 1999.

———. *1999 Agency Performance Report.* Washington, DC: USAID, Center for Development Information and Evaluation, 28 February 2000.

———. *1997 Agency Performance Report.* Washington, DC: USAID, Center for Development Information and Evaluation, January 1998.

———. *Results Review and Resource Request (R4).* Manila: USAID, 31 March 2000.

———. *The 2000 NGO Sustainability Index for Central and Eastern Europe and Eurasia,* 4th ed. Washington, DC: Bureau for Europe and Eurasia, Office of Democracy and Governance, January 2001.

Vallely, Richard M. "Couch Potato Democracy?" *The American Prospect* (March–April 1996): 25–26.

Van de Walle, Nicolas. *African Economies and the Politics of Permanent Crisis.* New York: Cambridge University Press, 2001.

Verba, Sidney and Norman H. Nie. *Participation in America: Political Democracy and Social Equality.* New York: Harper and Row, 1972.

Verba, Sidney, Kay Lehman Schlozman, and Henry Brady. *Voice and Equality: Civic Voluntarism and American Politics.* Cambridge, MA: Harvard University Press, 1995.

Vercier, Jean. *La justice criminelle dans le département de l'Hérault pendant la Révolution, 1789–1800.* Montpellier: Imprimerie Causse, Graille et Castelnau, 1926.

Vines, Alex. *Renamo: From Terrorism to Democracy in Mozambique?* London: James Currey, 1996.

Vogel, Frank E. "The Closing of the Door of Ijtihad and the Application of the Law." *American Journal of Islamic Social Sciences* 10 (Fall 1993): 396–401.

Vovelle, Michel. "Massacreurs et massacrés. Aspects sociaux de la contre-révolution en Provence après Thermidor." In *Les résistances à la Révolution,* ed. F. Lebrun and R. Dupuy. Paris: Éditions Imago, 1987.

Wade, Robert. "Globalization and Its Limits: Reports of the Death of the National Economy Are Greatly Exaggerated." In *National Diversity and Global Capitalism*, ed. Suzanne Berger and Ronald Dore. Ithaca, NY: Cornell University Press, 1996.

Wallon, Henri. *Les Représentants du peuple en mission et la justice révolutionnaire dans les départements en l'an II*. Paris: Hachette et Cie., 1890.

Walther, Ted. *The World Economy*. New York: Wiley, 1997.

Walton, John and David Seddon. *Free Markets and Food Riots: The Politics of Global Adjustment*. Oxford: Blackwell, 1994.

Walzer, Michael. "The Idea of Civil Society: A Path to Social Reconstruction." *Dissent* 38, no. 2 (Spring 1991): 293.

Ware, Alan. *The Breakdown of Democratic Party Organization, 1940–1980*. New York: Oxford University Press, 1985.

Warkentin, Craig. *Reshaping World Politics: NGOs, the Internet, and Global Civil Society*. Lanham, MD: Rowman and Littlefield, 2001.

Weinstein, Jeremy M. "Abandoning the Polity: Political Parties and Social Capital in American Politics." Paper presented at the meeting of the American Political Science Association, Atlanta, 1999.

Weisband, Edward and Christopher J. Colvin. "An Empirical Analysis of International Confederation of Free Trade Unions (ICFTU) Annual Surveys." *Human Rights Quarterly* 22, no. 1 (2000): 167–186.

Weiss, Carol F. and Michael J. Bucuvalas. *Social Science Research and Decision-Making*. New York: Columbia University Press, 1980.

Weiss, Linda. *The Myth of the Powerless State*. Ithaca, NY: Cornell University Press, 1998.

West, Tina. *The Consolidation of Democratic Governance in Ghana: How Can USAID Respond?* Burlington, VT: Associates in Rural Development, 1992.

———. *The Transition to Democratic Governance in Tanzania: An Assessment and Guidelines for Near-Term Action*. Burlington, VT: Associates in Rural Development, 1994.

White, Gordon. "Civil Society, Democratization and Development (I): Clearing the Analytic Ground." *Democratization* 1, no. 3 (Autumn 1994): 379.

Whitehead, Laurence. "Bolivia and the Viability of Democracy." *Journal of Democracy* (April 2001).

Wiebe, Robert H. *The Search for Order, 1877–1920*. New York: Hill and Wang, 1967.

Wildavsky, Aaron. *Speaking Truth to Power: The Art and Craft of Policy Analysis*. Boston: Little, Brown, 1979.

Williams, Pat A. T. "Religion, Violence, and Displacement in Nigeria." *Journal of Asian and African Studies* 32, no. 1–2 (June 1997): 33–49.

Williams, Pat A. T. and Toyin Falola. *Religious Impact on the Nation State: The Nigerian Predicament*. Aldershot, U.K., and Brookfield, VT: Avebury Press, 1995.

Willis, John R. *Islam and the Ideology of Slavery*. Vol. 1 of *Slaves and Slavery in Muslim Africa*. Totowa, NJ, and London: Frank Cass, 1985.

Wilson, James Q. *The Amateur Democrat: Club Politics in Three Cities*. Chicago: University of Chicago Press, 1962.

Wolfinger, Raymond. "The Influence of Precinct Work on Voting Behavior." *Public Opinion Quarterly* 27 (1963): 387–398.

Woloch, Isser. *Jacobin Legacy: The Democratic Movement under the Directory*. Princeton, NJ: Princeton University Press, 1970.

Woodward, Susan L. *Balkan Tragedy: Chaos and Dissolution after the Cold War*. Washington, DC: Brookings Institution, 1995.

————. "Bosnia and Herzegovina: How Not to End Civil War." In *Civil Wars, Insecurity, and Intervention*, ed. Barbara F. Walter and Jack Snyder. New York: Columbia University Press, 1999.

World Bank. *The East Asian Miracle: Economic Growth and Public Policy*. Washington, DC: World Bank, 1993.

————. *Global Economic Prospects and the Developing Countries, 1996*. Washington, DC: World Bank, 1996.

Wu Yu-Shan. "Comparing Third-Wave Democracies." *Issues and Studies* 37, no. 4 (Taipei, Taiwan) (July/August 2001): 1–37.

Zileinski, Jakub. "Transitions from Authoritarian Rule and the Problem of Violence." *Journal of Conflict Resolution* 43, no. 2 (April 1999): 213.

Zisk, Betty H. *The Politics of Transformation: Local Activism in the Peace and Environmental Movements*. Westport, CT: Praeger, 1992.

Index

About the Contributors

KRISTI ANDERSEN is Professor of Political Science at the Maxwell School of Syracuse University. In 1999 she was named Maxwell Professor of Teaching Excellence. Her research and teaching interests are in the areas of women and politics, American political parties, and public opinion. In 1996 she published *After Suffrage: Women in Partisan and Electoral Politics before the New Deal*, which won the Victoria Schuck Award from the American Political Science Association for the best book on women and politics published in 1996. Her earlier book, *The Creation of a Democratic Majority, 1928–1936* (1979), has been influential in shaping political scientists' thinking about the New Deal realignment. She has also published articles on such topics as the gender gap, voting for male and female candidates, the effects of entering the work force on women's political participation, the prospects for electing more women to Congress, and the changing meanings of U.S. elections.

ERIC BJORNLUND is a lawyer and a former Fellow of the Woodrow Wilson International Center for Scholars. He is former senior associate and Asia Director of the National Democratic Institute for International Affairs, where he worked from 1989 until 2000. During his eleven years at the National Democratic Institute he also served at various times as Mission Director in Indonesia, Mission Director in the West Bank and Gaza, Director of Program Development, General Counsel, and Senior Program Officer. Bjornlund developed and directed international and domestic election monitoring, civic education and civil society advocacy, political party building, legislative development, constitutional and electoral reform, and civil-military programs in twenty-five countries in Africa, Asia, and the Middle East. He has written and spoken extensively about elections, democratization, and democracy assistance, and has appeared on television and radio in the United States and abroad.

HARRY BLAIR is Senior Research Scholar and Lecturer in Political Science at Yale University and Senior Democracy Associate for Management Systems International of Washington, D.C., for whom he has been working as a consultant with the United States Agency for International Development's (USAID) Center for Democracy and Governance and its Center for Development Information and Evaluation. At Yale, he has been teaching courses on democratization and world food issues. At USAID, he is presently working on several civil society assessments and has recently completed an analysis of civic education programs in three other nations. He has also worked on assessing democratic decentralization, rule of law programs, and "results management" in the democracy sector. His earlier work centered mainly on the areas of political behavior, rural development, and natural resources management, principally in South Asia.

MICHAEL BRATTON is Professor of Political Science at the Department of Political Science and African Studies Center, Michigan State University. His articles on democratization in Africa have appeared in *World Politics*, *Comparative Politics*, *Comparative Political Studies*, the *British Journal of Political Science*, and *The Journal of Democracy*. He is co-author of *Democratic Experiments in Africa* (1997). He currently co-directs the Afrobarometer, a comparative series of national public attitude surveys on democracy, markets, and civil society in Africa.

HOWARD G. BROWN is Associate Professor of History, Binghamton University, State University of New York. His most direct experience with "democratic performance" was serving as Chair of the Faculty Senate, Binghamton University, in 1999–2000. He is currently Vice-Chair and Director of Graduate Studies in History. His areas of teaching and research are Early Modern Europe, France, the French Revolution, state formation, criminal justice, politicized violence, and state repression. He is the author of *War, Revolution and the Bureaucratic State* (1995) and co-editor of *Taking Liberties: Problems of a New Order from the French Revolution to Napoleon* (2003), and is currently completing a book entitled *Ending the French Revolution: Violence, Justice and Repression, 1795–1802*. His papers and articles have appeared in *The Journal of Modern History* and *The Historical Journal*.

DAVID L. CINGRANELLI is Professor of Political Science, Department of Political Science, Binghamton University, State University of New York. His research is focused on the human rights practices of governments from a cross-national comparative perspective. He conducts research on the measurement of human rights practices, the effect of the end of the Cold War on government respect for human rights, the relationships among different types of human rights, the dissent/repression linkage, and the relationship between the human rights practices of the governments of developing countries and the amounts and types of foreign aid they receive. His early published work focused on the issue of equity and urban service delivery policies. He is the author of *Ethics and American Foreign Policy toward the Third World* (1993) and editor of *Human Rights: Theory and Measurement* (1988) and *Human Rights and the Developing Countries* (1996).

ELIZABETH SPIRO CLARK is an Associate at the Institute for the Study of Diplomacy at Georgetown University. During 1998–2000 she was a Visiting Fellow with the International Forum for Democratic Studies at the National Endowment for Democracy. Two publications, "Why Elections Matter," *The Washington Quarterly* (Summer 2000) and "A Tune-up Not an Overhaul," *Journal of Democracy* (October 1999), resulted from her fellowship, as well as development of a workshop on democratic innovation for the second assembly of the World Movement for Democracy in São Paolo in November 2000 and a workshop on elections and legislatures for the Emerging Democracies Forum in Yemen in 1999. A retired Foreign Service Officer, she headed the Office of Democracy Promotion in the Bureau of Democracy, Human Rights, and Labor from 1995 to 1998.

EDWARD FRIEDMAN is the Hawkins Chair Professor of Political Science at the University of Wisconsin-Madison, where he has been teaching undergraduate and graduate courses on the challenges of democratization for many years. He the author of *National Identity and Democratic Prospects in Socialist China* (1995), the editor of *The Politics of Democratization: Generalizing East Asian Experiences* (1994), and co-editor of *What If China Doesn't Democratize? Implications for War and Peace* (2001). His articles include "The Painful Gradualness of Democratization: Proceduralism as a Necessarily Discontinuous Revolution," in *Democracy and Its Limits*, ed. Howard Handelman and Mark Tessler (2000) and "Development, Revolution, Democracy and Dictatorship: China versus India?" in *Democracy, Revolution and History*, ed. Theda Skocpol (1998).

JOHN W. HARBESON is Professor of Political Science in the Graduate School and recently Chair of the Department of Political Science at City College, City University of New York. He has authored/edited nine books and seventy articles, including *The Ethiopian Transformation* (1988), *Civil Society and the State*, ed. with Donald Rothchild and Naomi Chazan (1994), and three editions of *Africa in World Politics*, ed. with Donald Rothchild. He was Senior Fellow at United States Institute of Peace (1998–1999) and Visiting Research Fellow at the Center for International Studies, Princeton University (2001–2002). From 1993 to 1995 he was Regional Democracy and Governance Advisor for Eastern and Southern Africa, United States Agency for International Development.

TERRENCE LYONS is Assistant Professor in the Institute for Conflict Analysis and Resolution at George Mason University. From 1990 until 1998 he served as coordinator of the Conflict Resolution in Africa project at the Brookings Institution and conducted research on African security, humanitarian intervention, democratization, and U.S. foreign policy. He served as a Senior Researcher and Program Leader for Conflict Resolution and Peacebuilding at the International Peace Research Institute, Oslo, from 1998 to 1999. His published works include *African Foreign Policies: Power and Process*, ed. with Gilbert M. Khadiagala (2001), *Voting for Peace: Postconflict Elections in Liberia* (1999), *Sovereignty as Responsibility: Conflict Management in Africa*, with Francis M. Deng and Sadikiel Kimaro (1996), and *Somalia: State Collapse, Multilateral Intervention, and Strategies for Political Reconstruction*, with Ahmed I. Samatar (1995), as well as articles in the *Journal of Democracy* and the *Journal of Modern African Studies*.

ALI A. MAZRUI is Albert Schweitzer Professor in the Humanities and Director of the Institute of Global Cultural Studies at Binghamton University, State University of New York. He is also Senior Scholar in Africana Studies at Cornell University in Ithaca, New York and Chair of the Center for the Study of Islam and Democracy in Washington, D.C. Mazrui is Albert Luthuli Professor-at-Large at the University of Jos in Nigeria. He has written more than twenty books about government and politics in Africa and in parts of the Muslim world. His television work includes the widely discussed nine-part television series *The Africans: A Triple Heritage* (PBS/BBC, 1986). He has also written for newspapers in different parts of the world, as well as for major scholarly journals in the social sciences. His latest book is *The Power of Babel: Language and Governance in Africa's Experience*, with Alamin M. Mazrui (1999).

EDWARD R. McMAHON is Dean's Professor of Applied Politics and Director of the Center on Democratic Performance at Binghamton University, State University of New York. Prior to joining Binghamton in 1999, McMahon served for nine years as a senior staff member of the National Democratic Institute for International Affairs, where he designed, implemented, and evaluated projects designed to support democratic institution-building, especially in Africa. He also spent ten years as a diplomat with the State Department and with the United States Agency for International Development. He serves as a consultant to the Freedom House's Annual Survey of Political Rights and Civil Liberties and is also a Contributing Editor of the *Political Handbook of the World*.

SHAHEEN MOZAFFAR is Professor of Political Science at Bridgewater State College and Research Fellow of the African Studies Center at Boston University.

During the 1999–2000 academic year he was an American Association for the Advancement of Science Diplomacy Fellow in the United States Agency for International Development's Bureau for Latin America and the Caribbean (Office of Regional Sustainable Development), where he worked on democracy and human rights issues. He was also a member of the U.S. delegation to the Organization of American States election observation team to Haiti for the legislative elections in May 2000. He has written widely on the colonial state, ethnic politics, institutional choice, electoral systems and democratic transitions in Africa. He is a recipient of a National Science Foundation research grant and is completing a book manuscript on institutional choice and political consequences in Africa's emerging democracies. His publications have appeared in *Nationalism and Ethnic Politics*, *Comparative Political Studies*, and *International Political Science Review*.

BRIAN NUSSBAUM is a student in political science and a research assistant of the Center on Democratic Performance at Binghamton University, State University of New York.

THOMAS A.P. SINCLAIR is Director and Assistant Professor of the Master in Public Administration Program at Binghamton University, State University of New York. He has managed parliamentary development projects in Ukraine and participated in legislative consulting activities on oversight and committee operations in both Eastern Europe and Africa. He has also assisted county legislatures and administrative departments in restructuring their taxation and purchasing systems. His teaching and research interests include comparative administration, contract management and procurement, public budgeting, policy analysis, and policy implementation.

NICOLAS VAN DE WALLE is Professor of Political Science at Michigan State University. From 1994 to 2000 he was also a Fellow at the Overseas Development Council in Washington, D.C. In recent years he has conducted field research in Botswana, Cameroon, Senegal, Uganda, and Zambia. He has published widely on democratization issues as well as on the politics of economic reform in Africa. He is the author of *African Economies and the Politics of Permanent Crisis, 1979–1999* (2001) as well as co-author of three books: *Democratic Experiments in Africa: Regime Transitions in Comparative Perspectives* (1997), *Improving Aid to Africa* (1996), and *Of Time and Power: Leadership Duration in the Modern World* (1991). He is co-editor of *Agenda for Africa's Economic Renewal* (1996) and *Foreign Aid in Africa: Learning from Country Experiences* (1998).